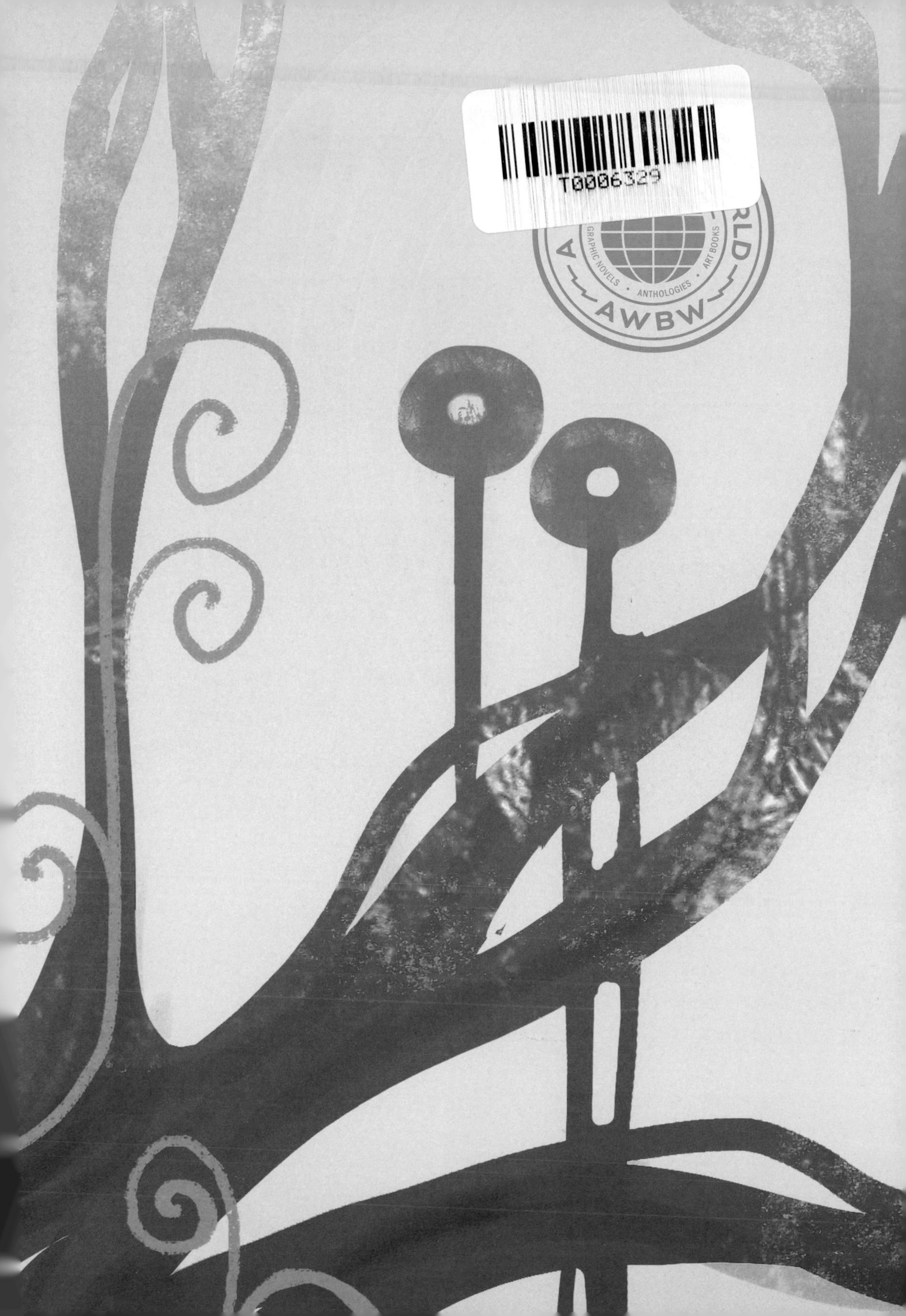
GRAPHIC NOVELS • ANTHOLOGIES • ART BOOKS
AWBW

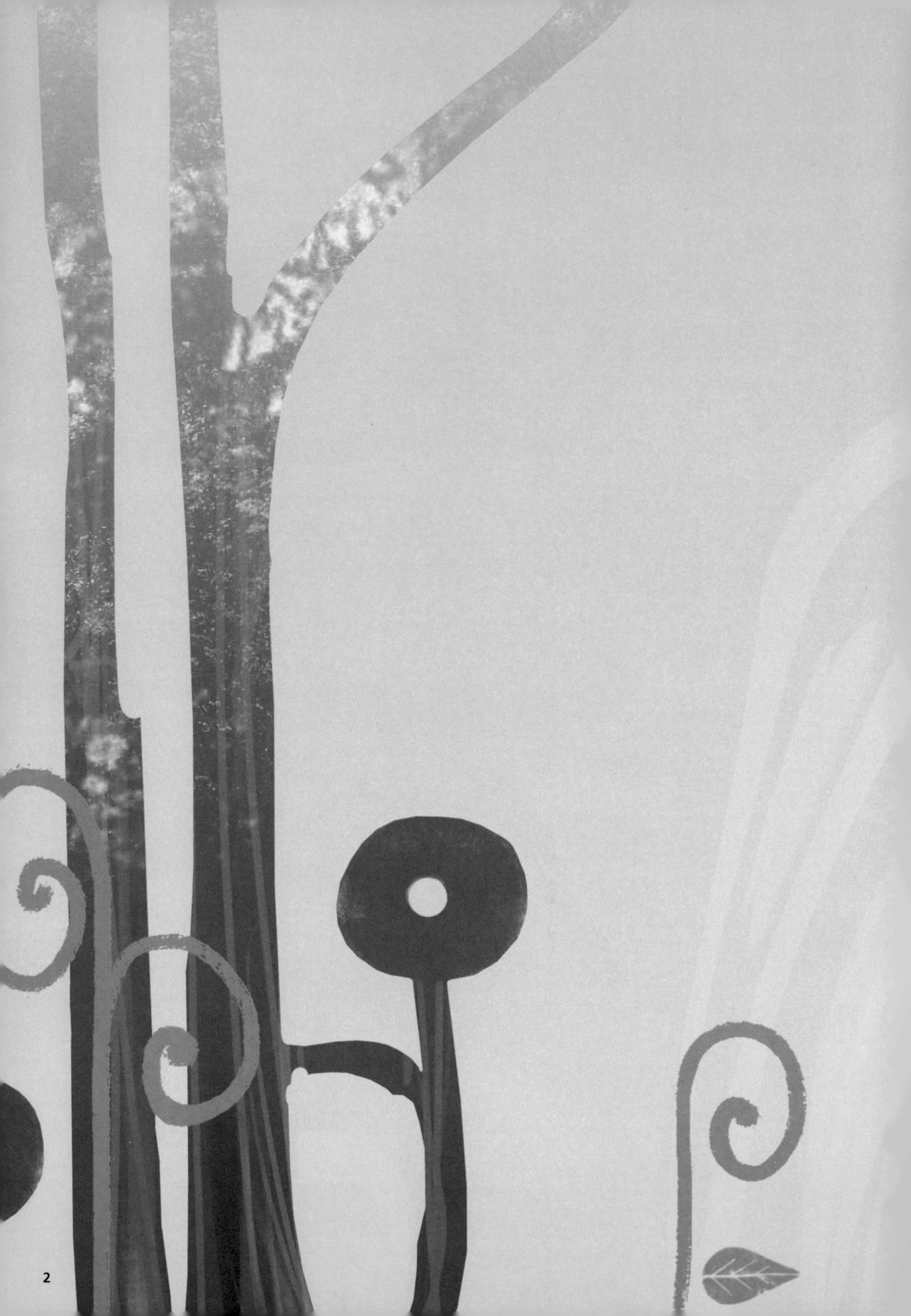

EMBODIED

AN INTERSECTIONAL FEMINIST COMICS POETRY ANTHOLOGY

EDITED BY WENDY & TYLER CHIN-TANNER

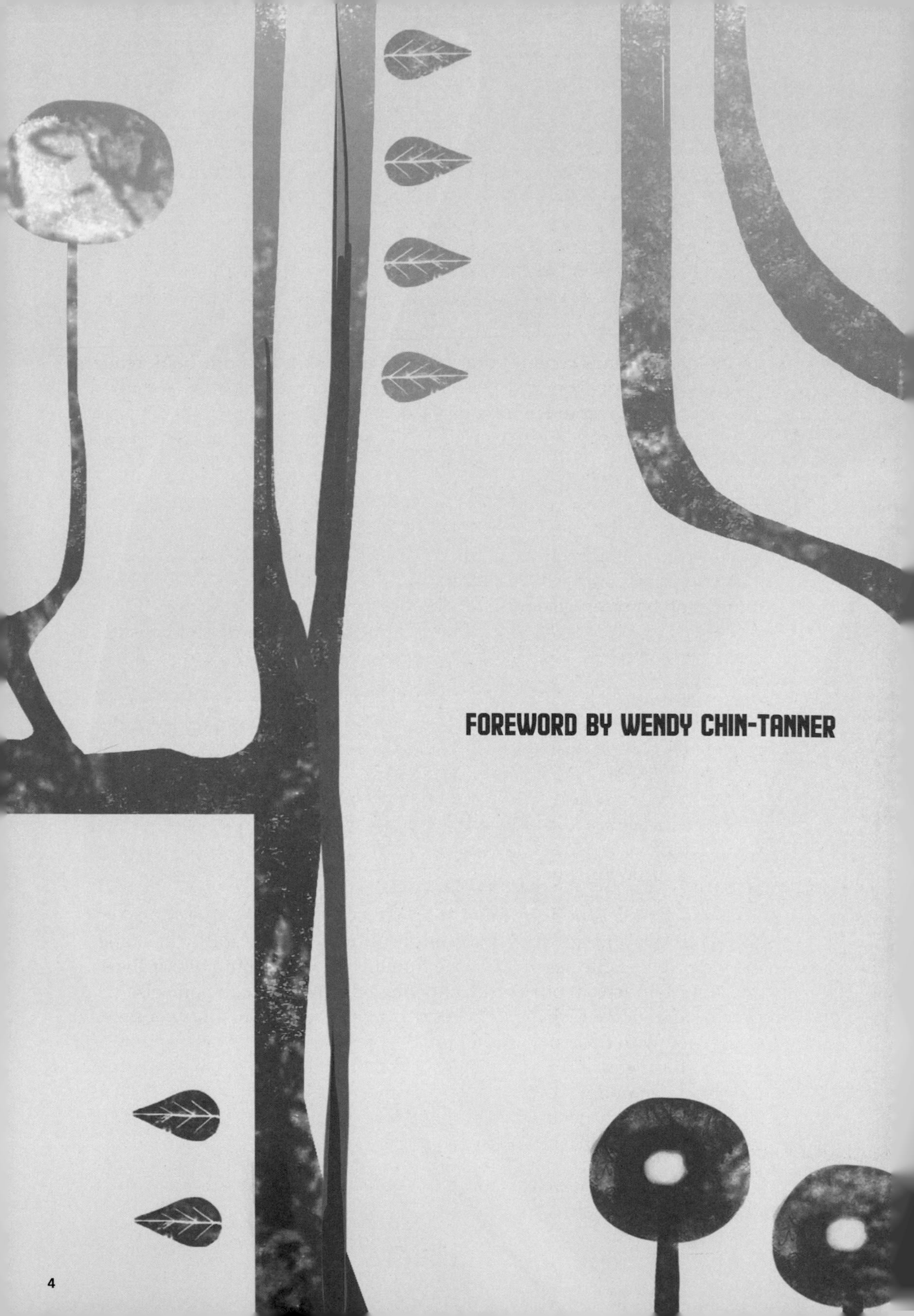

FOREWORD BY WENDY CHIN-TANNER

EMBODIED is the first comics poetry anthology that marries the unique aspects of poetry with those of sequential art in a collection of stories focused on gender, identity, and the body. My co-editor Tyler and I have gathered new work by an ethnically, regionally, and generationally diverse array of America's premier cis female, trans, and non-binary poets and adapted it into sequential art narratives drawn, colored, and lettered by top non-cis male artists. The result is a book that continually awes and surprises me with its many nuanced layers, and is truly greater than the sum of its parts.

EMBODIED brings contemporary American poetry to comic book readers and comics to poetry readers in a hybrid form that showcases the relevance, urgency, and power of both media. Comics and poetry have always been at the cutting edge of political commentary, inspiring and bearing witness to social movements.

As both a poet and a co-publisher at A Wave Blue World, I'm drawn to poetry and comics for many of the same reasons. While their tool kits might look different at first glance, both forms engage with distillation, the use of silence, the relationship between different parts of the page, and the interaction between visual content and negative space. In EMBODIED, dramatic tension is created not only within the narrative of the stories themselves, but in the interplay between form and content, different panels and pages, and the artwork and the script.

When reading comics poetry, what doesn't appear on the page is just as important as what does. To understand the intersectional feminist literary praxis at work in this anthology, Rachel Blau DuPlessis' notion of "writing between the lines" as a form of feminist literary language seems particularly apt. What is the meaning of what is said in the context of what is not said? Each of the comics poetry stories in EMBODIED answers this question in a variety of different ways.

At A Wave Blue World, we are first and foremost storytellers. Stories are the reflections and the driving forces of culture, with the ability to shape the way we live. Stories are how we humans make meaning of our lives and what happens in our world, allowing us to walk in someone else's shoes and identify with experiences we have never personally encountered. Our vision with this book is to provide a platform for poets and artists of marginalized genders and identities to tell their own stories, at a time when they are most under siege. To that end, the May 2021 release of EMBODIED coincides with International Women's Health Month and a portion of the proceeds will benefit International Women's Health Coalition.

We believe in the power of stories to create empathy, because empathy is the engine of change.

COVER ILLUSTRATION BY CLAUDIA IANNICIELLO
LOGO AND COVER DESIGN BY TIM DANIEL
BOOK AND PRODUCTION DESIGN BY PETE CARLSSON

Publisher's Cataloging-In-Publication Data
(Prepared by The Donohue Group, Inc.)

Names: Chin-Tanner, Wendy, editor, writer of supplementary textual content. | Chin-Tanner, Tyler, editor.
Title: Embodied : an intersectional feminist comics poetry anthology / edited by Wendy & Tyler Chin-Tanner
   [foreword by Wendy Chin-Tanner].
Description: [Rhinebeck, New York] : A Wave Blue World, 2021. | Summary: "A unique collection of
   intersectional feminist poetry-in-comics, a collaboration between cis female, trans, and non-binary
   poets and comics artists"--Provided by publisher.
Identifiers: ISBN 9781949518139
Subjects: LCSH: Feminism--Comic books, strips, etc. | Women--Comic books, strips, etc. | Feminism--Poetry.
   Women--Poetry. | LCGFT: Graphic novels. | Poetry.
Classification: LCC PN6726 .E43 2021 | DDC 741.5973--dc23

TYLER CHIN-TANNER
CO-PUBLISHER

WENDY CHIN-TANNER
CO-PUBLISHER

JUSTIN ZIMMERMAN
DIRECTOR OF OPERATIONS AND MEDIA

PETE CARLSSON
PRODUCTION DESIGNER

DIANA KOU
DIRECTOR OF MARKETING

JESSE POST
BOOK PUBLICIST

HAZEL NEWLEVANT
SOCIAL MEDIA COORDINATOR

ERIN BEASLEY
SALES MANAGER

Regular edition: ISBN 978-1-949518-13-9   Independent Bookstore Day edition: ISBN 978-1-949518-16-0   AWBW.com

Printed in Canada

TABLE OF CONTENTS

Voyages

Poem by Miller Oberman
Art by Jen Hickman
Letters by Cardinal Rae

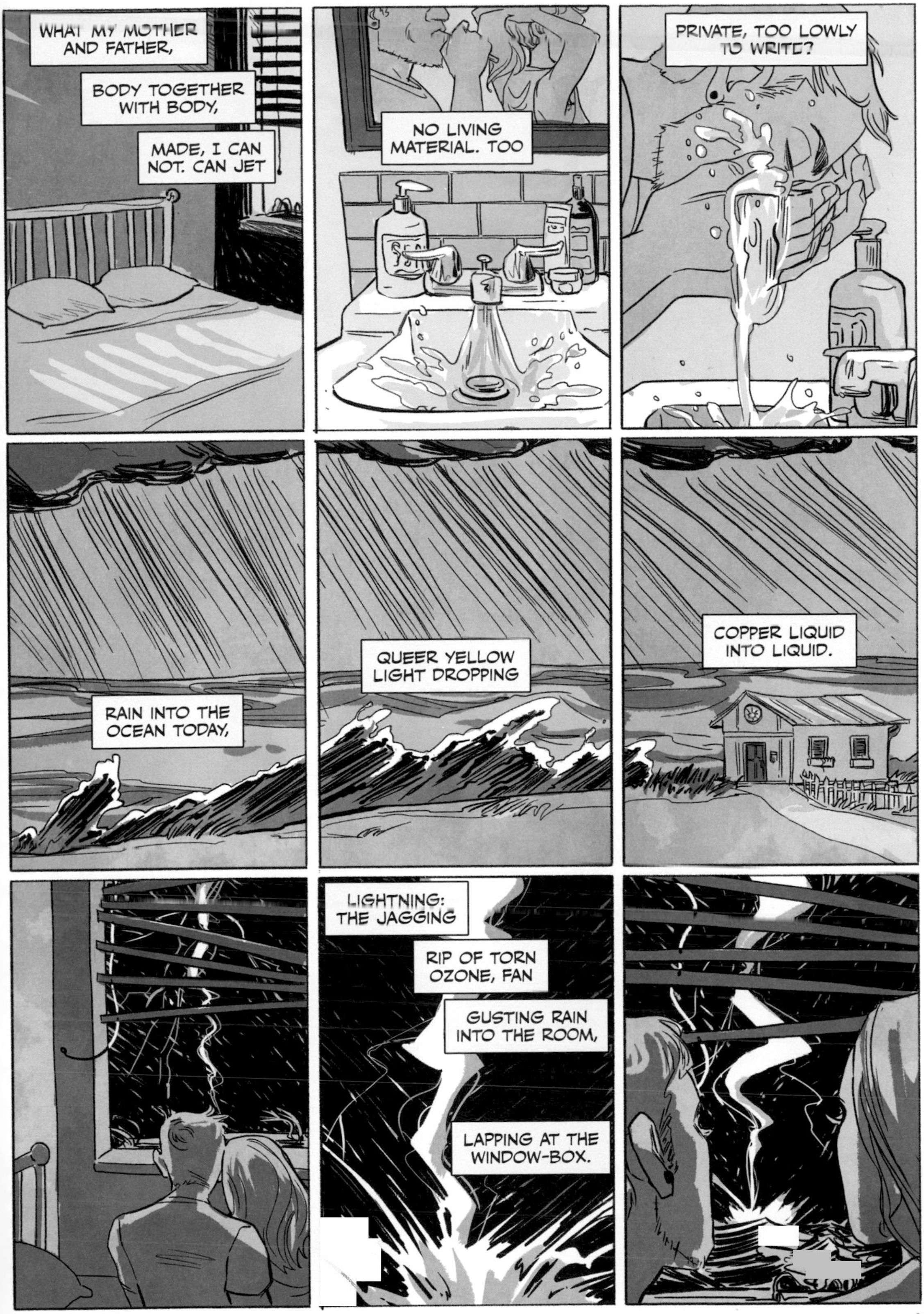
WHAT MY MOTHER AND FATHER,
BODY TOGETHER WITH BODY,
MADE, I CAN NOT. CAN JET
NO LIVING MATERIAL. TOO
PRIVATE, TOO LOWLY TO WRITE?
RAIN INTO THE OCEAN TODAY,
QUEER YELLOW LIGHT DROPPING
COPPER LIQUID INTO LIQUID.
LIGHTNING: THE JAGGING
RIP OF TORN OZONE, FAN
GUSTING RAIN INTO THE ROOM,
LAPPING AT THE WINDOW-BOX.

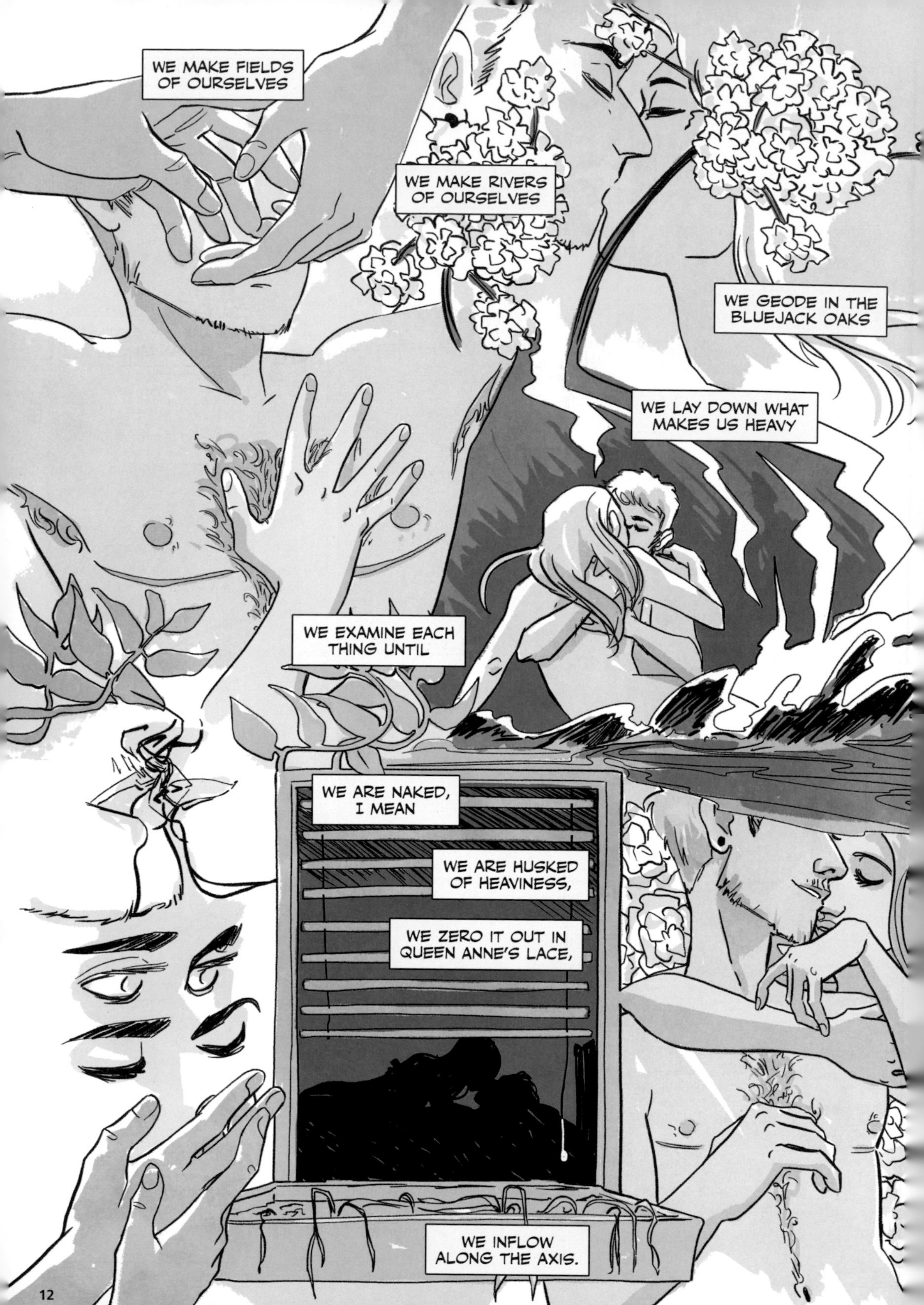

WE MAKE FIELDS OF OURSELVES
WE MAKE RIVERS OF OURSELVES
WE GEODE IN THE BLUEJACK OAKS
WE LAY DOWN WHAT MAKES US HEAVY
WE EXAMINE EACH THING UNTIL
WE ARE NAKED, I MEAN
WE ARE HUSKED OF HEAVINESS,
WE ZERO IT OUT IN QUEEN ANNE'S LACE,
WE INFLOW ALONG THE AXIS.

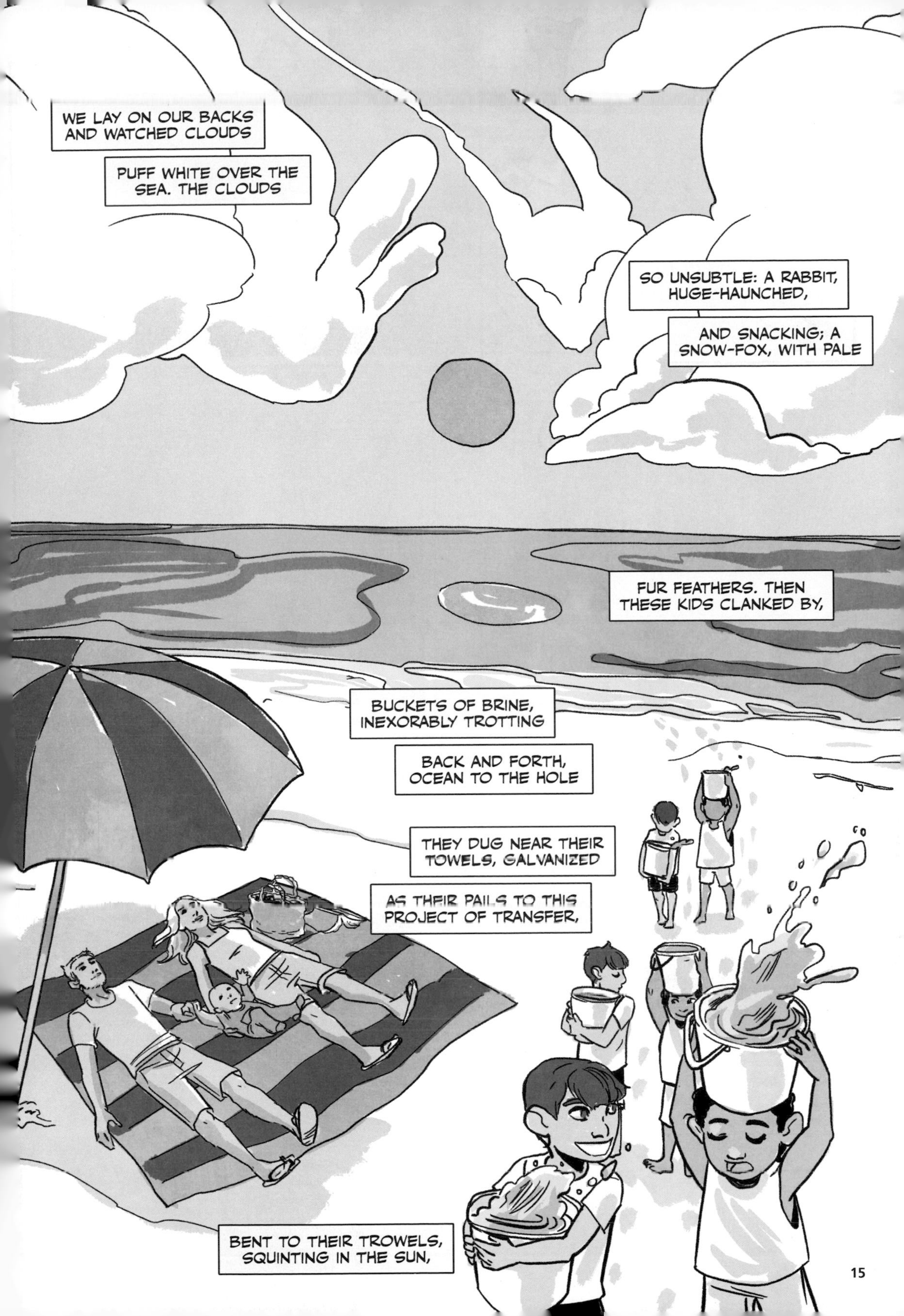
WE LAY ON OUR BACKS AND WATCHED CLOUDS
PUFF WHITE OVER THE SEA. THE CLOUDS
SO UNSUBTLE: A RABBIT, HUGE-HAUNCHED,
AND SNACKING; A SNOW-FOX, WITH PALE
FUR FEATHERS. THEN THESE KIDS CLANKED BY,
BUCKETS OF BRINE, INEXORABLY TROTTING
BACK AND FORTH, OCEAN TO THE HOLE
THEY DUG NEAR THEIR TOWELS, GALVANIZED
AS THEIR PAILS TO THIS PROJECT OF TRANSFER,
BENT TO THEIR TROWELS, SQUINTING IN THE SUN,

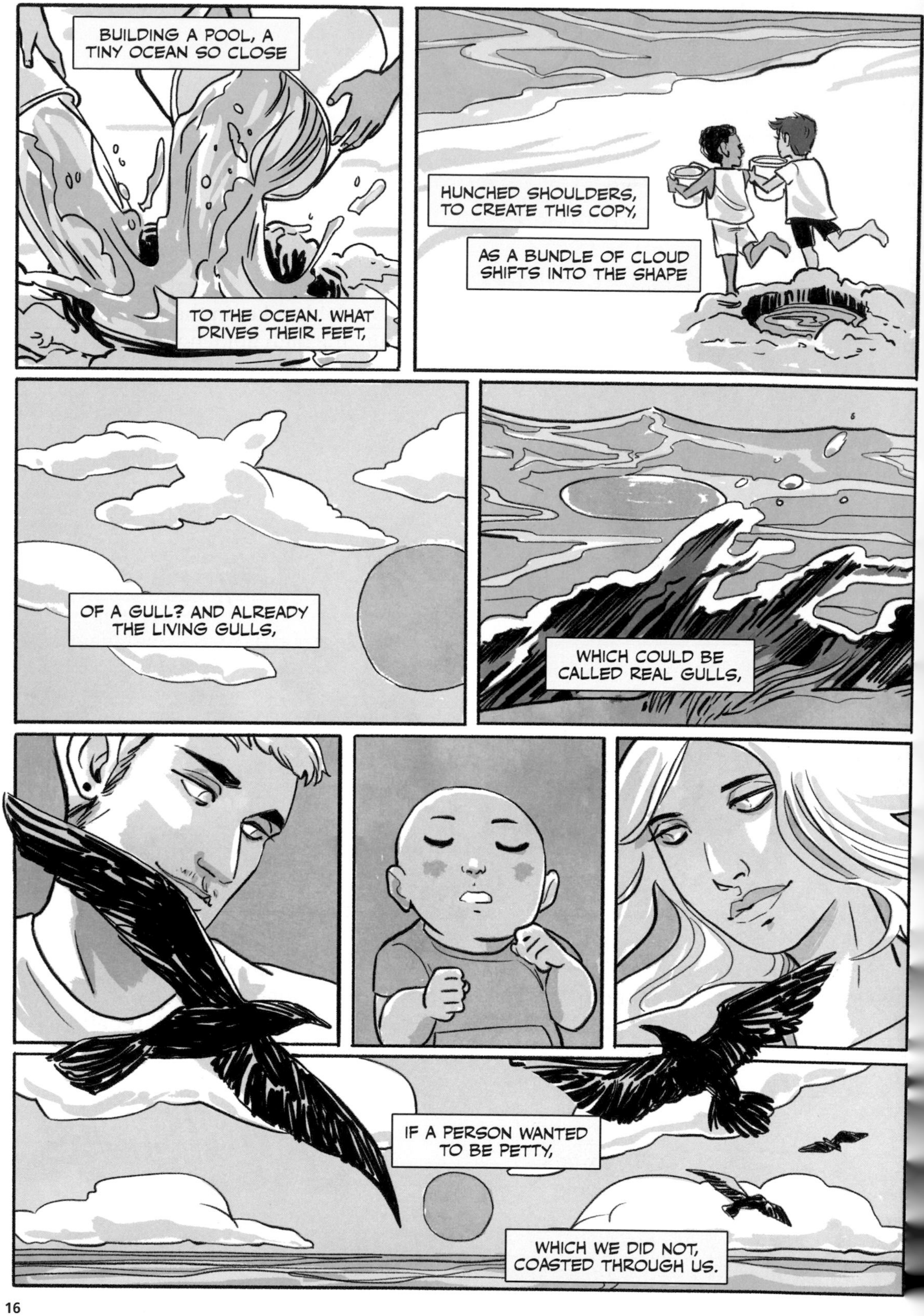
BUILDING A POOL, A TINY OCEAN SO CLOSE
TO THE OCEAN. WHAT DRIVES THEIR FEET,
HUNCHED SHOULDERS, TO CREATE THIS COPY,
AS A BUNDLE OF CLOUD SHIFTS INTO THE SHAPE
OF A GULL? AND ALREADY THE LIVING GULLS,
WHICH COULD BE CALLED REAL GULLS,
IF A PERSON WANTED TO BE PETTY,
WHICH WE DID NOT, COASTED THROUGH US.

Voyages
by Miller Oberman

"And could they hear me I would tell them:"
–Hart Crane

1.
What my mother and father,
body together with body,
made, I can not. Can jet
no living material. Too
private, too lowly to write?
Rain into the ocean today,
queer yellow light dropping
copper liquid into liquid.
Lightning: the jagging
rip of torn ozone, fan
gusting rain into the room,
lapping at the window-box.

2.
We make fields of ourselves
we make rivers of ourselves
we geode in the bluejack oaks
we lay down what makes us heavy
we examine each thing until
we are naked, I mean
we are husked of heaviness,
we zero it out in Queen Anne's lace,
we inflow along the axis.

3.
Who would find a way
into your body from this motion?
Who sink in and root, quilt-grass
morning-built, ajar as a song
vaulting from a passing ship,
drawn by distant human music?
How ordinary this day is,
gauzy sift of clouds, spill of wax on wood,
whorl of an old knot grown smooth
from sand and polish, from stain,
oil from our hands, how
ordinary, to want this.

4.
White blossoms of the Galax,
June vaulted spikes in the woods,
the sun, the high golden yolk,
black scent of soil. If what
comes from me is not life, it is
also not not life. Let me not
be questionless. Let me be
open as a vowel, wave-glazed.

5.
We lay on our backs and watched clouds
puff white over the sea. The clouds
so unsubtle: a rabbit, huge-haunched,
and snacking; a snow-fox, with pale
fur feathers. Then these kids clanked by,
buckets of brine, inexorably trotting
back and forth, ocean to the hole
they dug near their towels, galvanized
as their pails to this project of transfer,
bent to their trowels, squinting in the sun,
building a pool, a tiny ocean so close
to the ocean. What drives their feet,
hunched shoulders, to create this copy,
as a bundle of cloud shifts into the shape
of a gull? And already the living gulls,
which could be called real gulls,
if a person wanted to be petty,
which we did not, coasted through us.

[You know what living means? Tits out, tits in the rain. Tits]

Poem by Diane Seuss
Art by Liana Kangas
Letters by Cardinal Rae

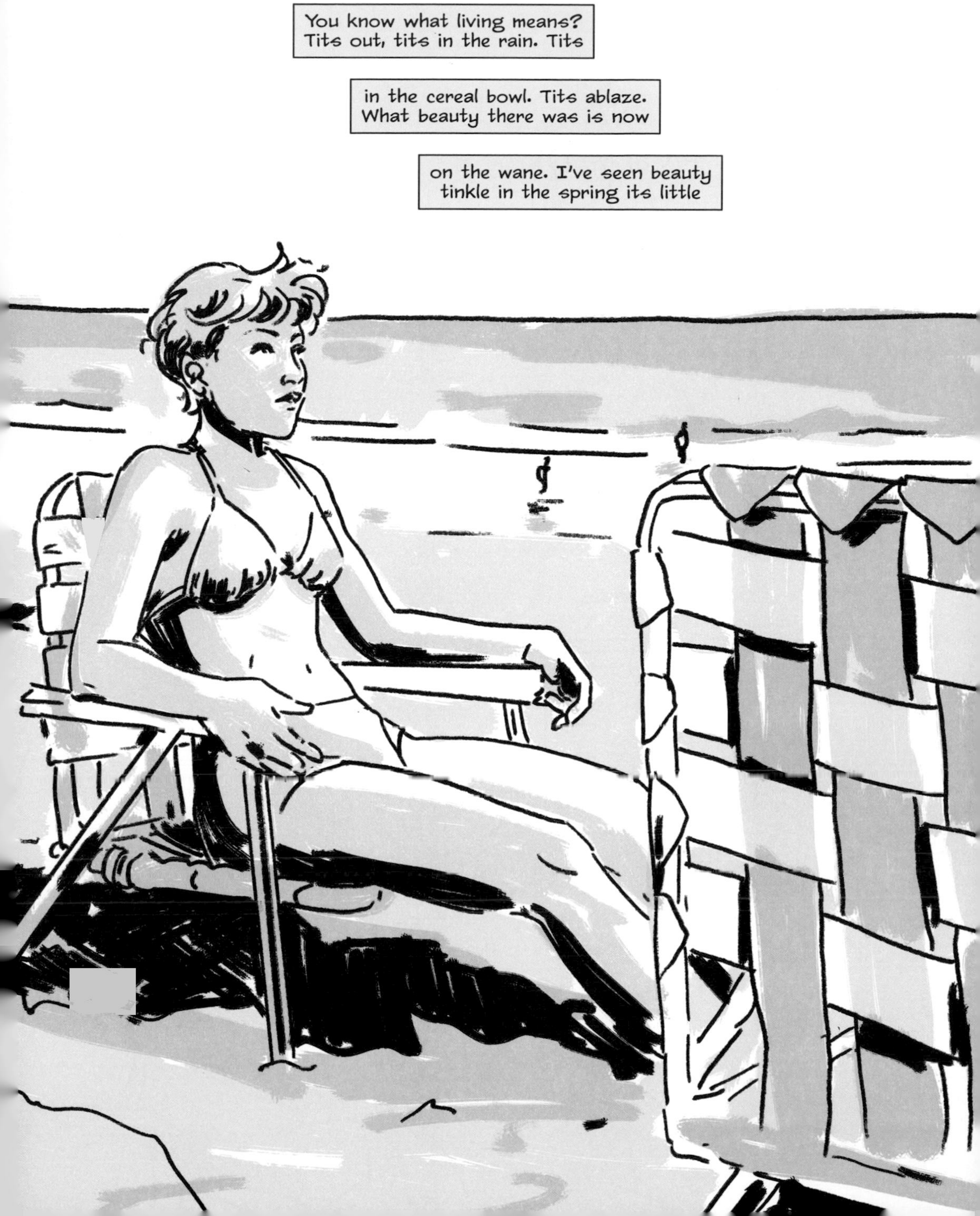
You know what living means? Tits out, tits in the rain. Tits
in the cereal bowl. Tits ablaze. What beauty there was is now
on the wane. I've seen beauty tinkle in the spring its little

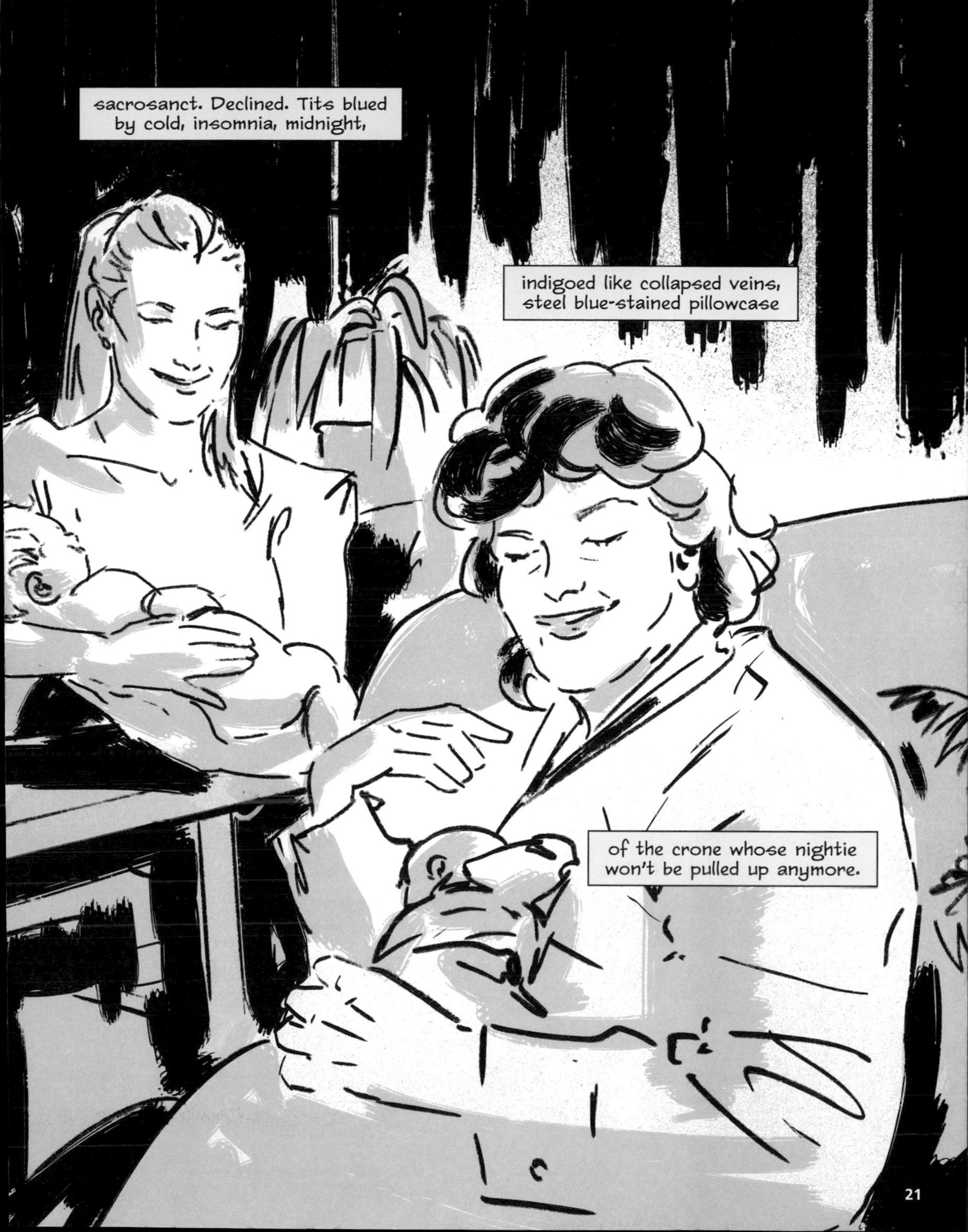
sacrosanct. Declined. Tits blued by cold, insomnia, midnight,
indigoed like collapsed veins, steel blue-stained pillowcase
of the crone whose nightie won't be pulled up anymore.

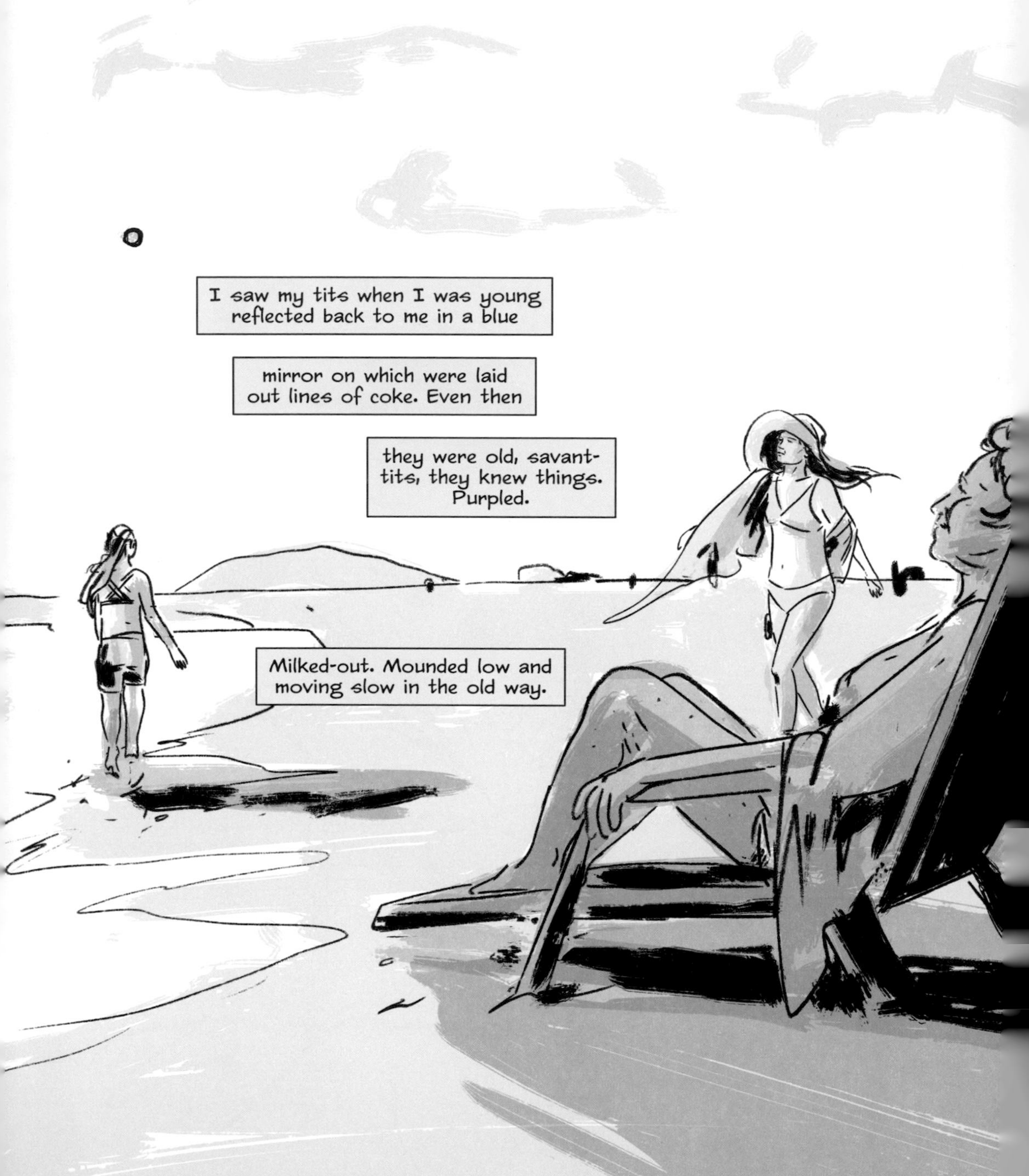
I saw my tits when I was young reflected back to me in a blue
mirror on which were laid out lines of coke. Even then
they were old, savant-tits, they knew things. Purpled.
Milked-out. Mounded low and moving slow in the old way.

[You know what living means? Tits out, tits in the rain. Tits]
By Diane Seuss

You know what living means? Tits out, tits in the rain. Tits
in the cereal bowl. Tits ablaze. What beauty there was is now
on the wane. I've seen beauty tinkle in the spring its little
breeze-borne bells. Summer's copper gong, heat frizzing
the wisteria until all that's left is rat hair. Winter, I think
there are ice flutes. I think blue lips of killed kids blow cold
notes from ice flutes. You know what living's for? Tits
sacrosanct. Declined. Tits blued by cold, insomnia, midnight,
indigoed like collapsed veins, steel blue-stained pillowcase
of the crone whose nightie won't be pulled up anymore.
I saw my tits when I was young reflected back to me in a blue
mirror on which were laid out lines of coke. Even then
they were old, savant-tits, they knew things. Purpled.
Milked-out. Mounded low and moving slow in the old way.

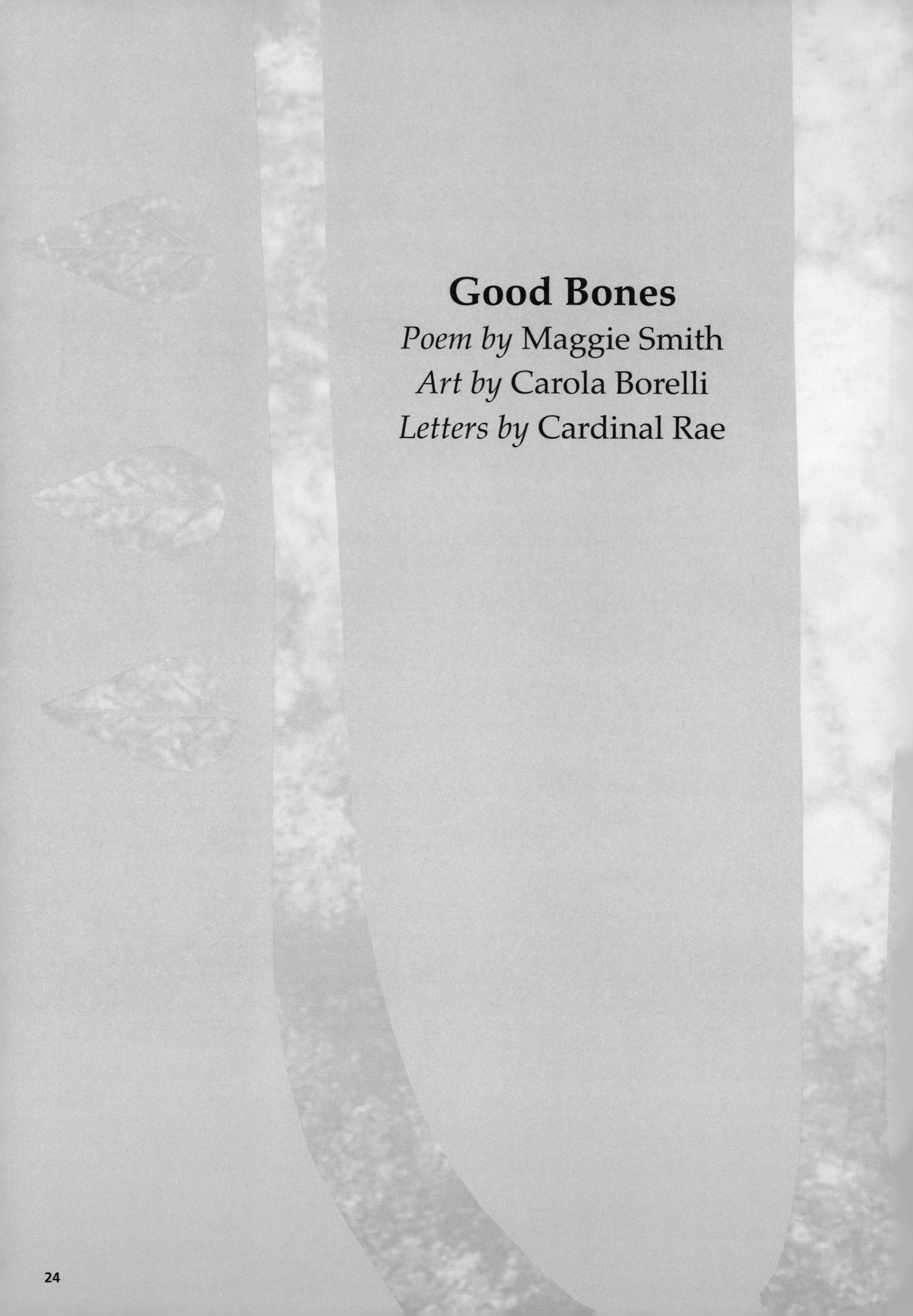

Good Bones

Poem by Maggie Smith

Art by Carola Borelli

Letters by Cardinal Rae

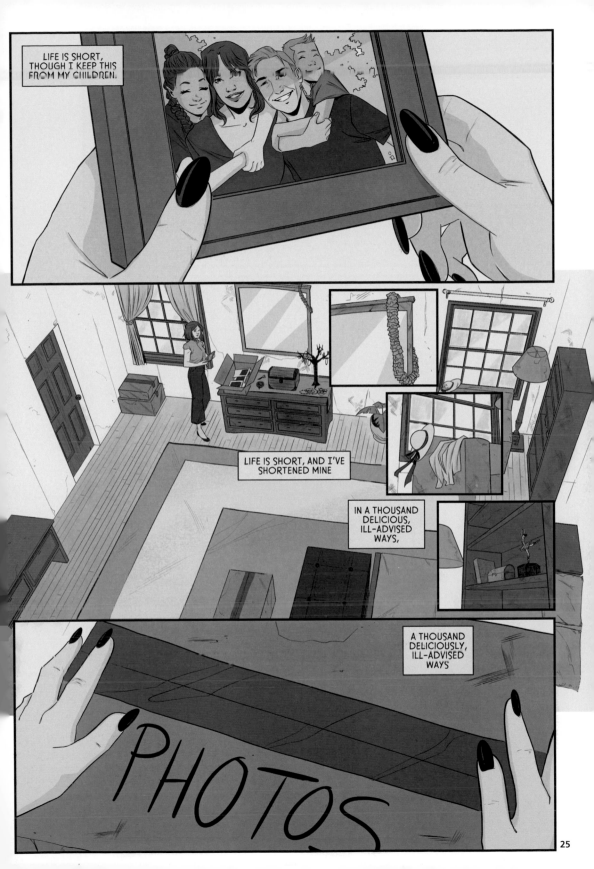

LIFE IS SHORT, THOUGH I KEEP THIS FROM MY CHILDREN.

LIFE IS SHORT, AND I'VE SHORTENED MINE

IN A THOUSAND DELICIOUS, ILL-ADVISED WAYS,

A THOUSAND DELICIOUSLY, ILL-ADVISED WAYS

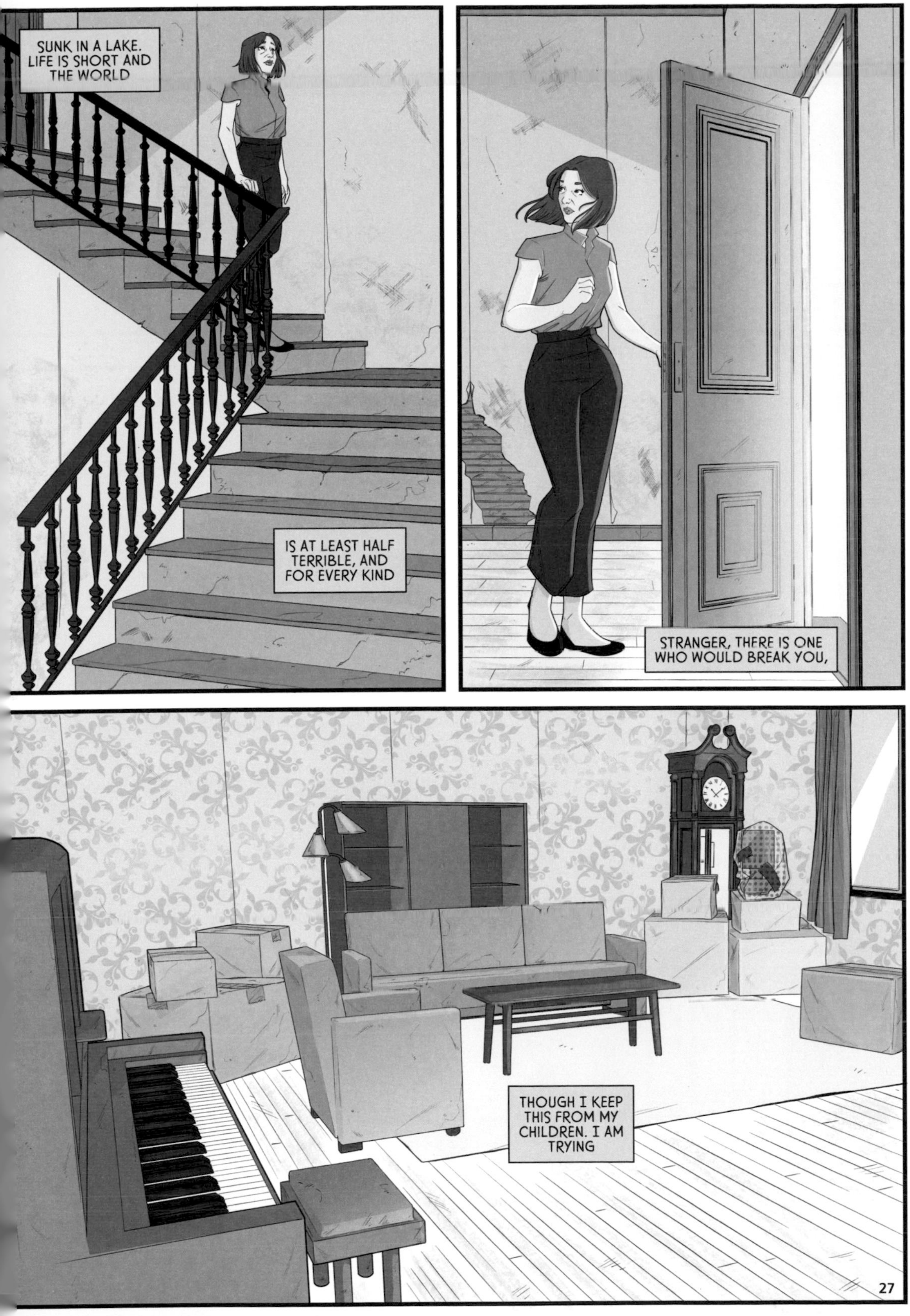
SUNK IN A LAKE. LIFE IS SHORT AND THE WORLD
IS AT LEAST HALF TERRIBLE, AND FOR EVERY KIND
STRANGER, THERE IS ONE WHO WOULD BREAK YOU,
THOUGH I KEEP THIS FROM MY CHILDREN. I AM TRYING

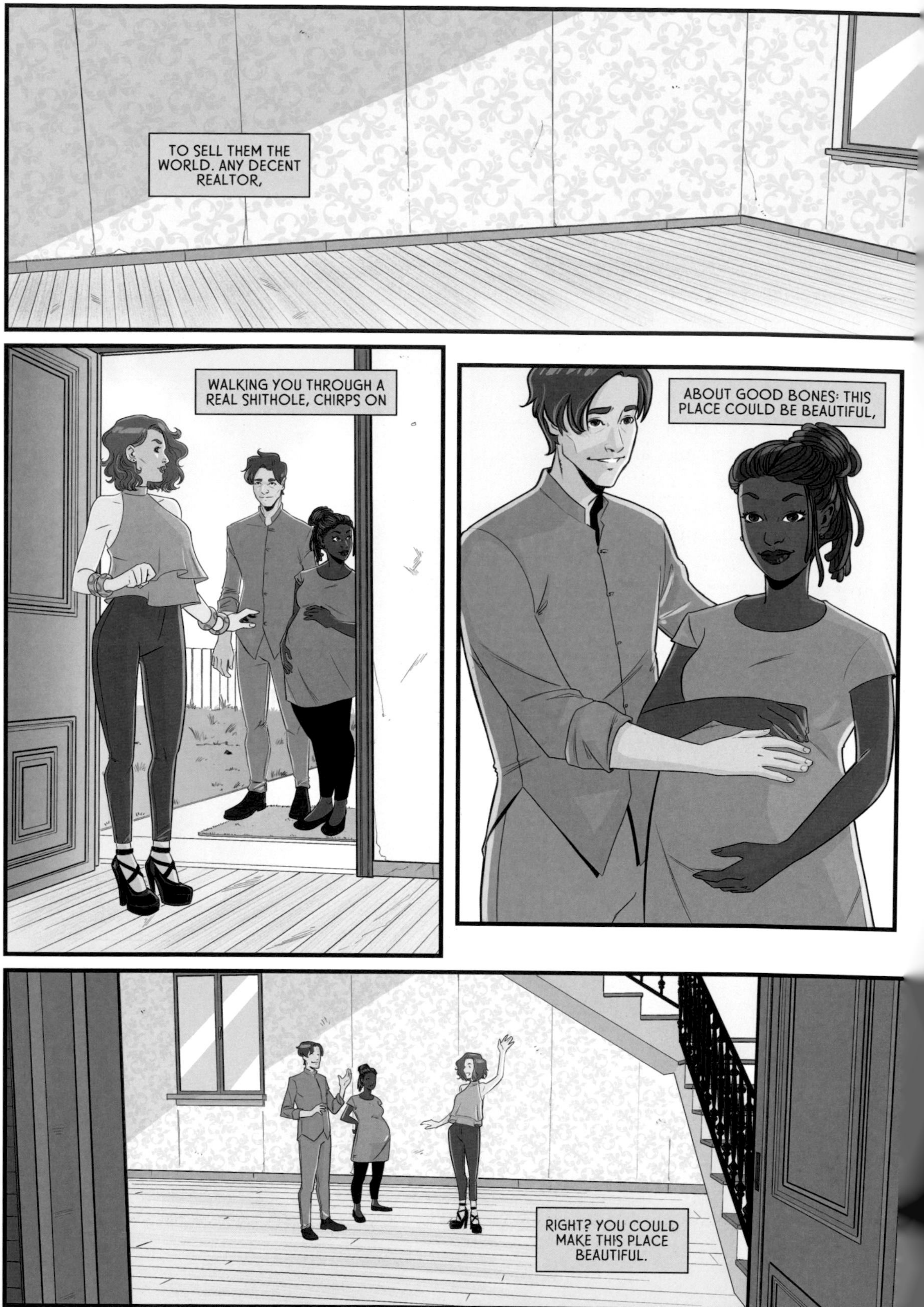
TO SELL THEM THE WORLD. ANY DECENT REALTOR,
WALKING YOU THROUGH A REAL SHITHOLE, CHIRPS ON
ABOUT GOOD BONES: THIS PLACE COULD BE BEAUTIFUL,
RIGHT? YOU COULD MAKE THIS PLACE BEAUTIFUL.

Good Bones
by Maggie Smith

Life is short, though I keep this from my children.
Life is short, and I've shortened mine
in a thousand delicious, ill-advised ways,
a thousand deliciously ill-advised ways
I'll keep from my children. The world is at least
fifty percent terrible, and that's a conservative
estimate, though I keep this from my children.
For every bird there is a stone thrown at a bird.
For every loved child, a child broken, bagged,
sunk in a lake. Life is short and the world
is at least half terrible, and for every kind
stranger, there is one who would break you,
though I keep this from my children. I am trying
to sell them the world. Any decent realtor,
walking you through a real shithole, chirps on
about good bones: This place could be beautiful,
right? You could make this place beautiful.

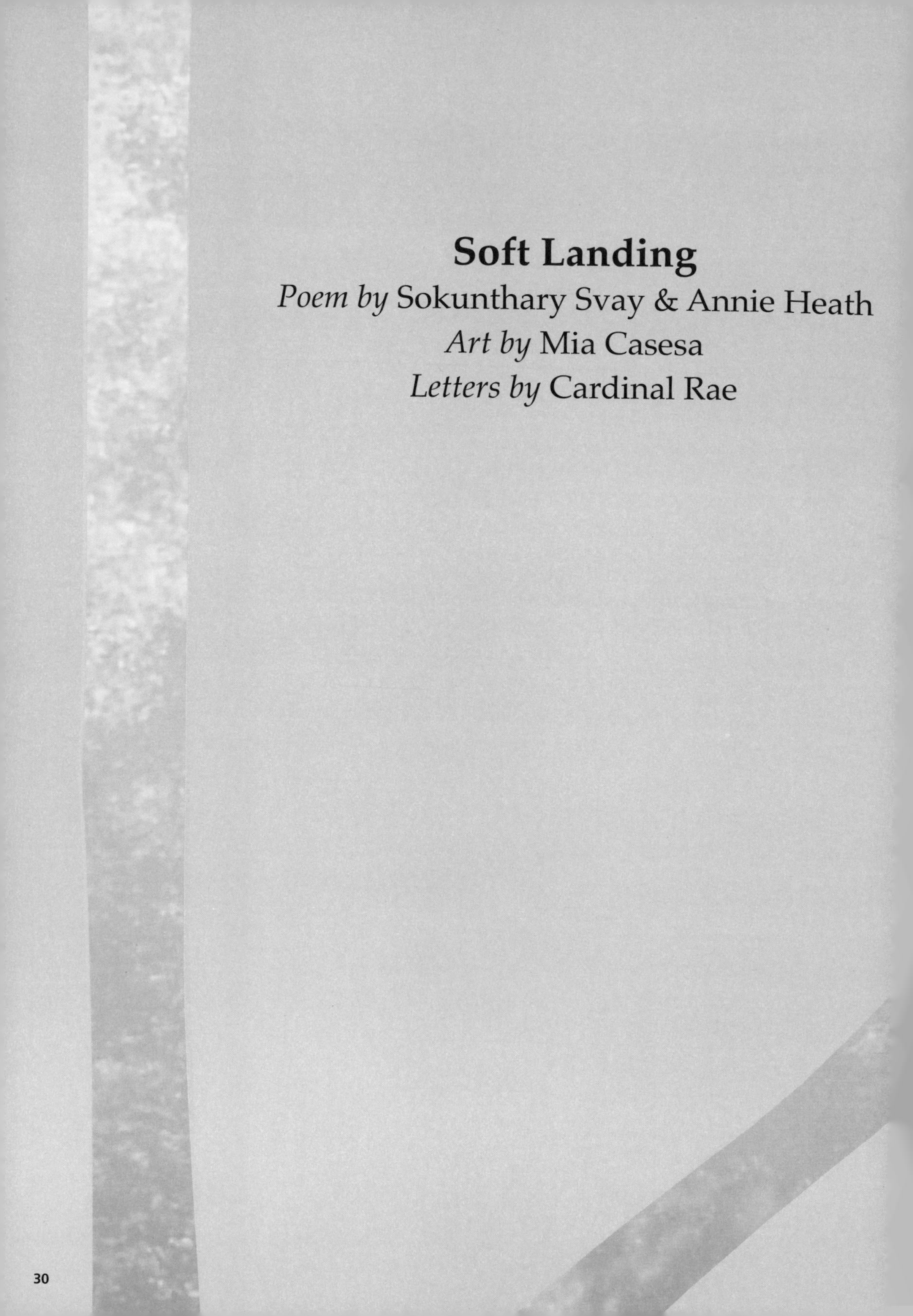

Soft Landing

Poem by Sokunthary Svay & Annie Heath

Art by Mia Casesa

Letters by Cardinal Rae

31

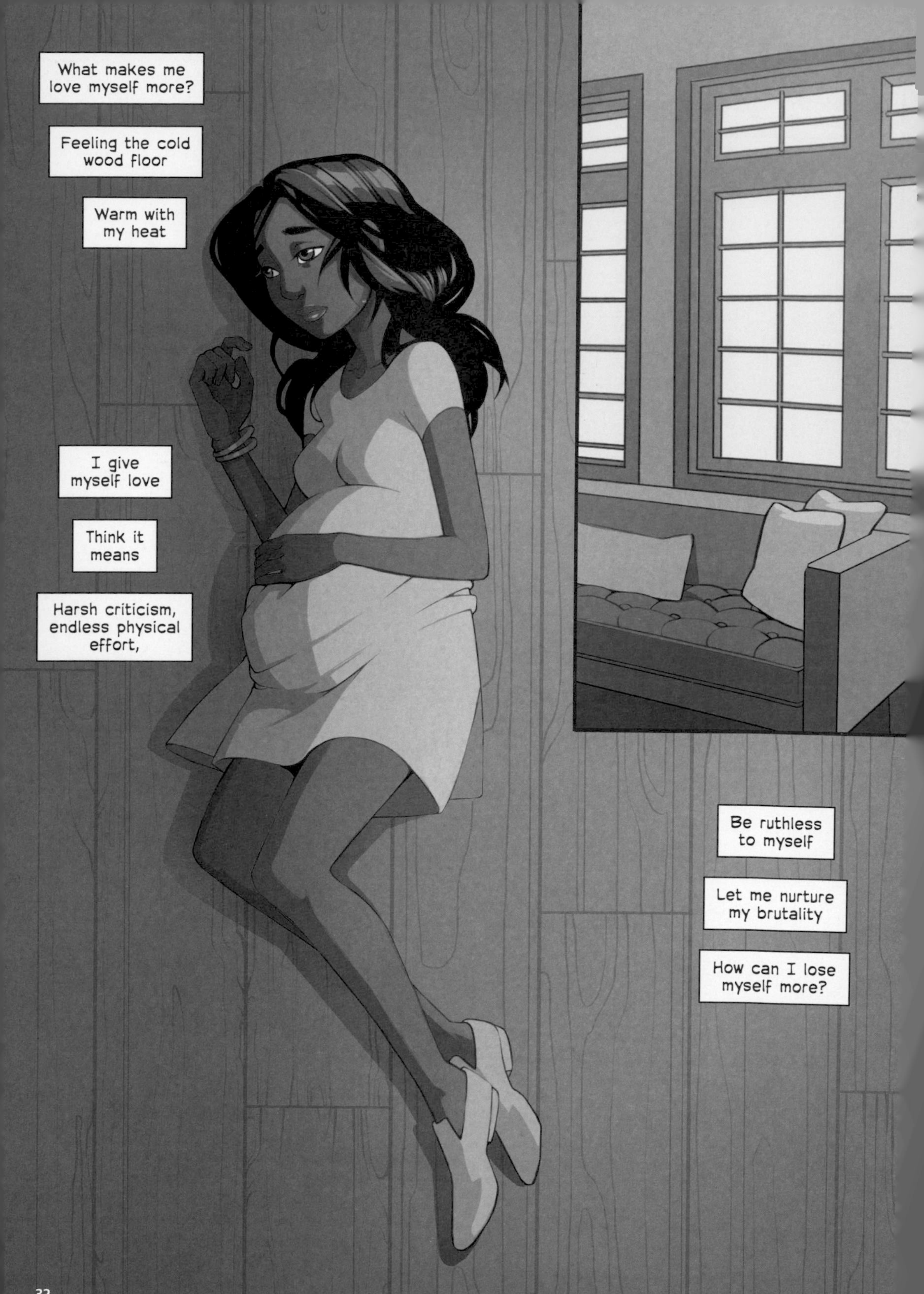
What makes me love myself more?
Feeling the cold wood floor
Warm with my heat
I give myself love
Think it means
Harsh criticism, endless physical effort,
Be ruthless to myself
Let me nurture my brutality
How can I lose myself more?

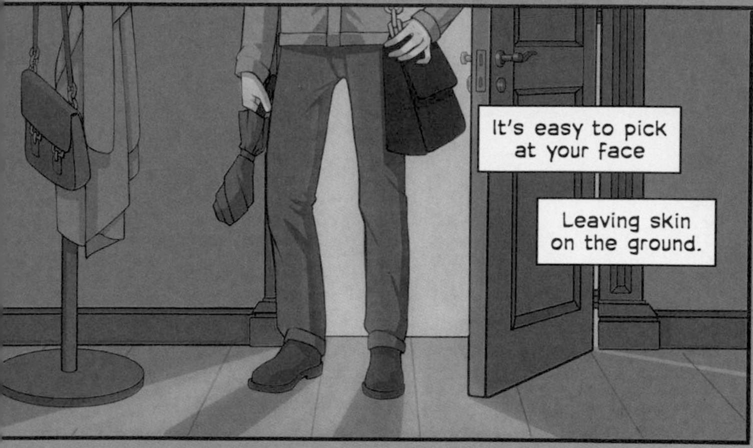
It's easy to pick at your face
Leaving skin on the ground.

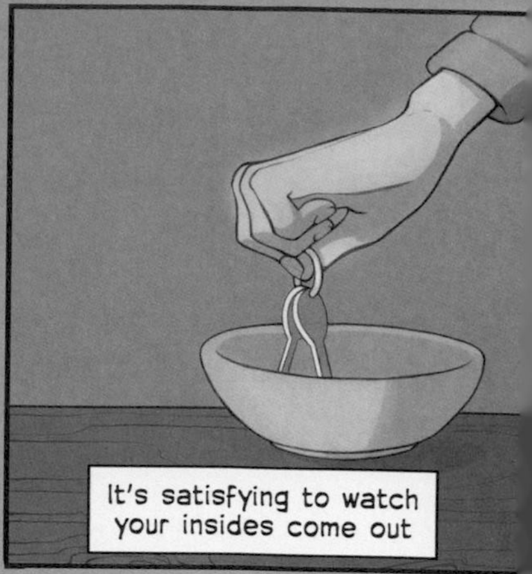
It's satisfying to watch your insides come out

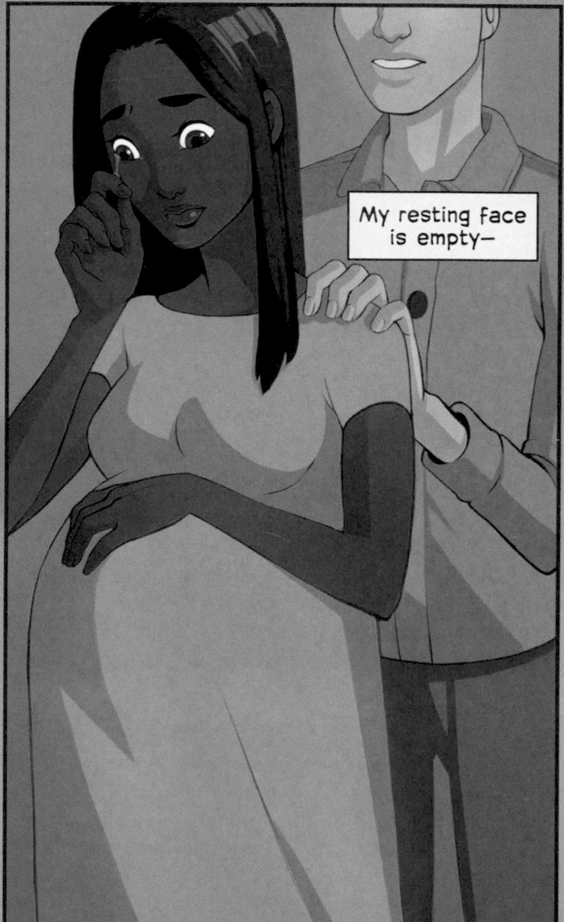
My resting face is empty—

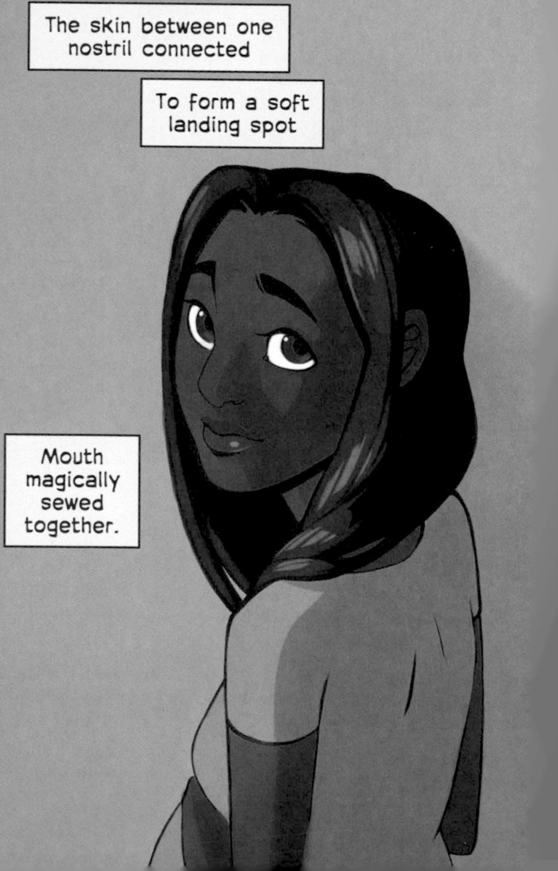
The skin between one nostril connected
To form a soft landing spot
Mouth magically sewed together.

Soft Landing
by Sokunthary Svay & Annie Heath

A belly expands and protrudes
Pushing out resting fabric
Trying to give more
I take in more air, so hoping to grasp

Beat myself into the ground
Into unforgiving cement

No amount of stretch can alleviate
Panic in open space

It's easy to pick at your face
Leaving skin on the ground.
It's satisfying to watch your insides come out

My resting face is empty

The skin between one nostril connected
To form a soft landing spot
Mouth magically sewed together.

**

What makes me love myself more?

Feeling the cold wood floor
Warm with my heat

I give myself love—
Think it means
Harsh criticism, endless physical effort,
Be ruthless to myself

Let me nurture my brutality

How can I lose myself more?

**

I wonder how people search
For something inaccessible
How to rip open a coarse wall
In the quiet black

Going back through an archived mind
Filled with shelves, empty pages
I wonder about capacity
That cavity that needs filling

**

Rubble Girl

Poem by Jenn Givhan
Art by Sara Woolley
Letters by Cardinal Rae

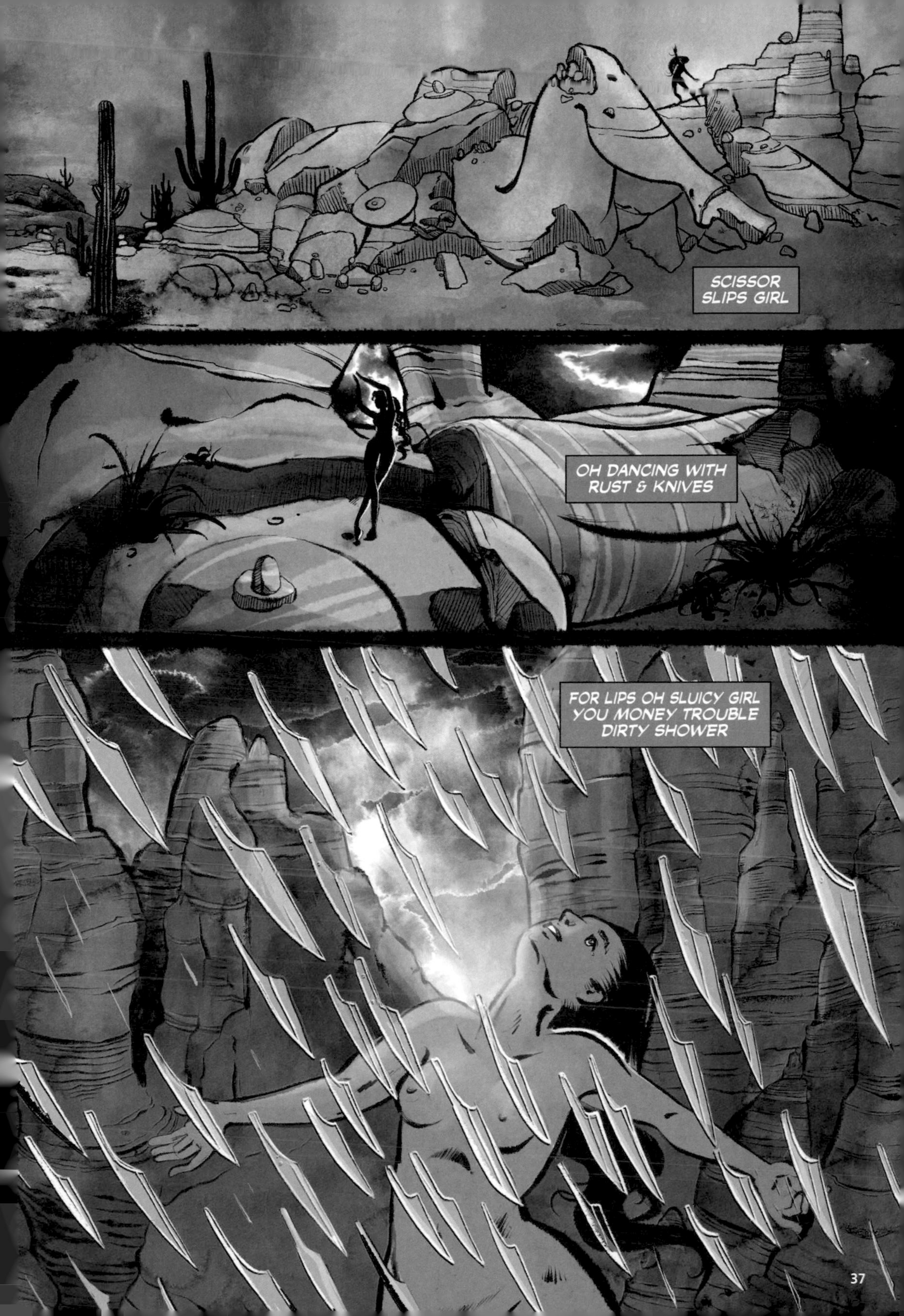
SCISSOR SLIPS GIRL
OH DANCING WITH RUST & KNIVES
FOR LIPS OH SLUICY GIRL YOU MONEY TROUBLE DIRTY SHOWER

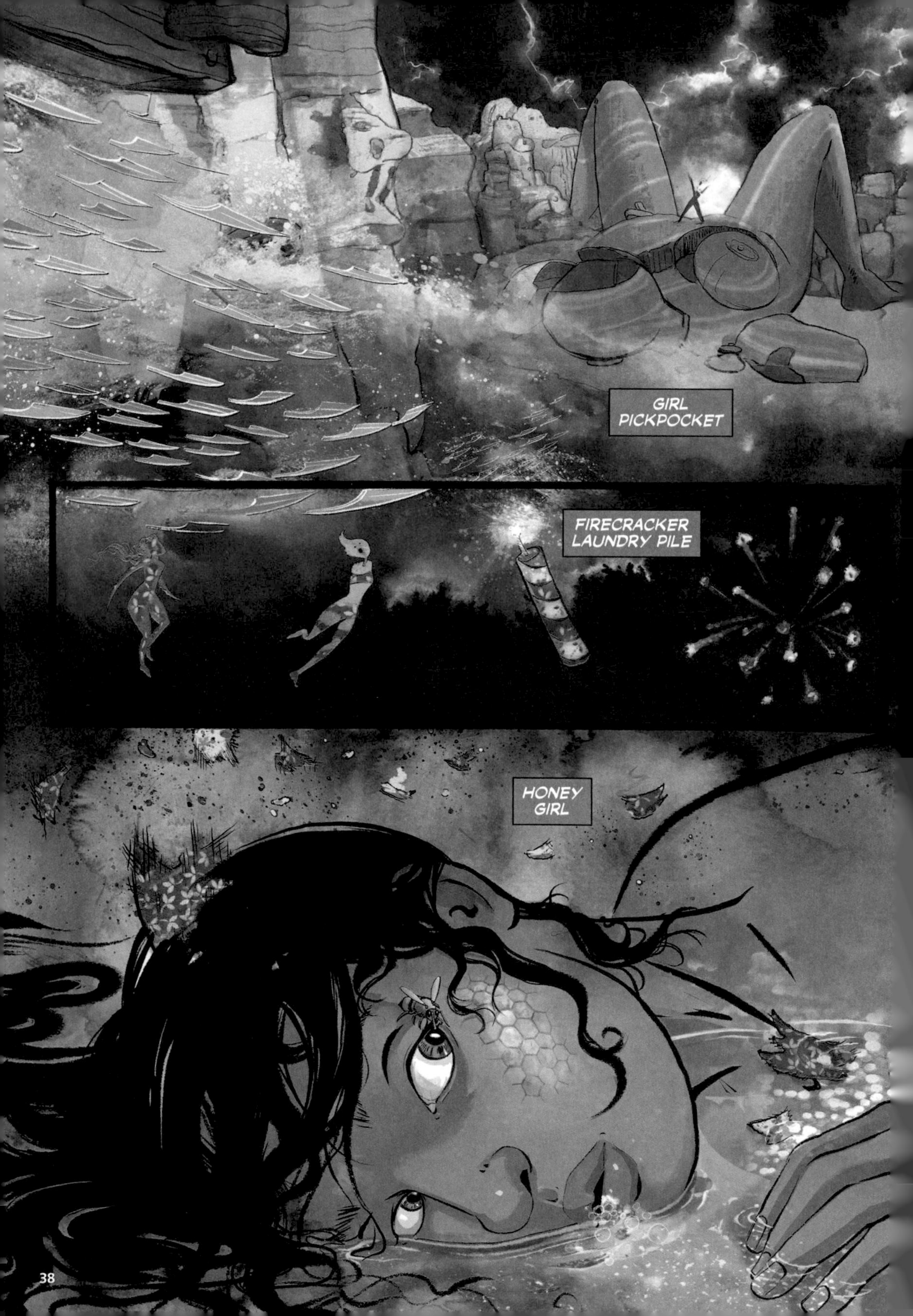
GIRL PICKPOCKET
FIRECRACKER LAUNDRY PILE
HONEY GIRL

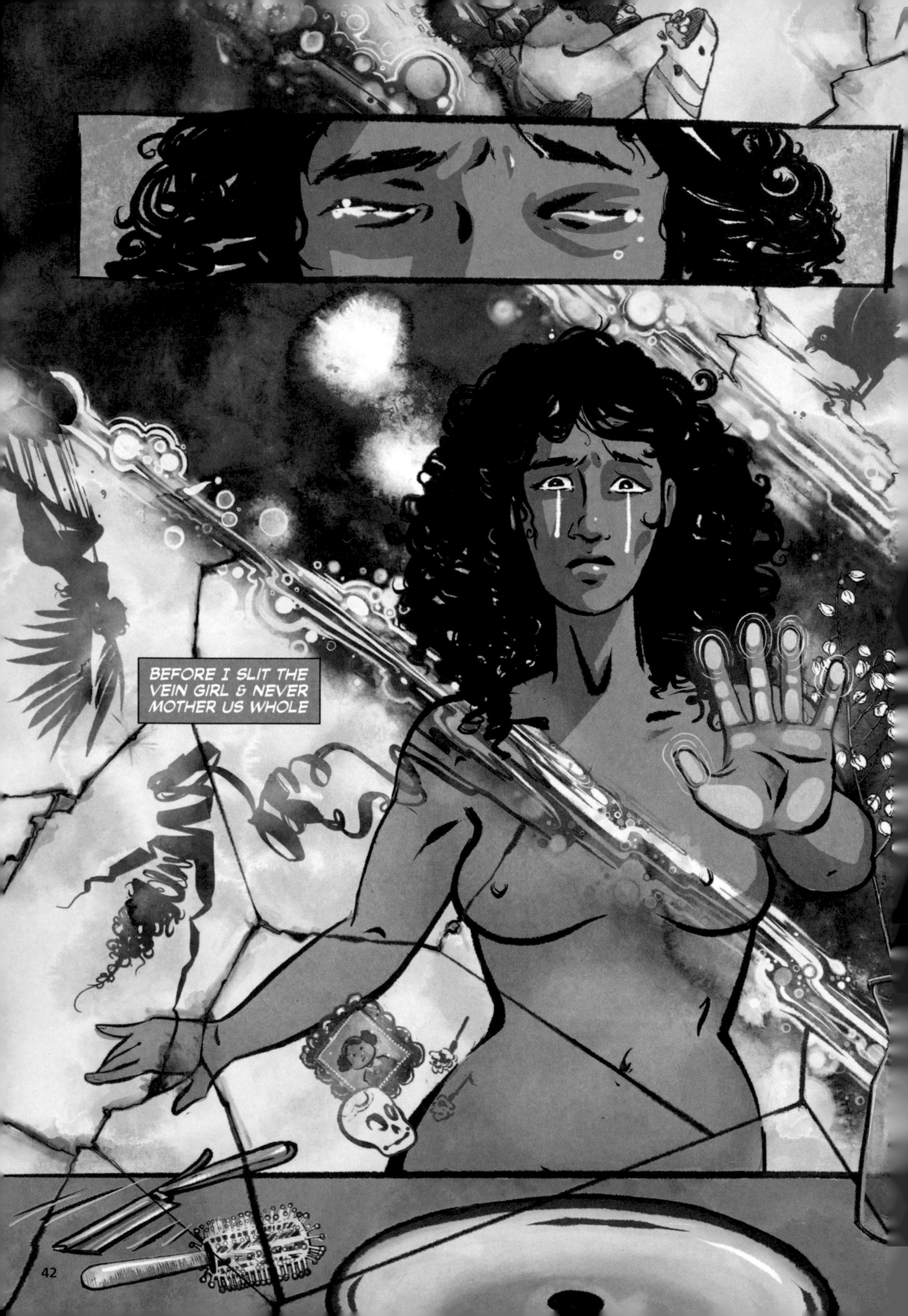
BEFORE I SLIT THE VEIN GIRL & NEVER MOTHER US WHOLE

Rubble Girl
by Jenn Givhan

Scissor slips girl oh dancing with rust & knives
for lips oh sluicy girl you money trouble dirty shower
girl pickpocket firecracker laundry pile honey girl

yucca-mouth girl cutting flowerheads & sewing candy skulls for
scrubbing memory's sugar girl tequila sick & toilet bowl again
girl hungry girl you unstitched razor girl

blade girl grubby necked & spitting girl or
swallowing headdown girl stomach pit
fine girl gumming to sidewalk catcalled girl escape girl

oh plucking bones from graves girl rising girl rising & rising
girl teach me again how to live that loose that tumble down girl
before I slit the vein girl & never mother us whole

Red Woman

Poem by Kenzie Allen
Art by Weshoyot Alvitre
Letters by Cardinal Rae

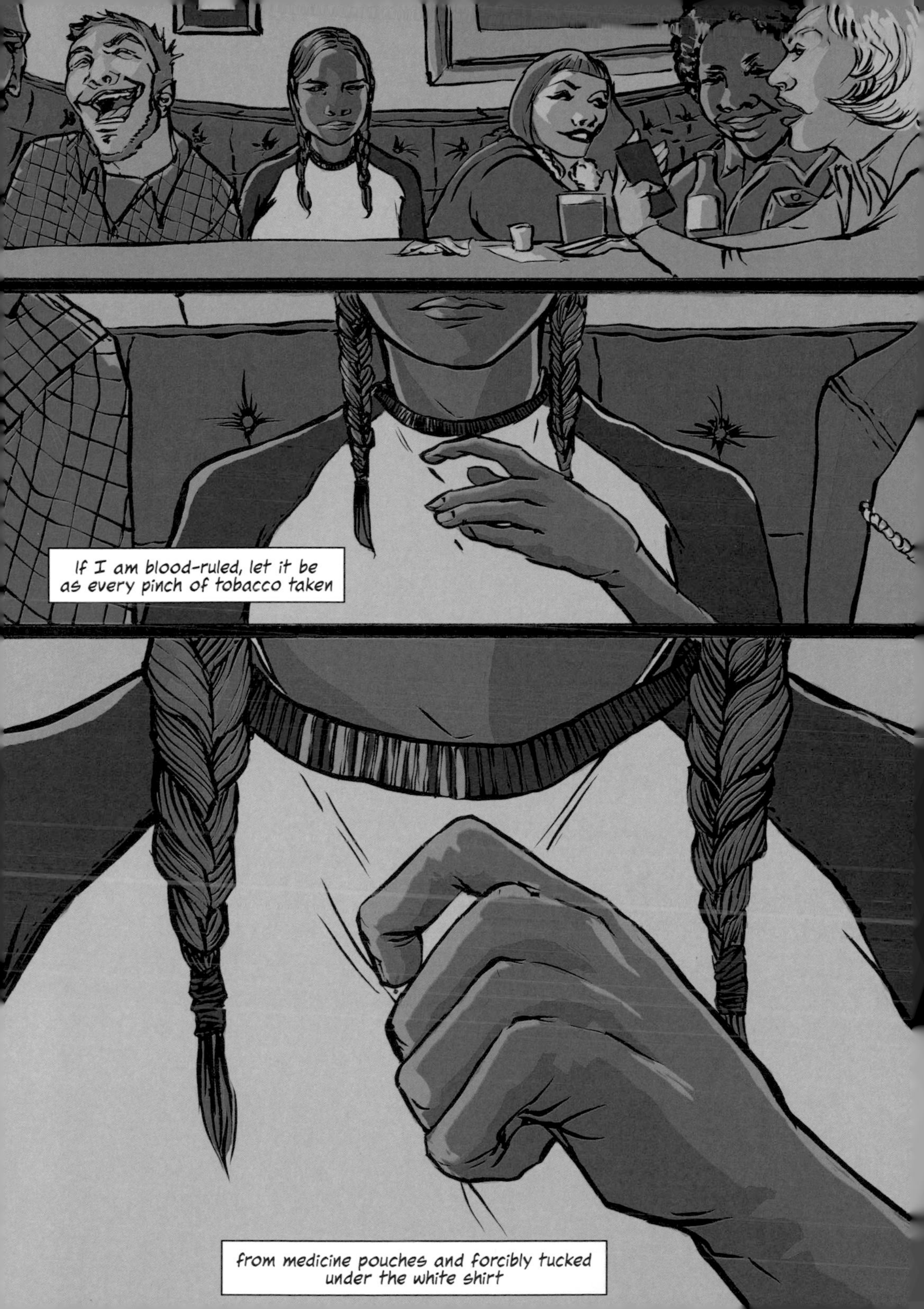
If I am blood-ruled, let it be
as every pinch of tobacco taken
from medicine pouches and forcibly tucked
under the white shirt

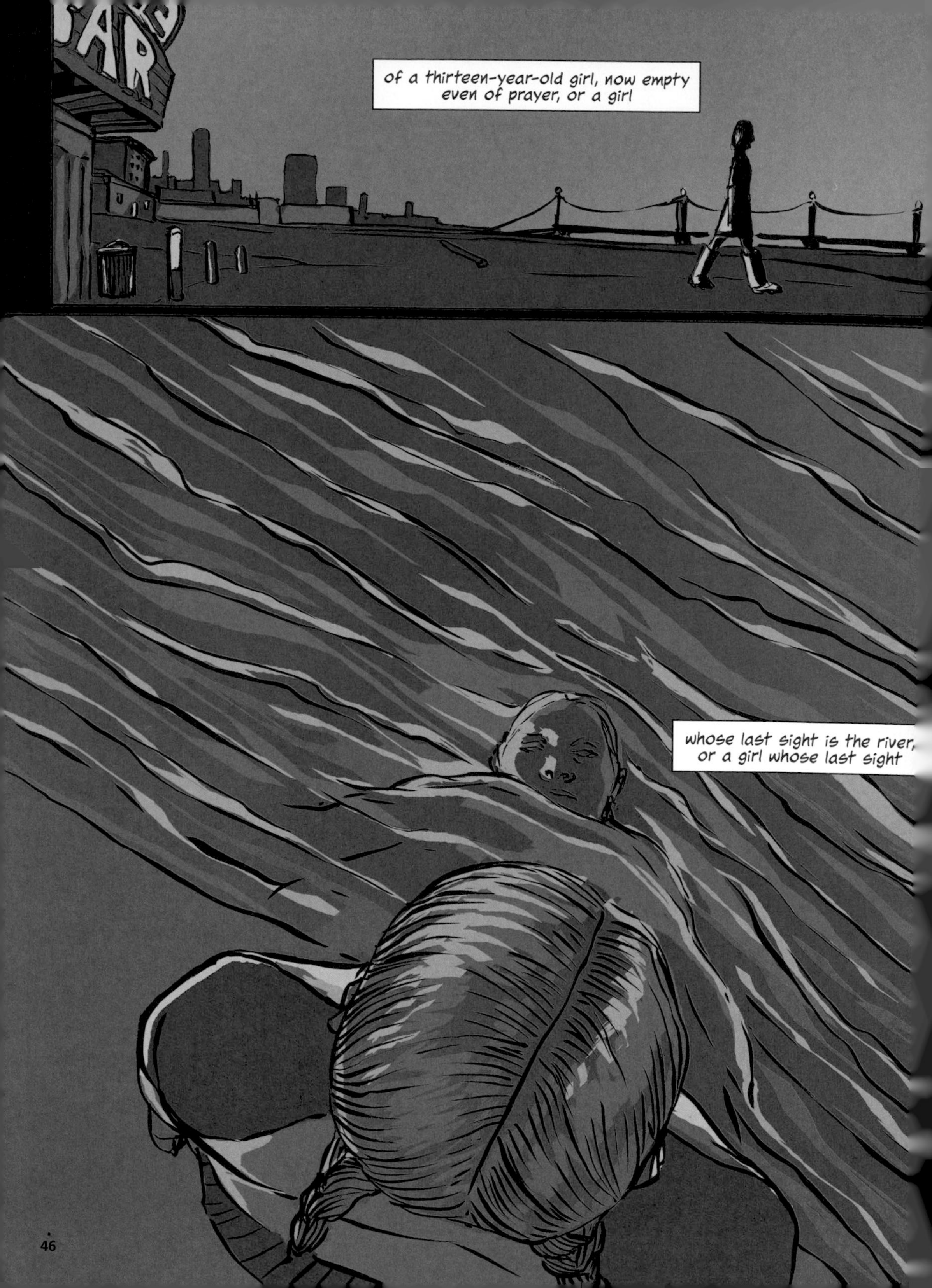

of a thirteen-year-old girl, now empty even of prayer, or a girl
whose last sight is the river, or a girl whose last sight

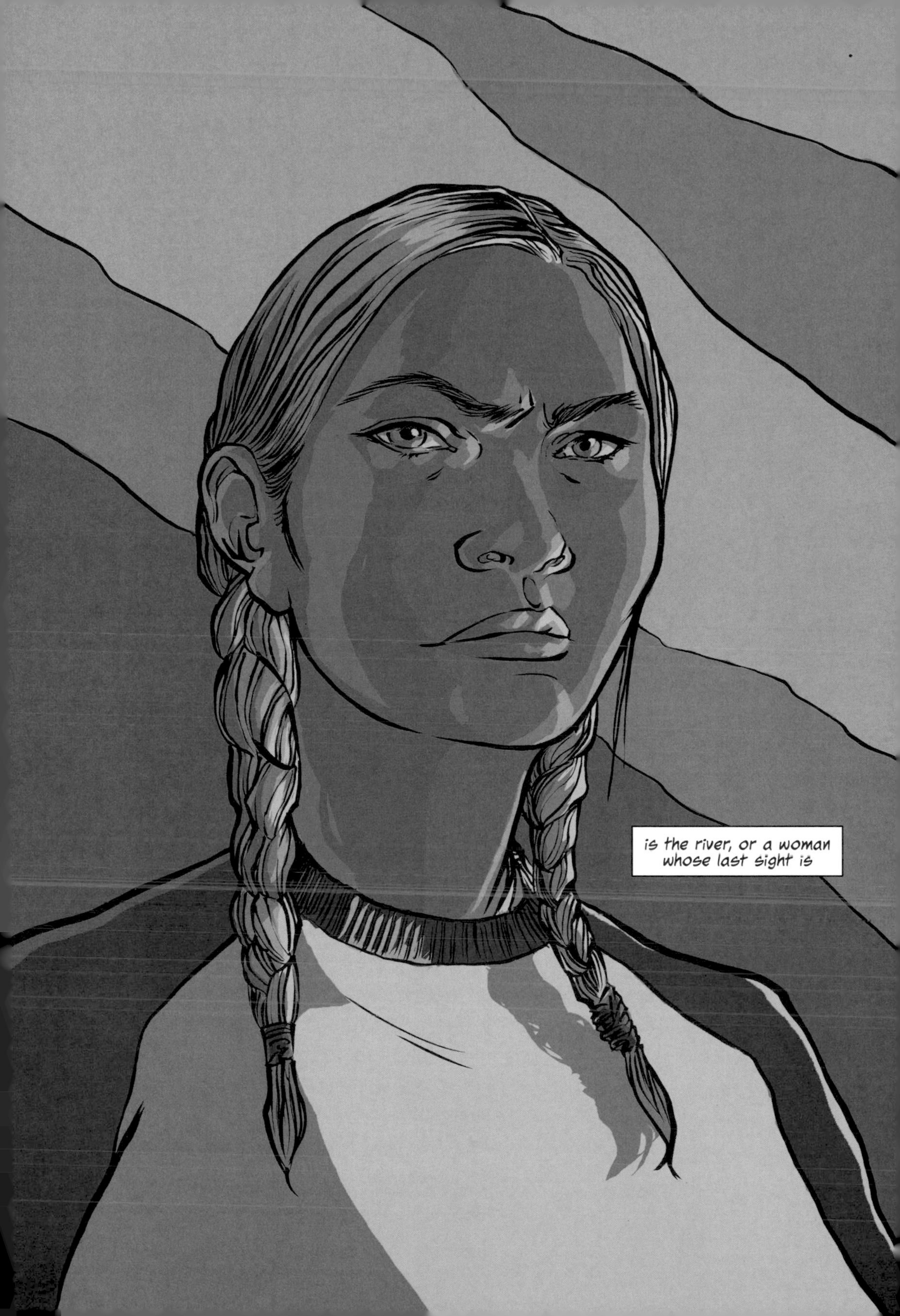
is the river, or a woman
whose last sight is

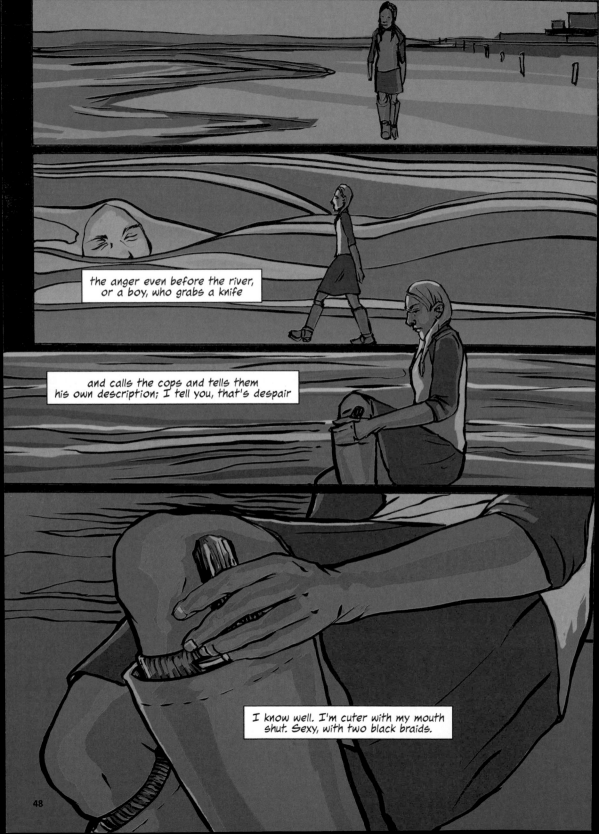

the anger even before the river,
or a boy, who grabs a knife

and calls the cops and tells them
his own description; I tell you, that's despair

I know well. I'm cuter with my mouth
shut. Sexy, with two black braids.

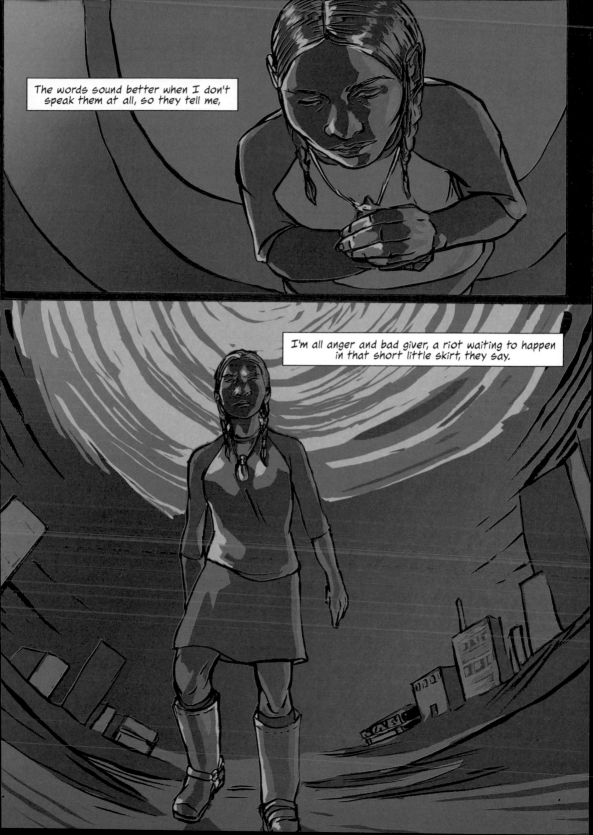

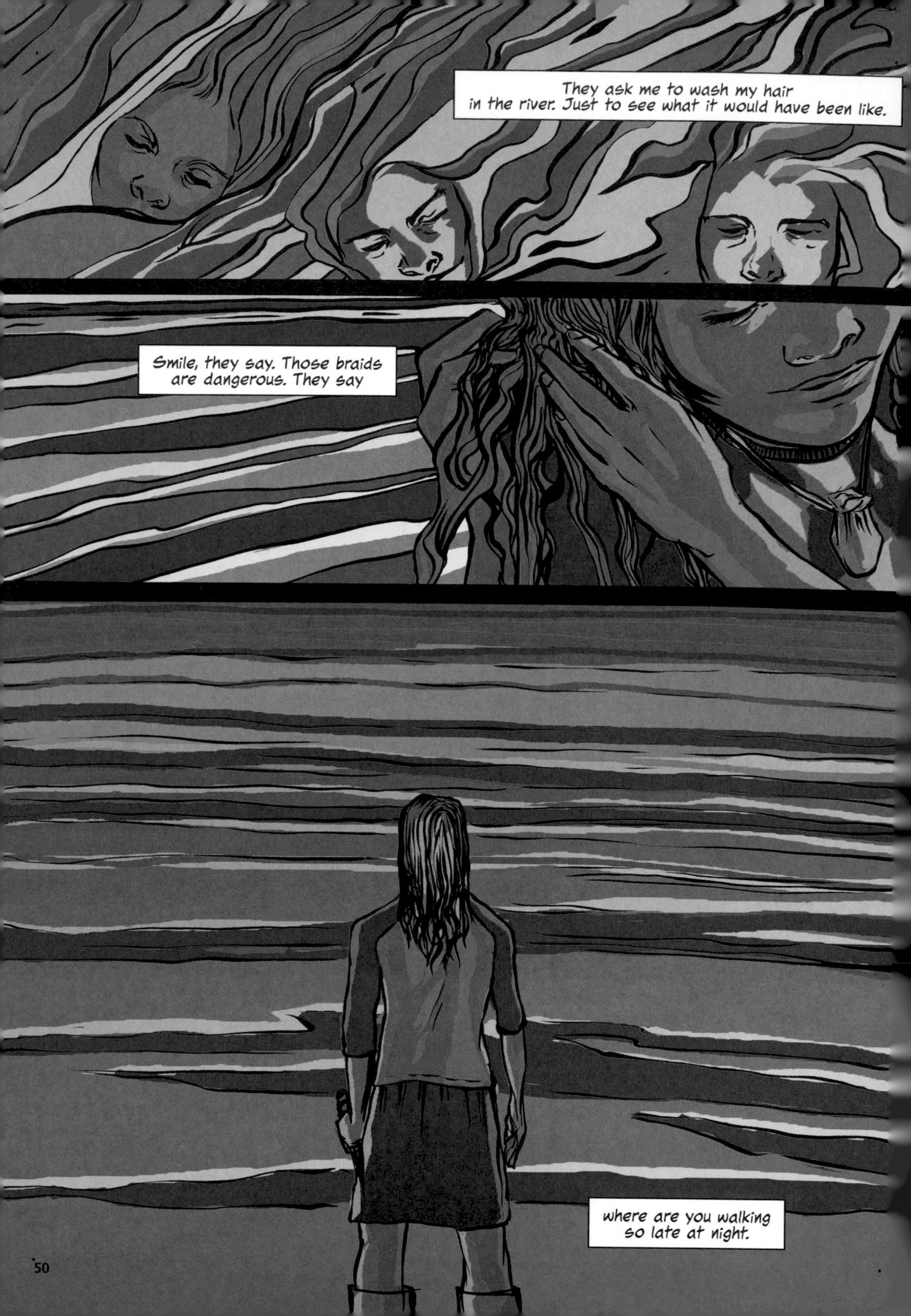
They ask me to wash my hair
in the river. Just to see what it would have been like.
Smile, they say. Those braids
are dangerous. They say
where are you walking
so late at night.

Red Woman
by Kenzie Allen

If I am blood-ruled, let it be
as every pinch of tobacco taken

from medicine pouches and forcibly tucked
under the white shirt

of a thirteen-year-old girl, now empty
even of prayer, or a girl

whose last sight is the river,
or a girl whose last sight

is the river, or a woman
whose last sight is

the anger even before the river,
or a boy, who grabs a knife

and calls the cops and tells them
his own description; I tell you, that's despair

I know well. I'm cuter with my mouth
shut. Sexy, with two black braids.

The words sound better when I don't
speak them at all, so they tell me,

I'm all anger and bad giver, a riot waiting to happen
in that short little skirt, they say.

They ask me to wash my hair
in the river. Just to see what it would have been like.

Smile, they say. Those braids are dangerous. They say
where are you walking so late at night.

Gender Studies

Poem by Caroline Hagood

Art by Stelladia

Letters by Cardinal Rae

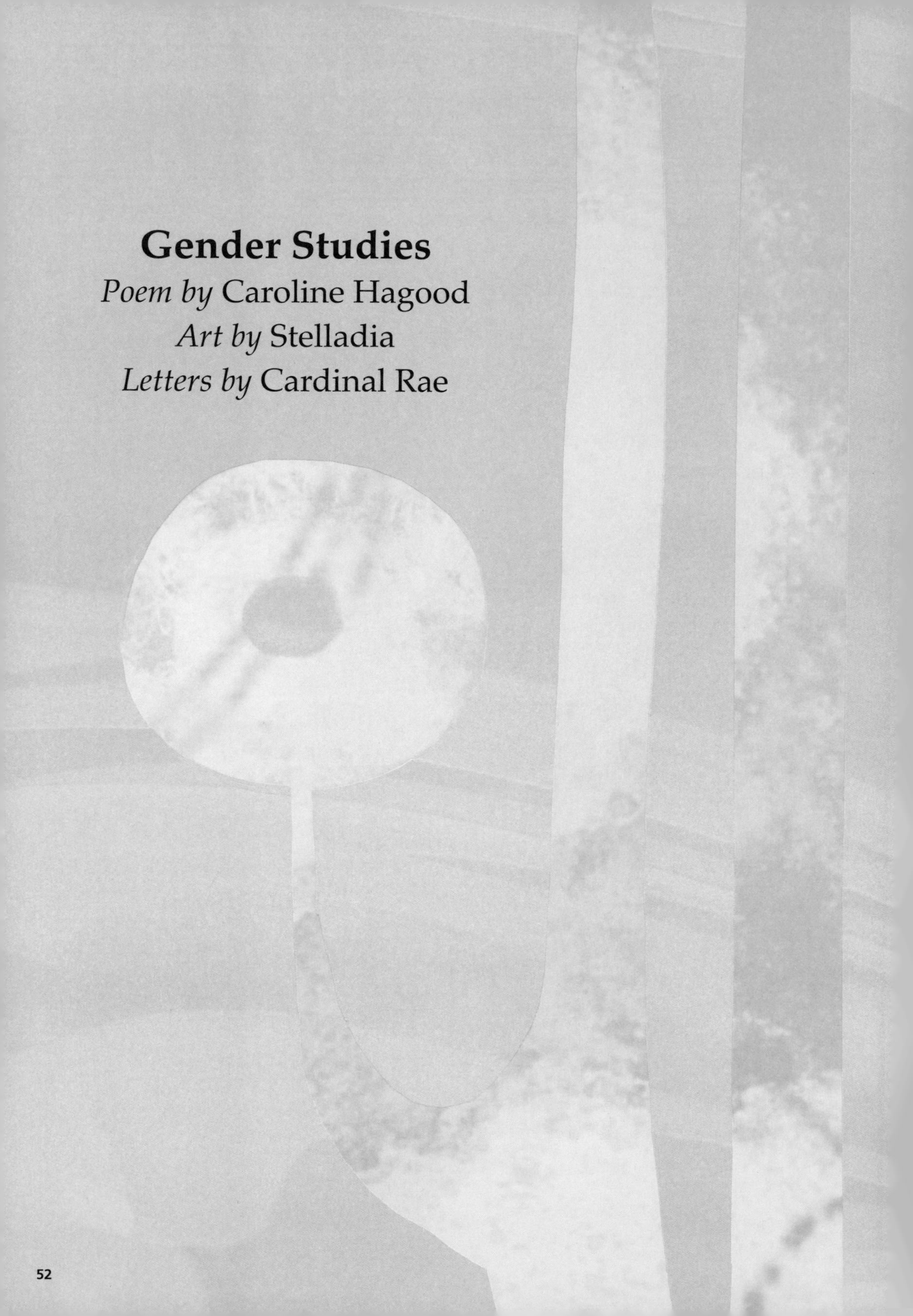

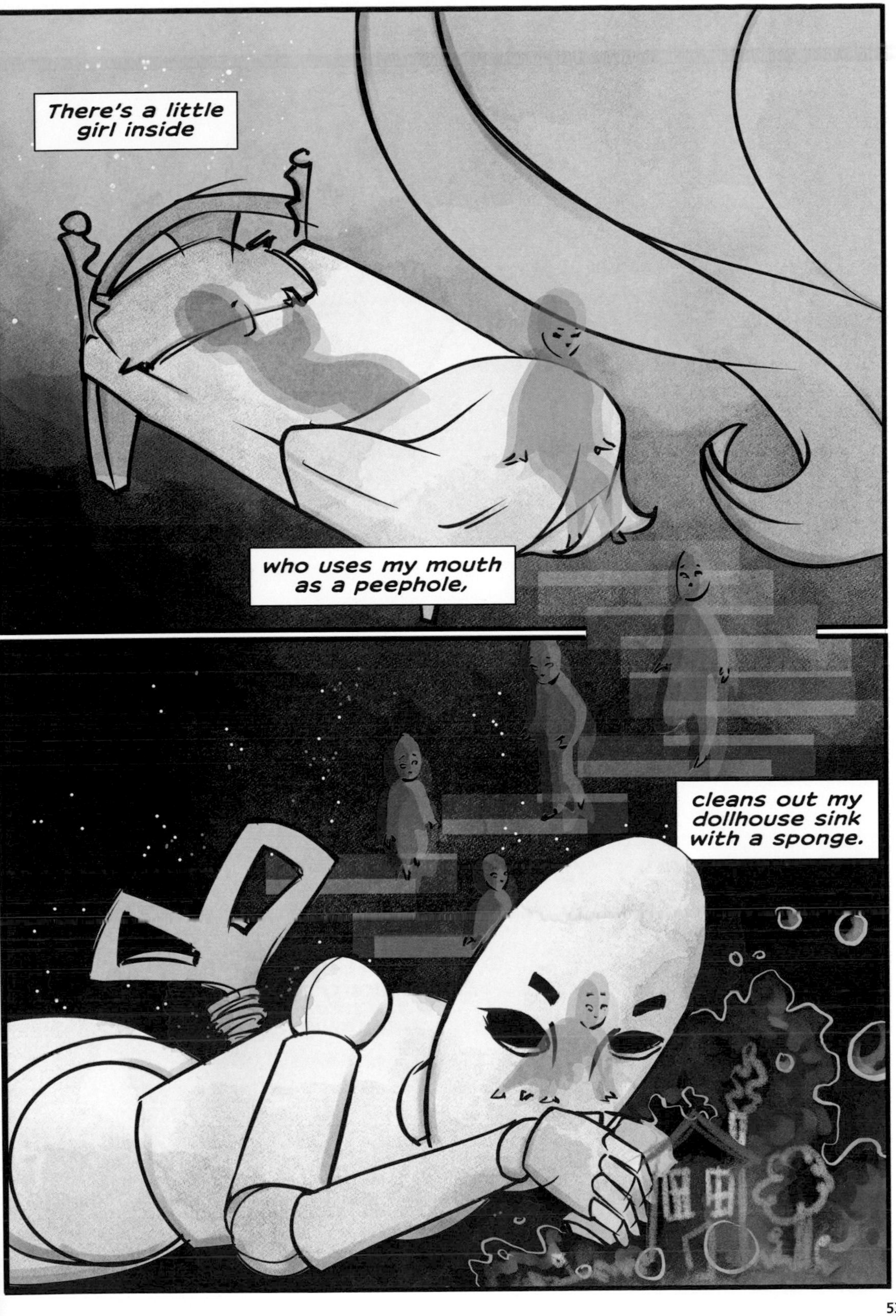
There's a little girl inside
who uses my mouth as a peephole,
cleans out my dollhouse sink with a sponge.

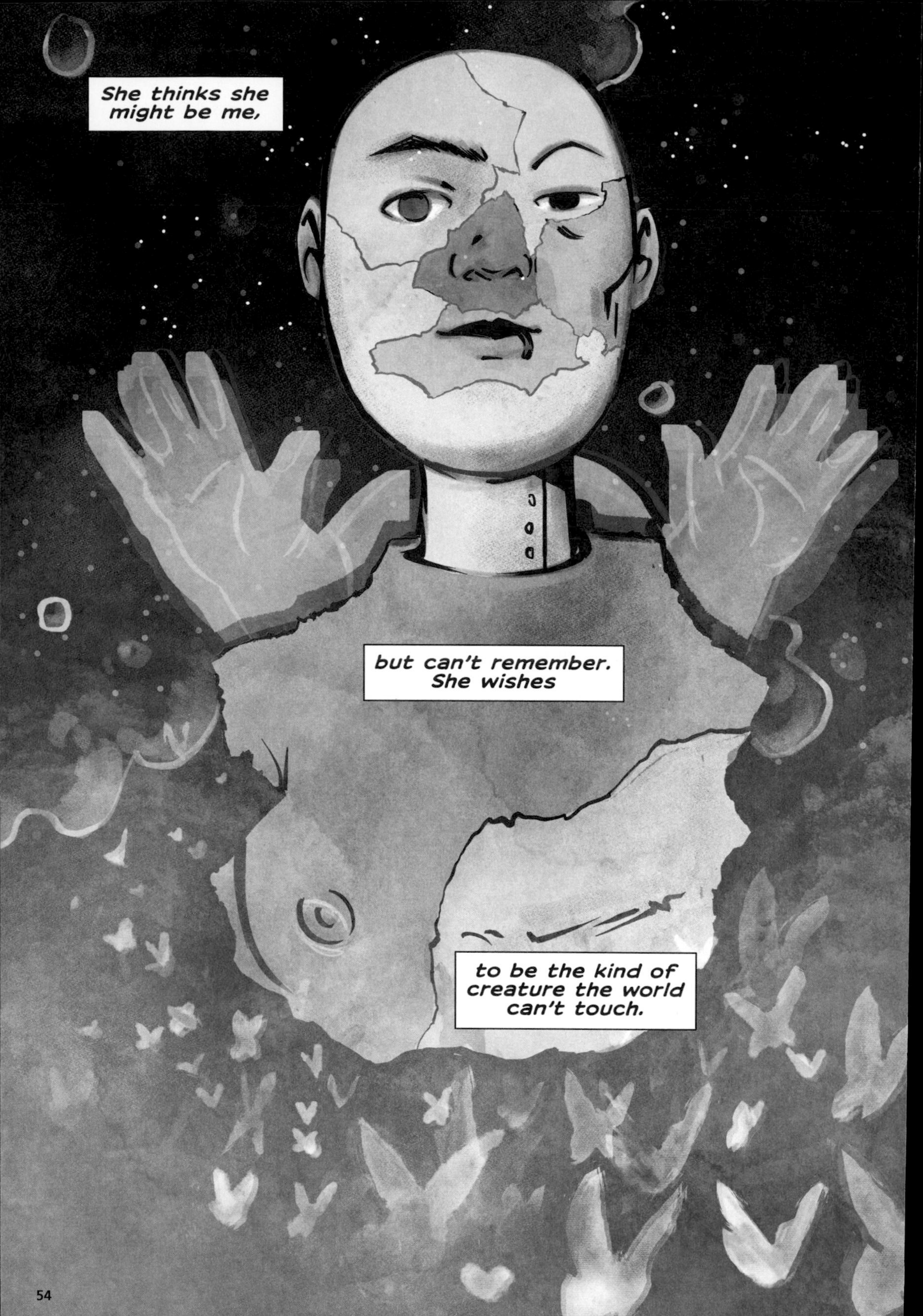
She thinks she might be me,
but can't remember. She wishes
to be the kind of creature the world can't touch.

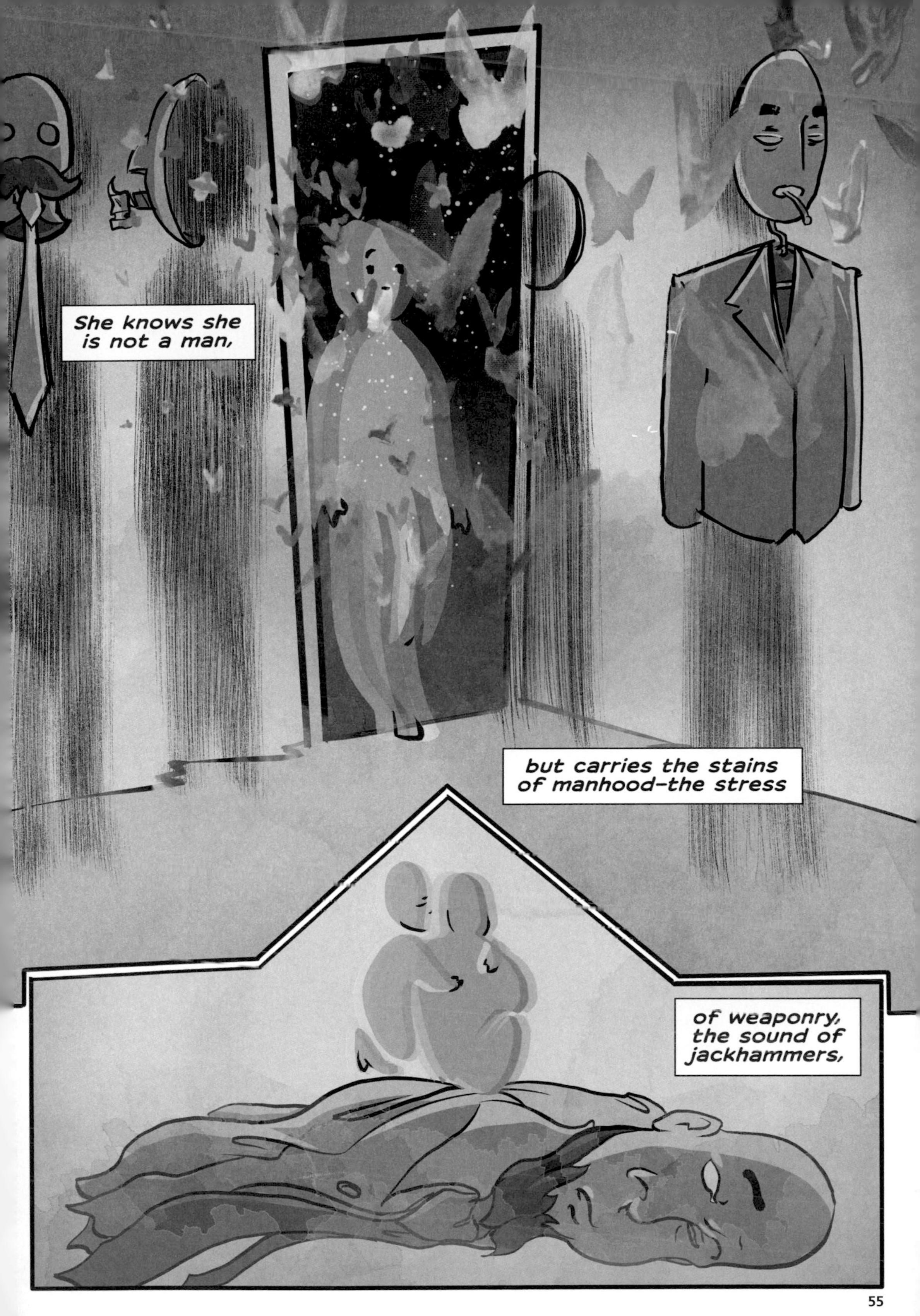
She knows she is not a man,
but carries the stains of manhood–the stress
of weaponry, the sound of jackhammers,

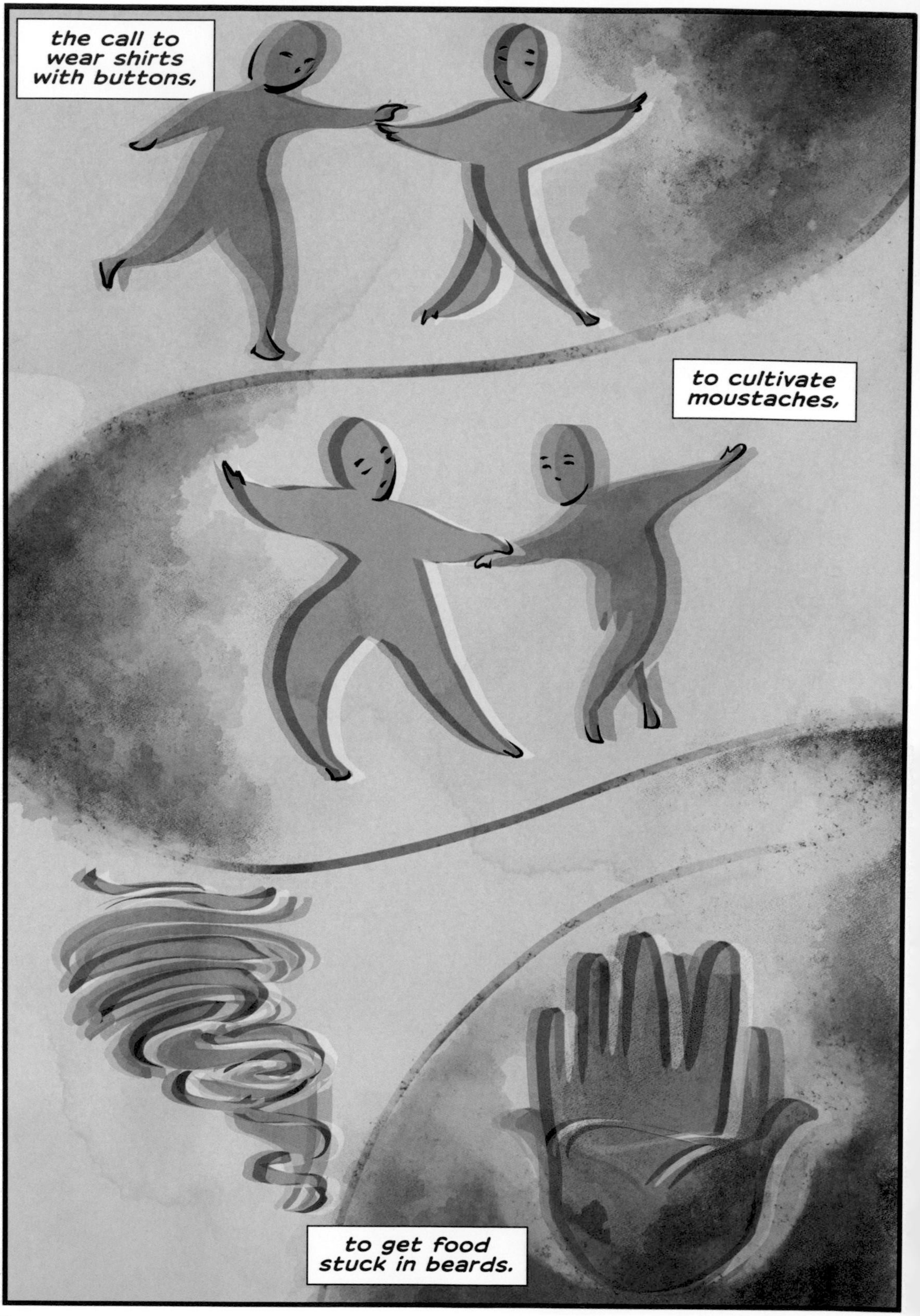
the call to wear shirts with buttons,
to cultivate moustaches,
to get food stuck in beards.

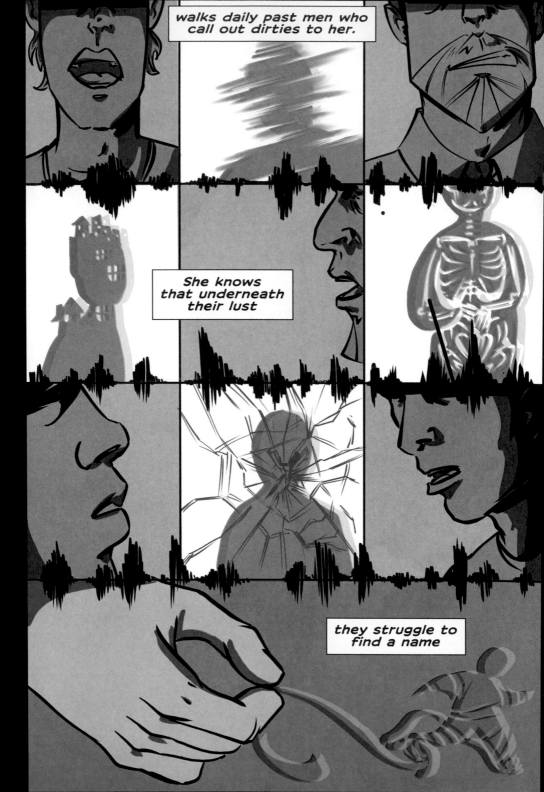

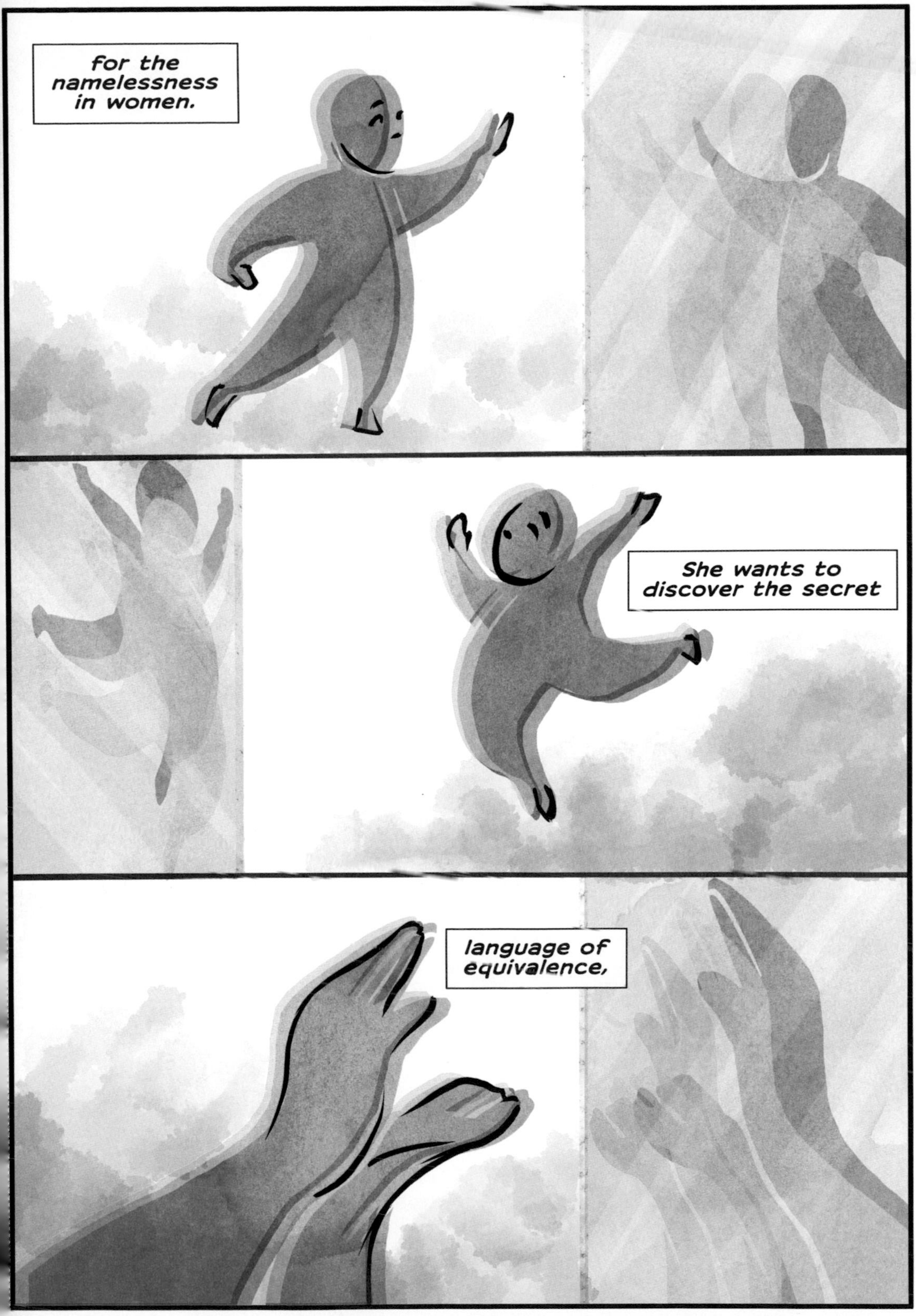
for the namelessness in women.
She wants to discover the secret
language of equivalence,

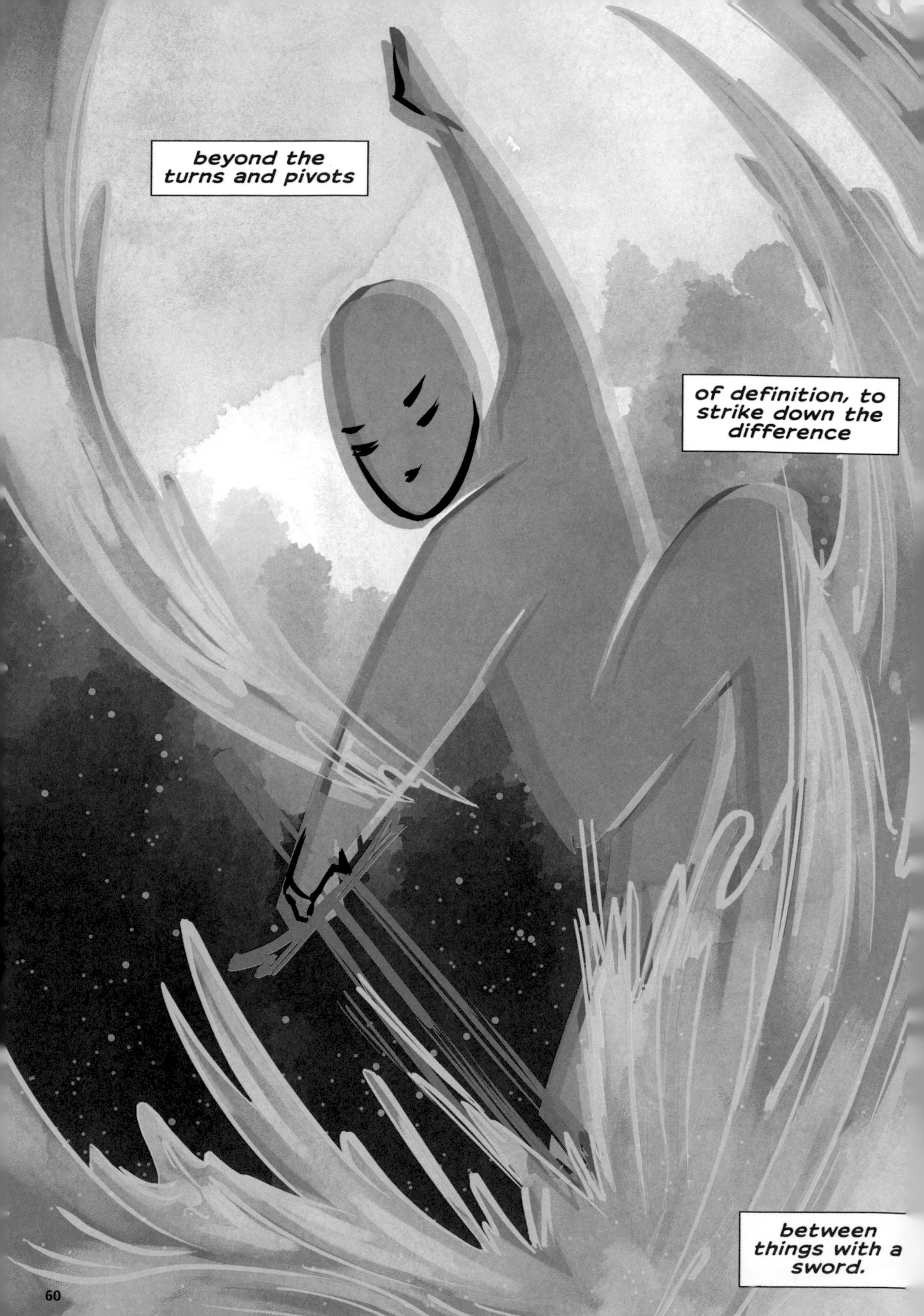
beyond the turns and pivots
of definition, to strike down the difference
between things with a sword.

Gender Studies
by Caroline Hagood

There's a little girl inside
who uses my mouth as a peephole,
cleans out my dollhouse sink with a sponge.

She thinks she might be me,
but can't remember. She wishes
to be the kind of creature the world can't touch.

She knows she is not a man,
but carries the stains of manhood—the stress
of weaponry, the sound of jackhammers,

the call to wear shirts with buttons,
to cultivate moustaches,
to get food stuck in beards.

Who is she if not a man?
She doesn't know, but sketches
pre-language possibilities on her thighs,

walks daily past men who call out dirties to her.
She knows that underneath their lust
they struggle to find a name

for the namelessness in women.
She wants to discover the secret
language of equivalence,

beyond the turns and pivots
of definition, to strike down the difference
between things with a sword.

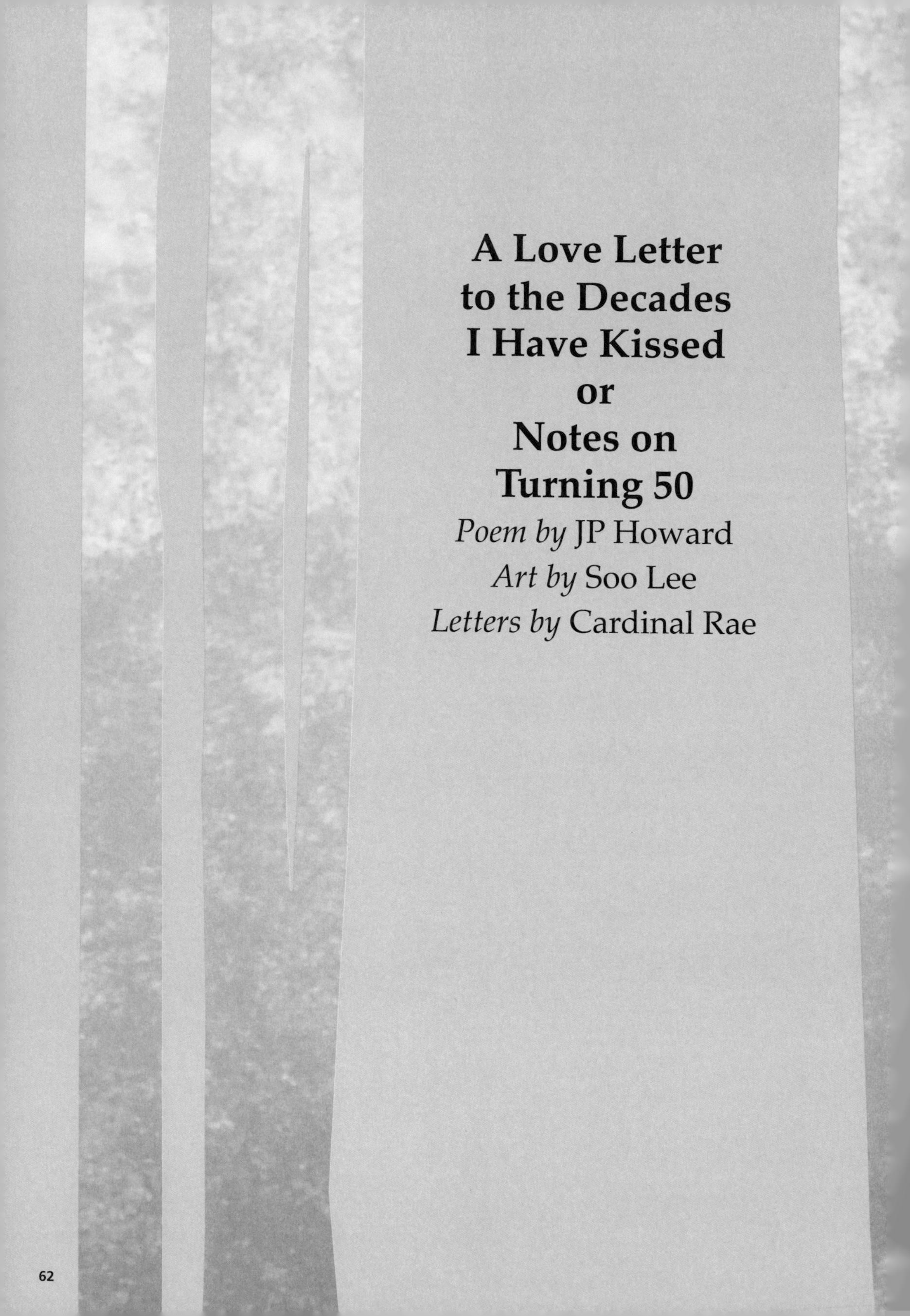

A Love Letter to the Decades I Have Kissed or Notes on Turning 50

Poem by JP Howard

Art by Soo Lee

Letters by Cardinal Rae

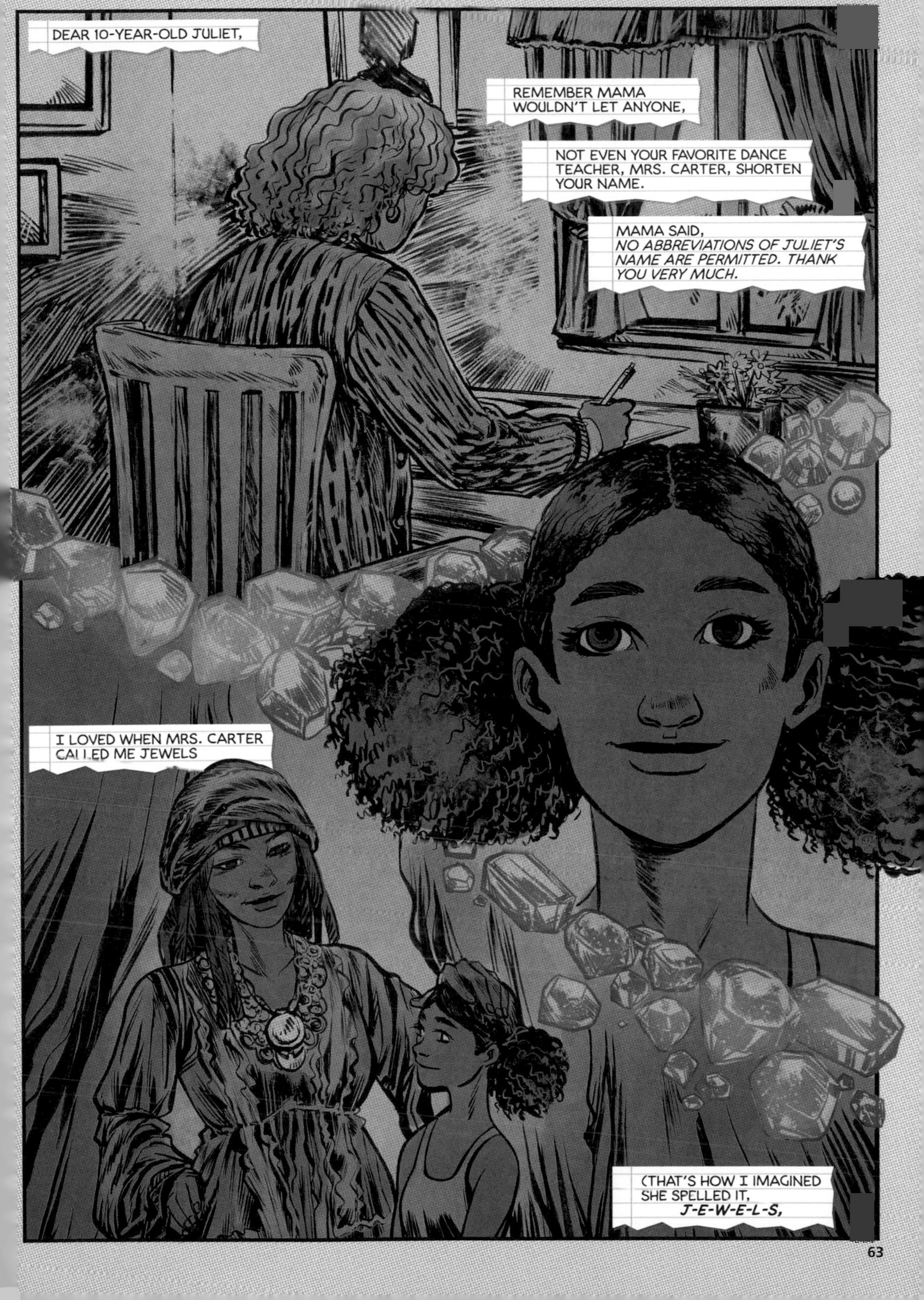
DEAR 10-YEAR-OLD JULIET,
REMEMBER MAMA WOULDN'T LET ANYONE,
NOT EVEN YOUR FAVORITE DANCE TEACHER, MRS. CARTER, SHORTEN YOUR NAME.
MAMA SAID, *NO ABBREVIATIONS OF JULIET'S NAME ARE PERMITTED. THANK YOU VERY MUCH.*
I LOVED WHEN MRS. CARTER CALLED ME JEWELS
(THAT'S HOW I IMAGINED SHE SPELLED IT, ***J-E-W-E-L-S,***

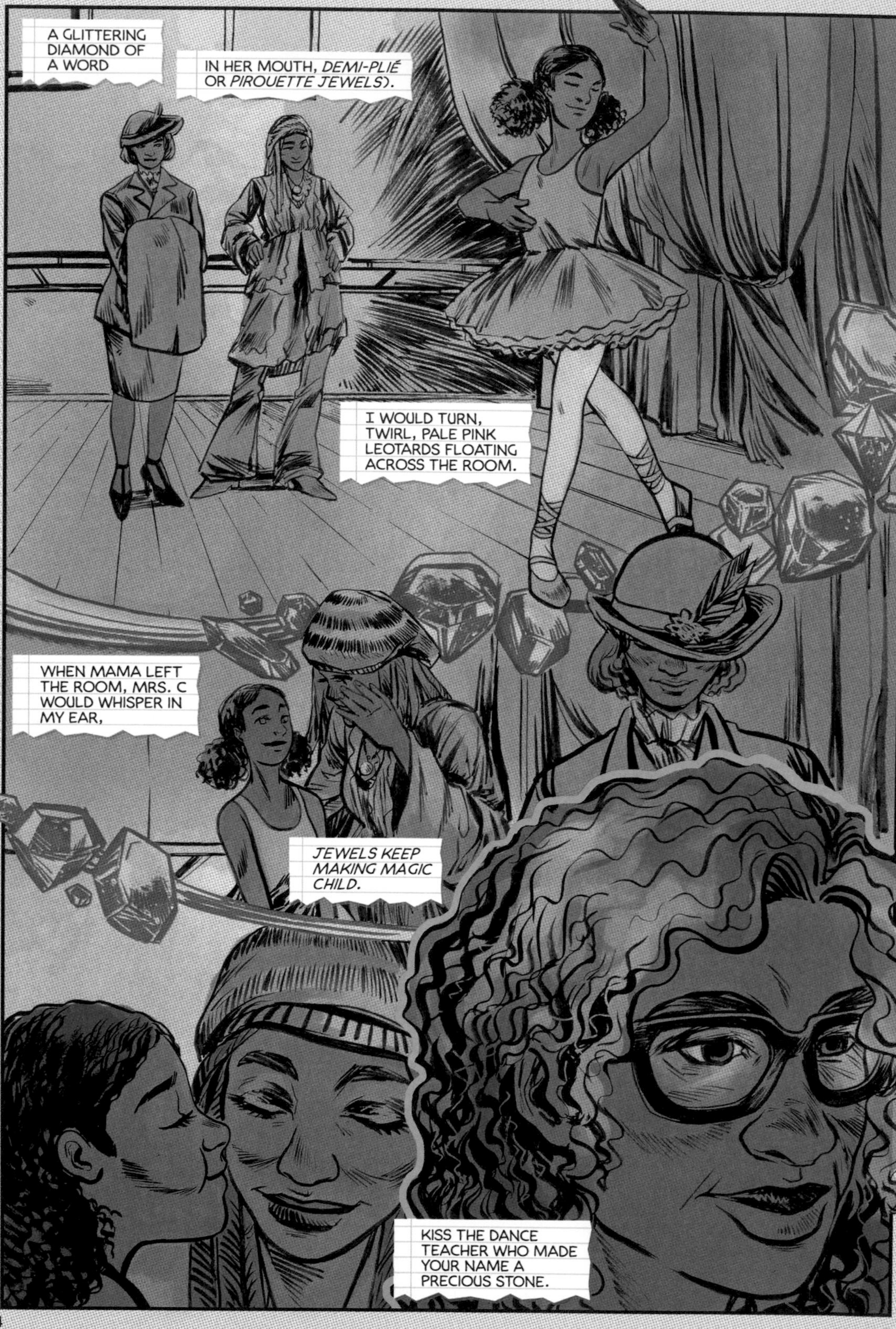
A GLITTERING DIAMOND OF A WORD
IN HER MOUTH, *DEMI-PLIÉ* OR *PIROUETTE JEWELS*).
I WOULD TURN, TWIRL, PALE PINK LEOTARDS FLOATING ACROSS THE ROOM.
WHEN MAMA LEFT THE ROOM, MRS. C WOULD WHISPER IN MY EAR,
JEWELS KEEP MAKING MAGIC CHILD.
KISS THE DANCE TEACHER WHO MADE YOUR NAME A PRECIOUS STONE.

A Love Letter to The Decades I Have Kissed or Notes on Turning 50 (excerpt)
by JP Howard

Dear 10-year-old Juliet,
remember Mama wouldn't let anyone,
not even your favorite dance teacher, Mrs. Carter, shorten your name.
Mama said, *No abbreviations of Juliet's name are permitted. Thank you very much.*
I loved when Mrs. Carter called me *Jewels*
(that's how I imagined she spelled it, J-E-W-E-L-S,
a glittering diamond of a word
in her mouth, *Demi-plié or pirouette Jewels*).
I would turn, twirl, pale pink leotards floating across the room.
When Mama left the room, Mrs. C would whisper in MY ear,
Jewels keep making magic child.
Kiss the dance teacher who made your name a precious stone.

Units & Increments

Poem by Shira Dentz
Art by Jessica Lynn
Colors by Kelly Fitzpatrick
Letters by Saida Temofonte

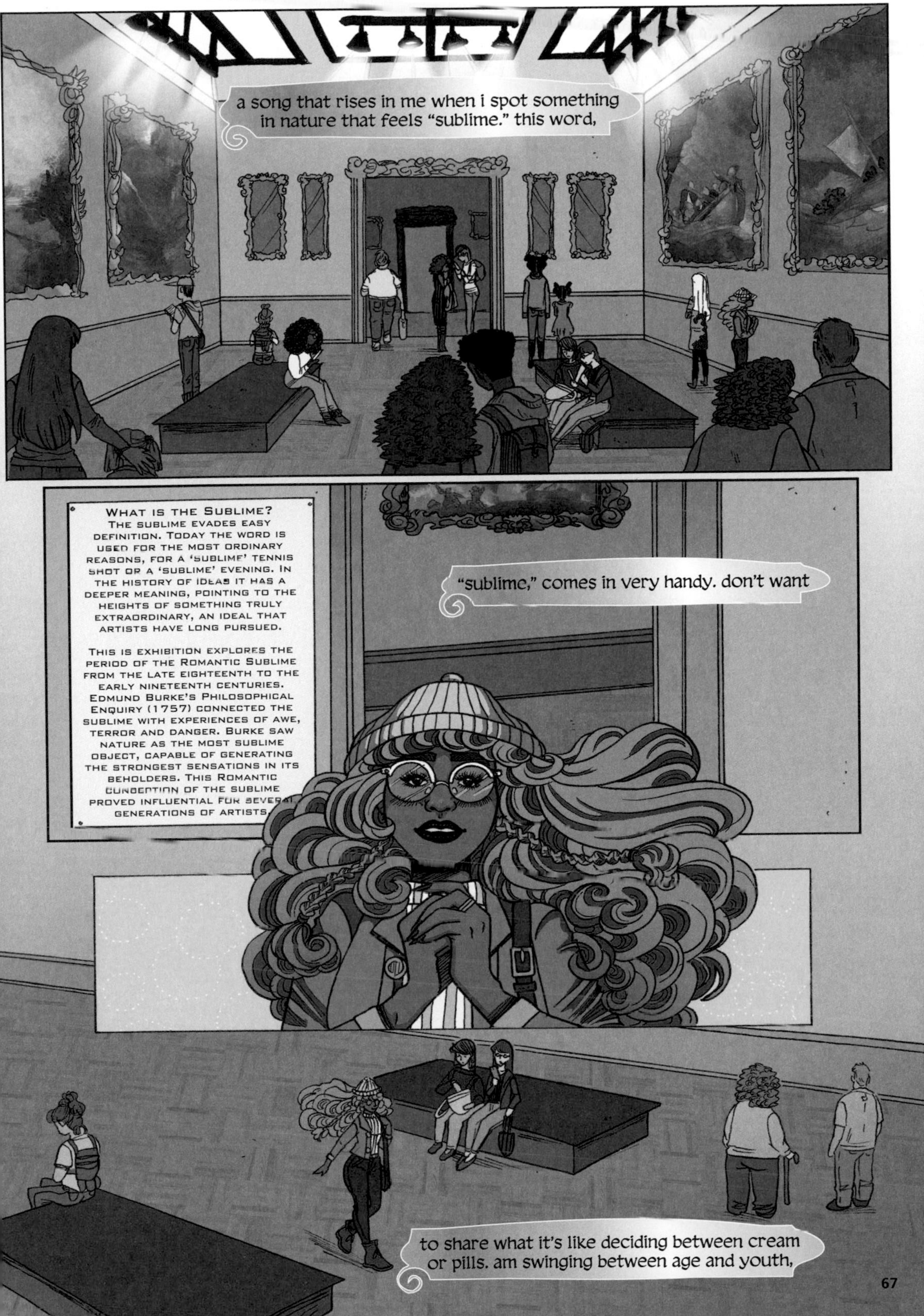
a song that rises in me when i spot something in nature that feels "sublime." this word,
WHAT IS THE SUBLIME?
THE SUBLIME EVADES EASY DEFINITION. TODAY THE WORD IS USED FOR THE MOST ORDINARY REASONS, FOR A 'SUBLIME' TENNIS SHOT OR A 'SUBLIME' EVENING. IN THE HISTORY OF IDEAS IT HAS A DEEPER MEANING, POINTING TO THE HEIGHTS OF SOMETHING TRULY EXTRAORDINARY, AN IDEAL THAT ARTISTS HAVE LONG PURSUED.
THIS IS EXHIBITION EXPLORES THE PERIOD OF THE ROMANTIC SUBLIME FROM THE LATE EIGHTEENTH TO THE EARLY NINETEENTH CENTURIES. EDMUND BURKE'S PHILOSOPHICAL ENQUIRY (1757) CONNECTED THE SUBLIME WITH EXPERIENCES OF AWE, TERROR AND DANGER. BURKE SAW NATURE AS THE MOST SUBLIME OBJECT, CAPABLE OF GENERATING THE STRONGEST SENSATIONS IN ITS BEHOLDERS. THIS ROMANTIC CONCEPTION OF THE SUBLIME PROVED INFLUENTIAL FOR SEVERAL GENERATIONS OF ARTISTS.
"sublime," comes in very handy. don't want
to share what it's like deciding between cream or pills. am swinging between age and youth,

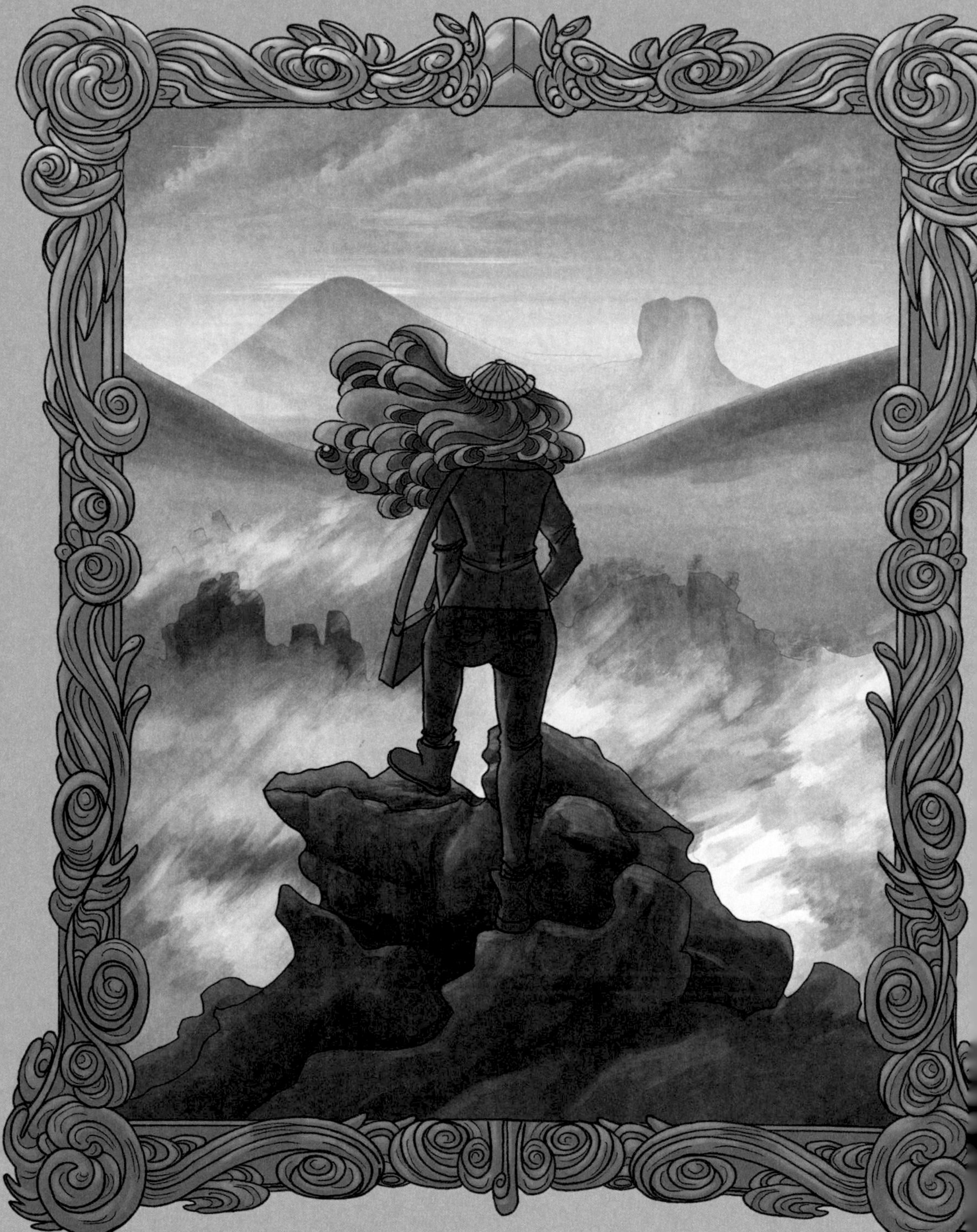

have to be able to imagine coming true to still

imagine it?

Units & Increments
(excerpt)
by Shira Dentz

1
a song that rises in me when i spot something
in nature that feels "sublime." this word,
"sublime," comes in very handy. don't want
to share what it's like deciding between cream
or pills. am swinging between age and youth,
trying to find a way to keep the blur rushing
towards me green and impressionistic. trying
to not lose "it." not ready to be encased like
an iridiscent gray branch. losing your period
is like losing someone to a freak accident.
one didn't know all the fantasies that one
can't have—how much of a fantasy do you
have to be able to imagine coming true to still
imagine it?

X

Poem by Khadijah Queen
Art by Ashley Woods
Letters by Cardinal Rae

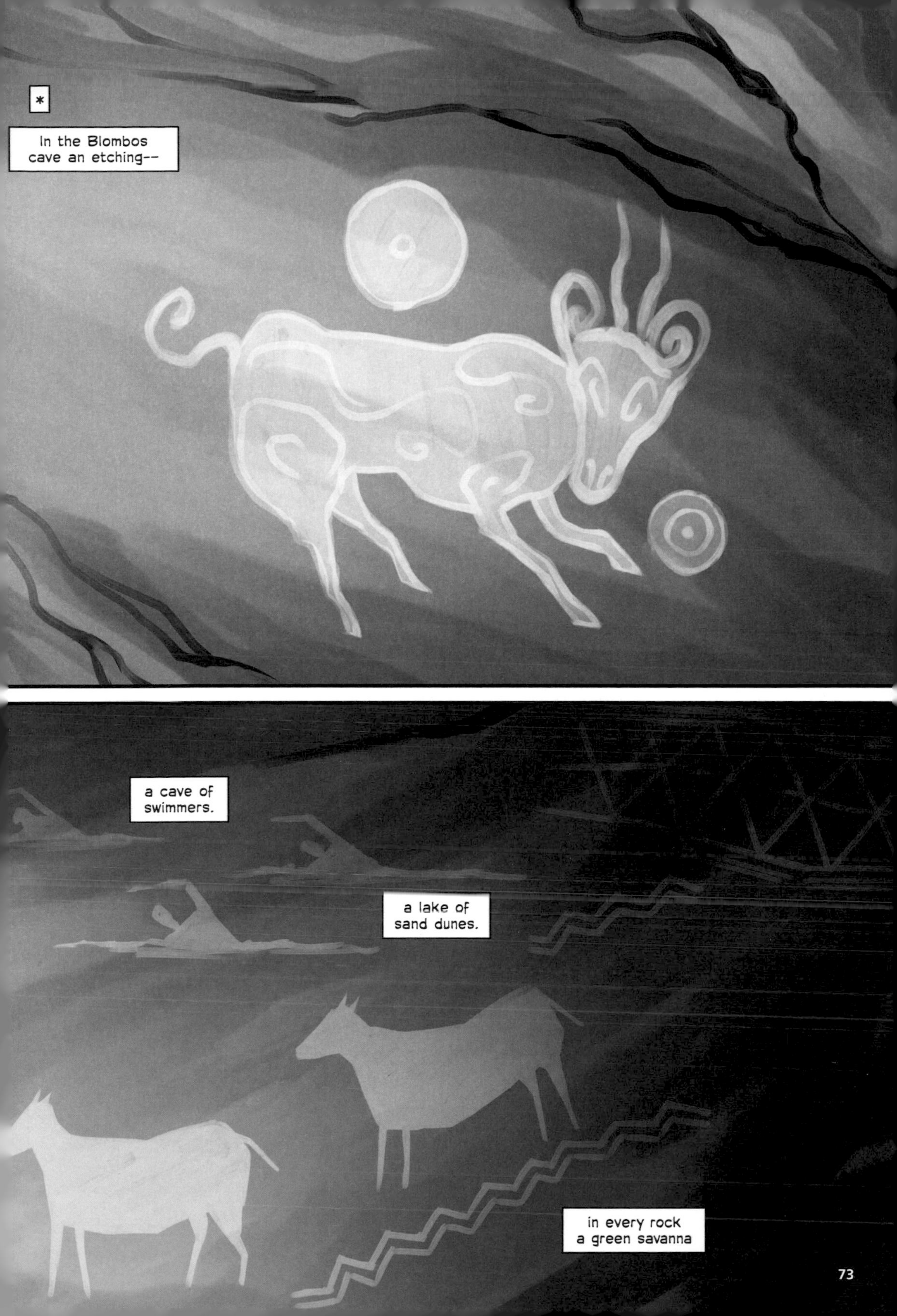
*
In the Blombos cave an etching--
a cave of swimmers.
a lake of sand dunes.
in every rock a green savanna

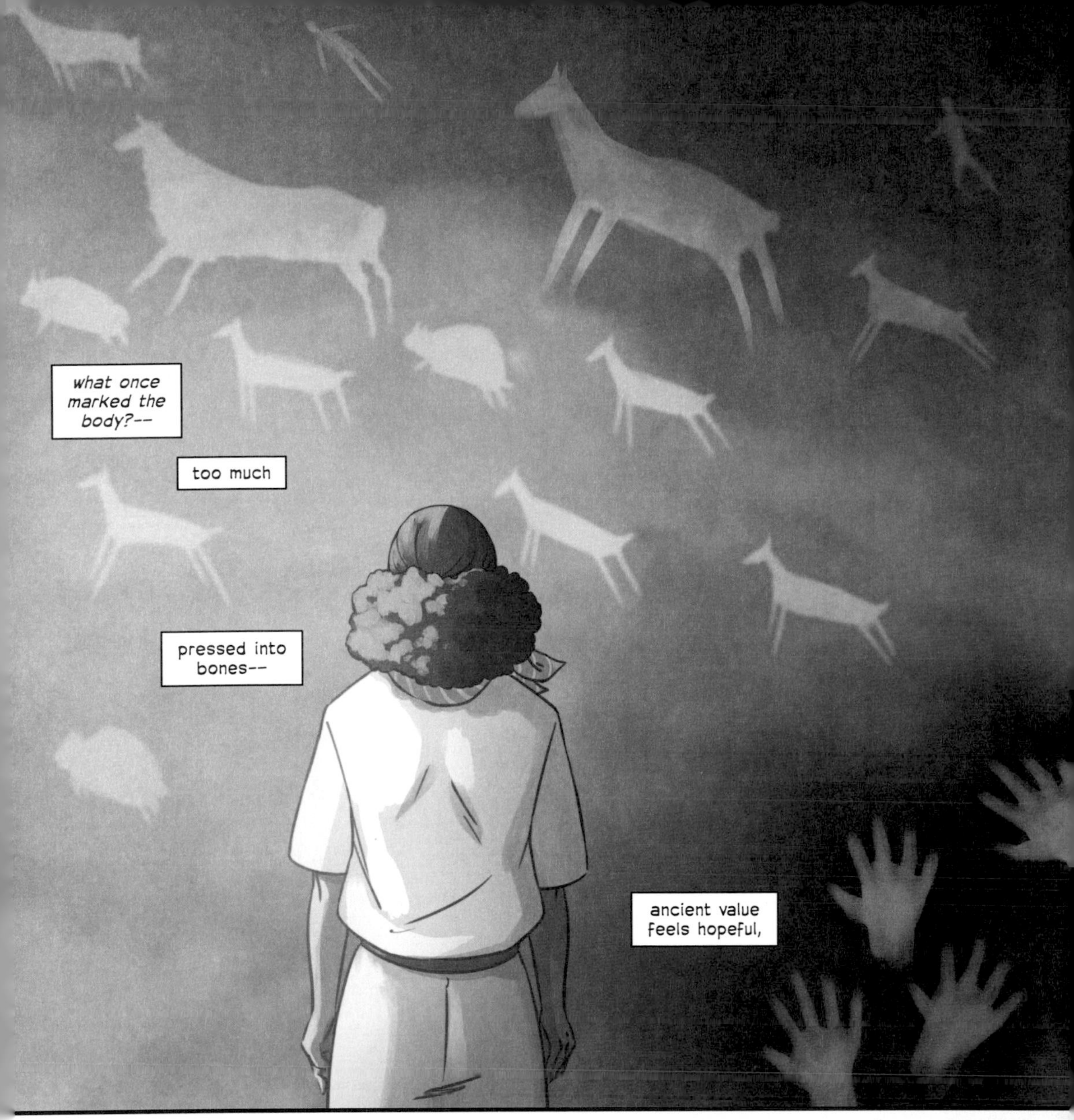
what once marked the body?--
too much
pressed into bones--
ancient value feels hopeful,
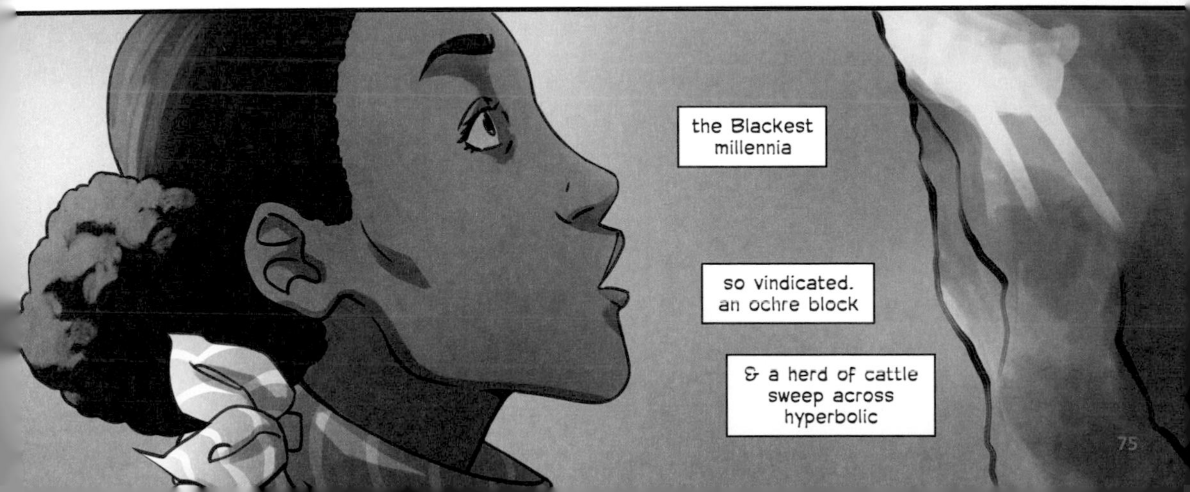
the Blackest millennia
so vindicated. an ochre block
& a herd of cattle sweep across hyperbolic

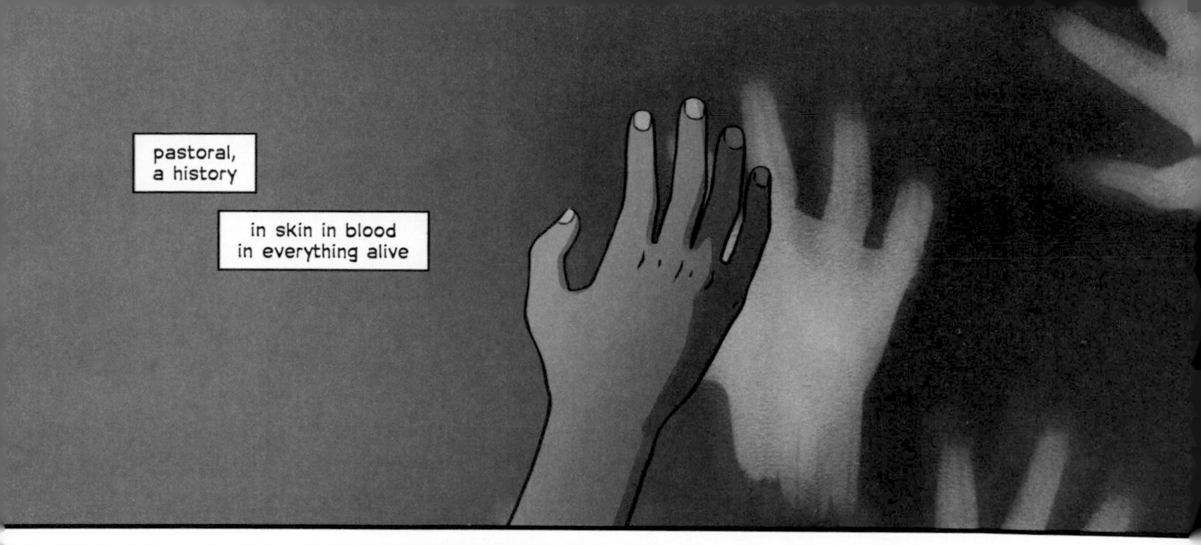
pastoral,
a history
in skin in blood
in everything alive

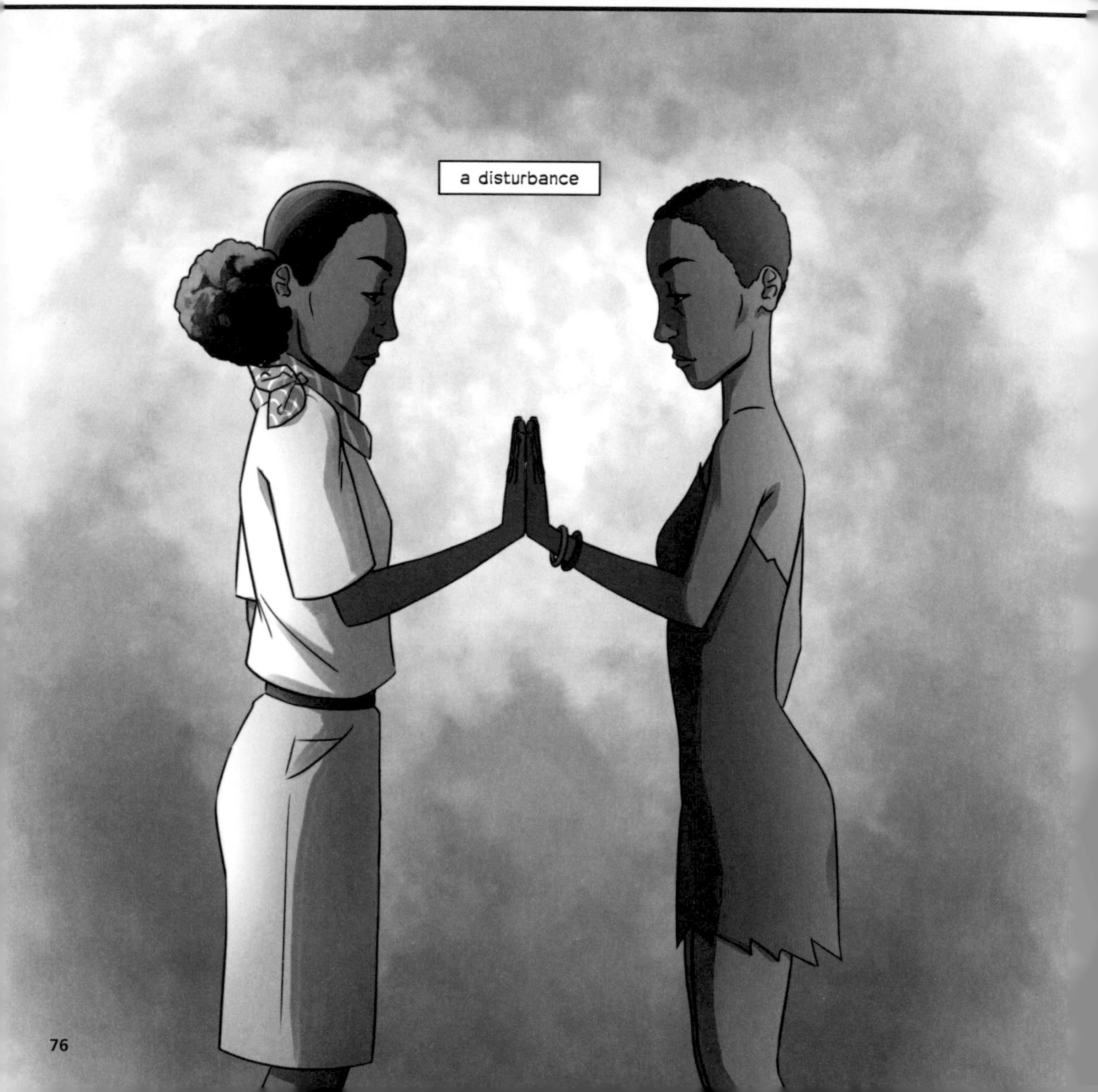
a disturbance

X
by Khadijah Queen

*

In the Blombos cave an etching—

a cave of swimmers. a lake of sand dunes. in every rock a green savanna
across the first continent.
100 years / 100,000—collapsed

gesture learned, the mark
of wanting to make marks in the surrounding
objects to say: what?

X

*

what once marked the body?—too much
pressed into bones—
ancient value feels hopeful, the Blackest millennia
so vindicated. an ochre block & a herd of cattle sweep across hyperbolic

pastoral, a history
in skin in blood in everything alive a disturbance

Tapestry

Poem by Khaty Xiong
Art by Morgan Beem
Letters by Cardinal Rae

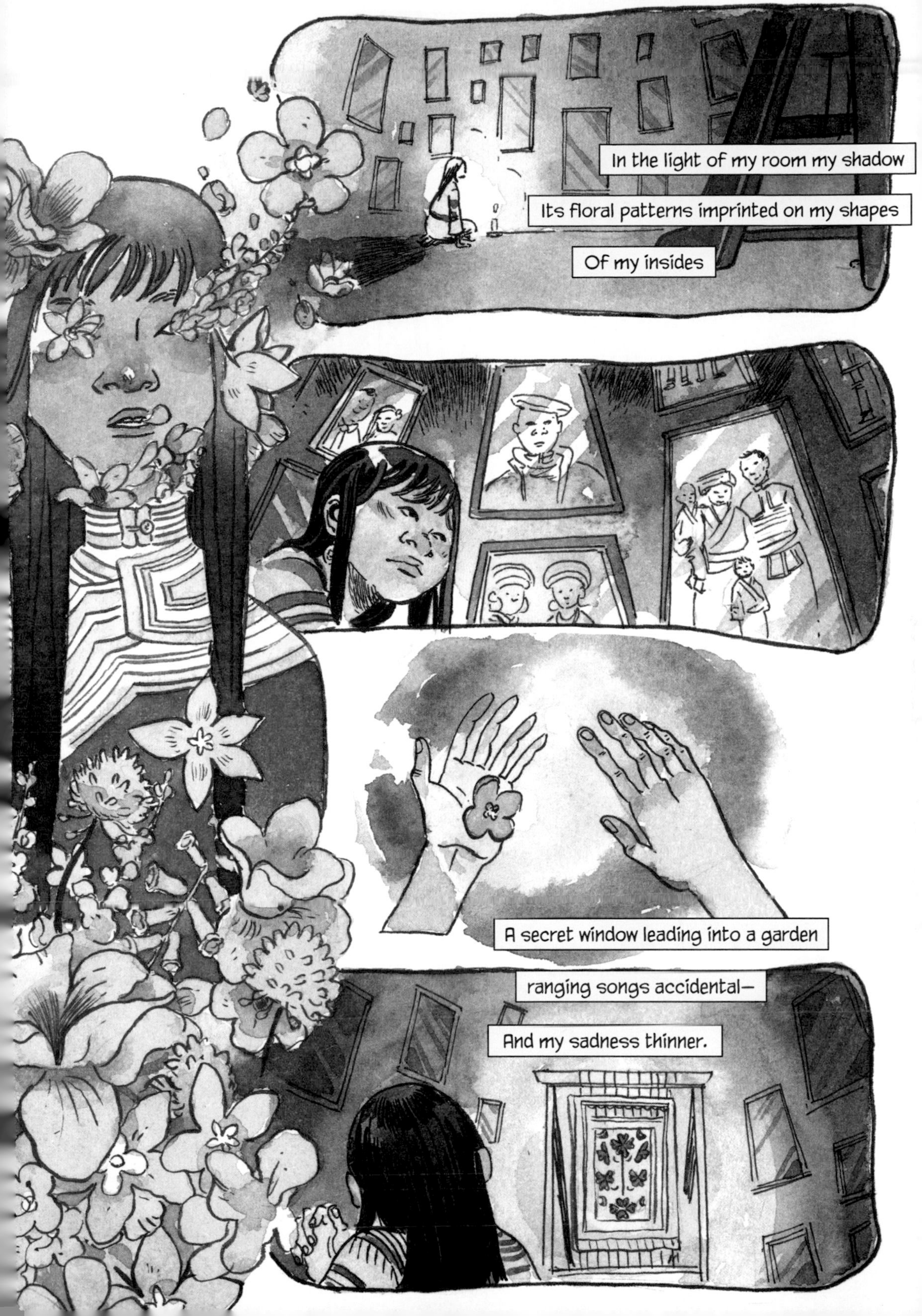
In the light of my room my shadow
Its floral patterns imprinted on my shapes
Of my insides
A secret window leading into a garden
ranging songs accidental—
And my sadness thinner.

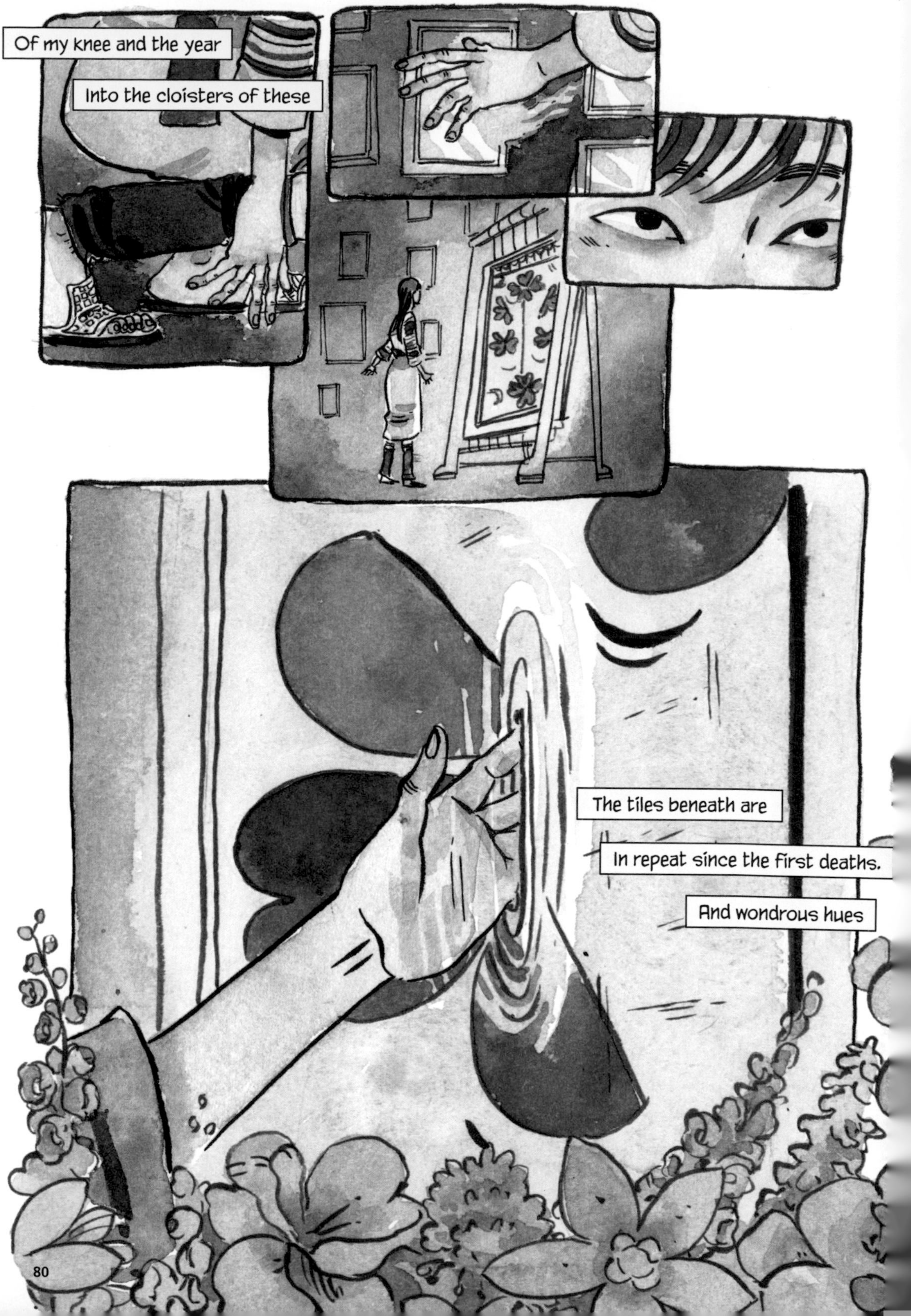
Of my knee and the year
Into the cloisters of these
The tiles beneath are
In repeat since the first deaths.
And wondrous hues

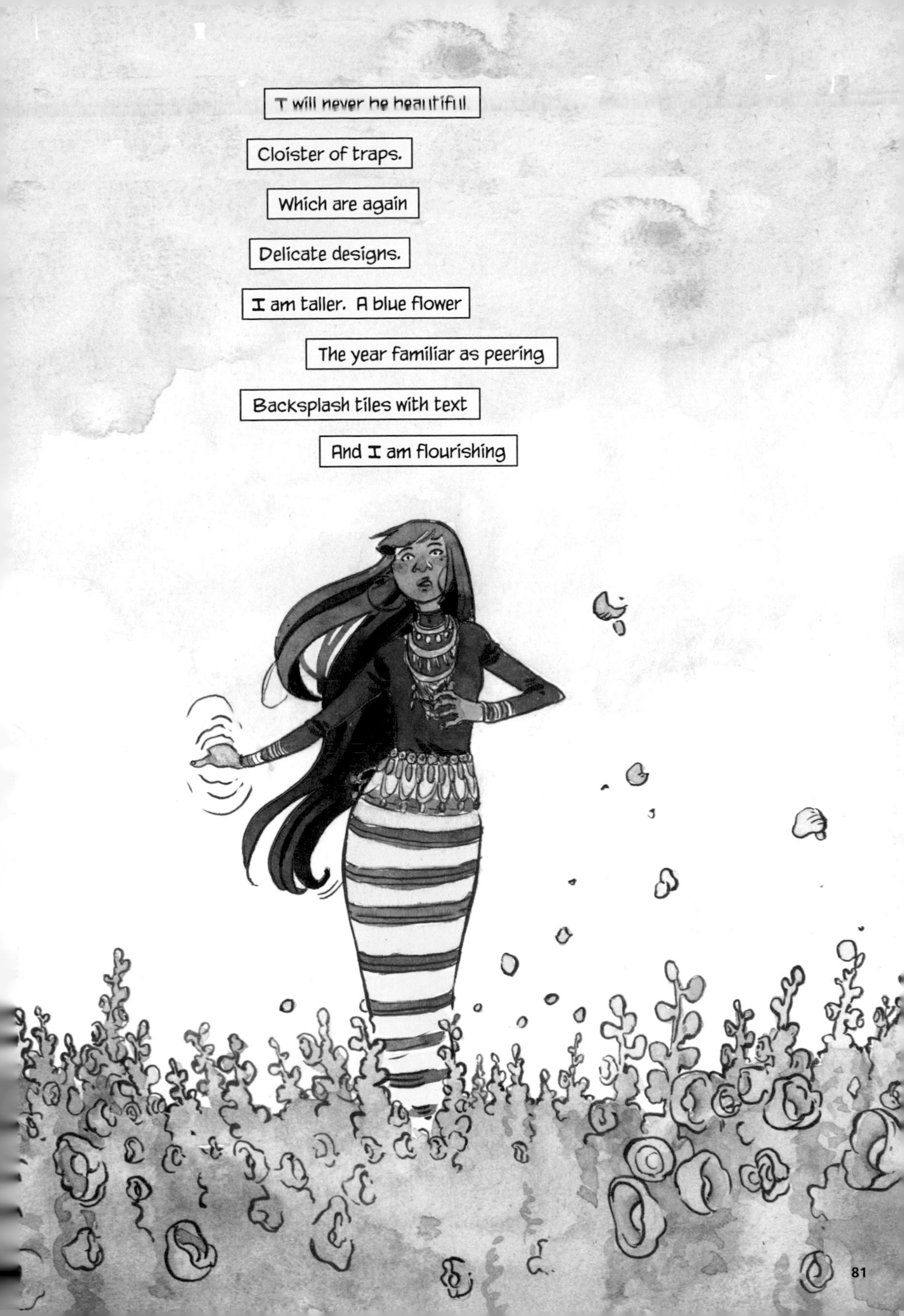
I will never be beautiful
Cloister of traps.
Which are again
Delicate designs.
I am taller. A blue flower
The year familiar as peering
Backsplash tiles with text
And I am flourishing

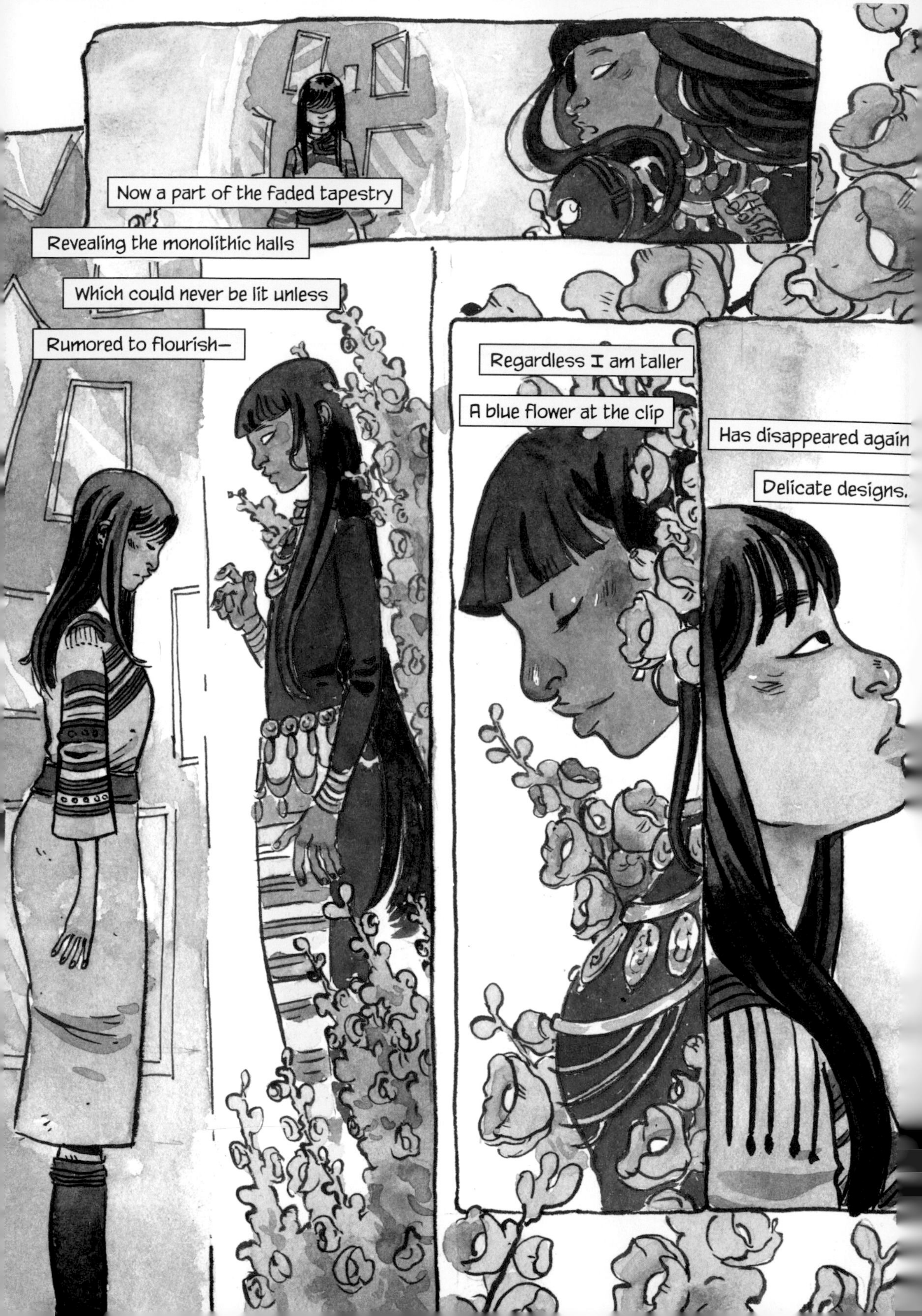
Now a part of the faded tapestry
Revealing the monolithic halls
Which could never be lit unless
Rumored to flourish—
Regardless I am taller
A blue flower at the clip
Has disappeared again
Delicate designs.

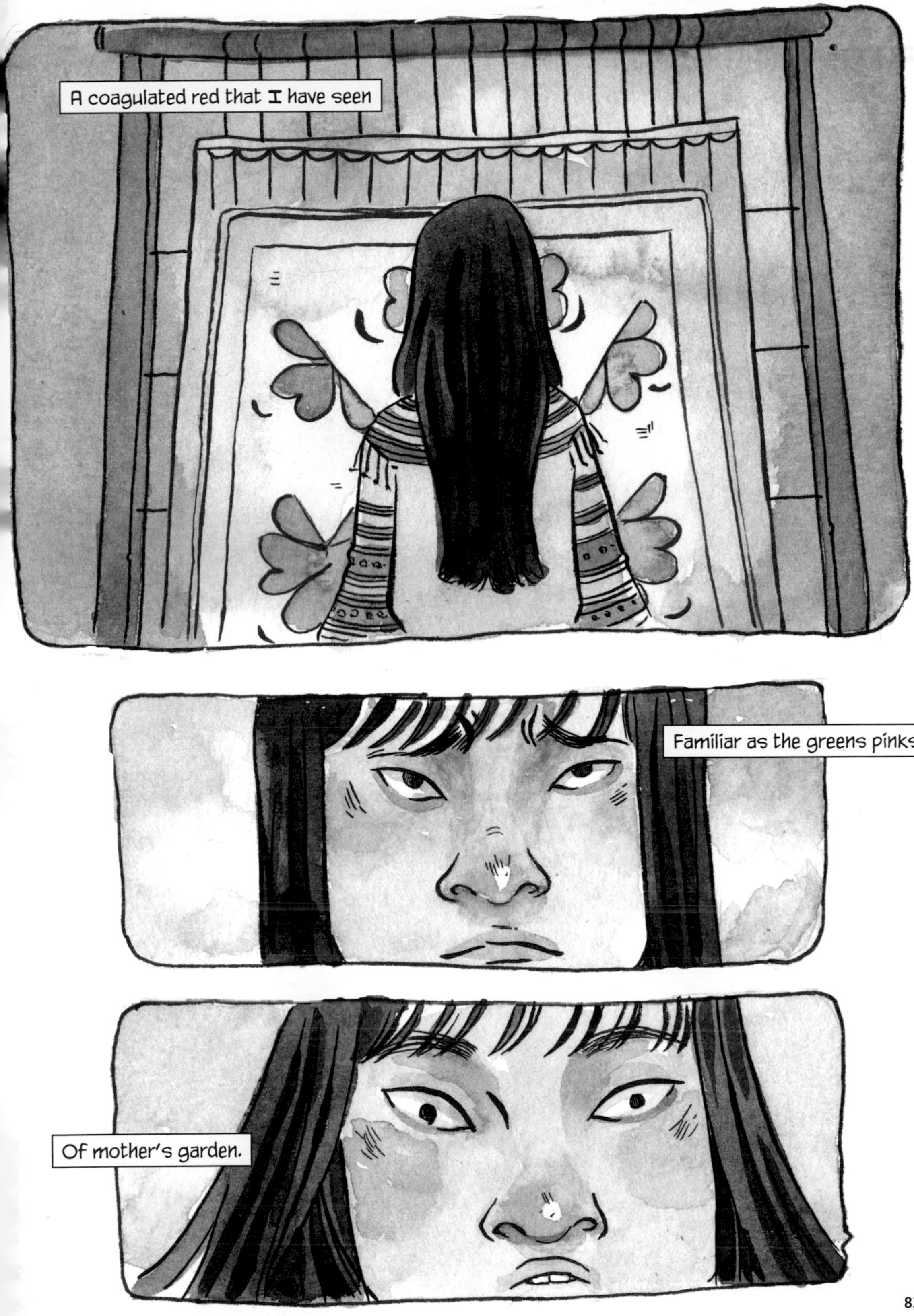
A coagulated red that I have seen
Familiar as the greens pinks
Of mother's garden.

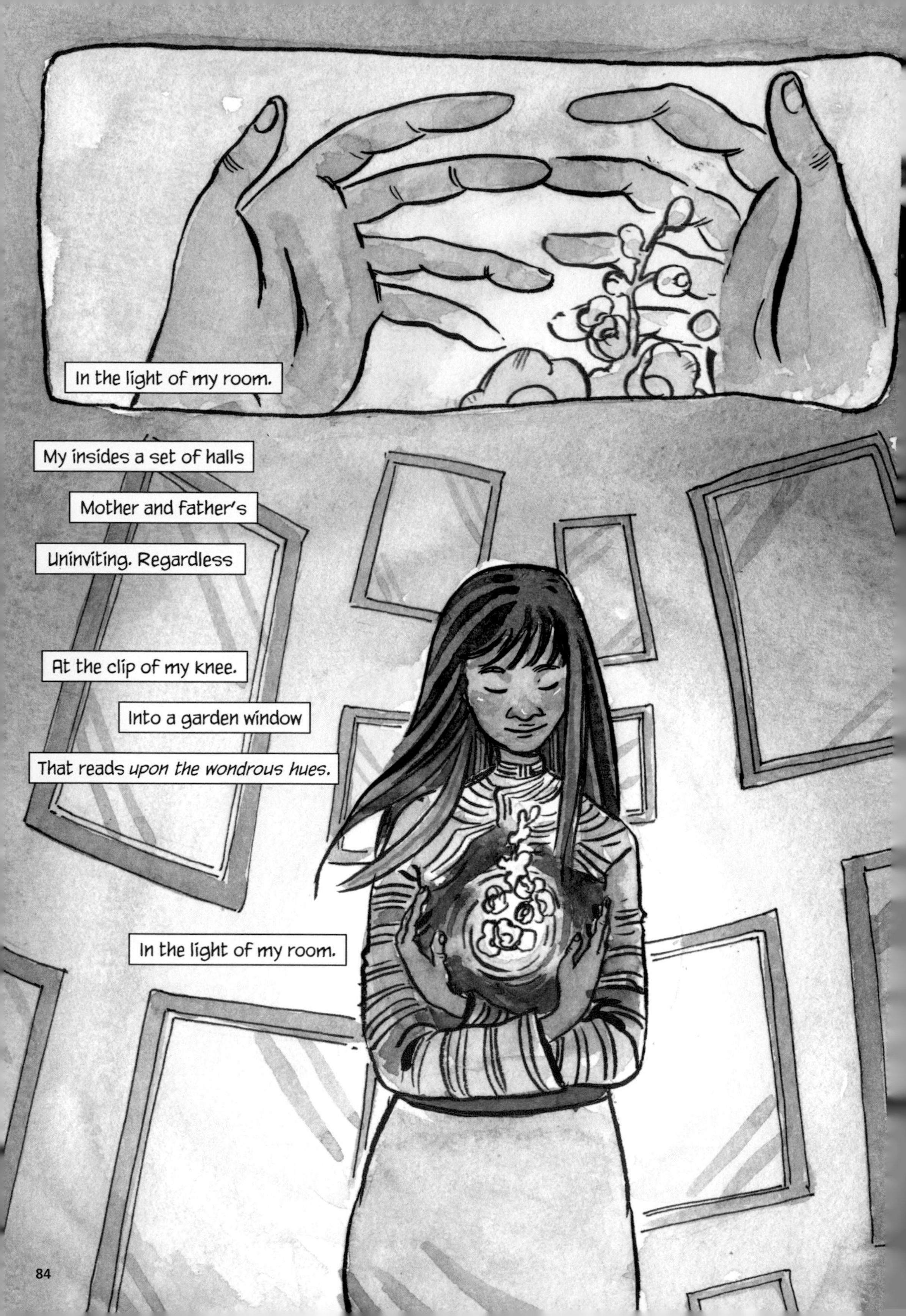
In the light of my room.
My insides a set of halls
Mother and father's
Uninviting. Regardless
At the clip of my knee.
Into a garden window
That reads *upon the wondrous hues.*
In the light of my room.

Tapestry
by Khaty Xiong

In the light of my room my shadow
Its floral patterns imprinted on my shapes
    Of my insides
A secret window leading into a garden
    ranging songs accidental—
And my sadness thinner.
Of my knee and the year
    Into the cloisters of these

    The tiles beneath are
        In repeat since the first deaths.
    And wondrous hues

I will never be beautiful.
Cloister of traps.
    Which are again
Delicate designs.
I am taller. A blue flower
        The year familiar as peering
Backsplash tiles with text
    And I am flourishing

    Now a part of the faded tapestry
Revealing the monolithic halls
    Which could never be lit unless
Rumored to flourish—
    Regardless I am taller
A blue flower at the clip
Has disappeared again
        Delicate designs...

        A coagulated red that I have seen
            Familiar as the greens pinks
        Of mother's garden.

    In the light of my room.
My insides a set of halls
    Mother and father's
Uninviting. Regardless
At the clip of my knee.
        Into a garden window
That reads *upon the wondrous hues.*
        In the light of my room.

Half Girl, Then Elegy

Poem by Omotara James
Art by Ayşegül Sınav
Color flats by Alexia Veldhuisen
Letters by Cardinal Rae

Half Girl, Then Elegy
by Omotara James

Having fallen while no one was looking
Having borne what fell through
Having fallen early

/

Having barely fallen through myself
My luck, so close to catching,
Having caught the worst of it

/

Having fallen from the sky, and then
Through it. Having landed to realize
I had been part

/

Having parted the late sky, partly
Sky where I am delicate, I took
A tumble through the night bloom

/

I took the night with me as I tumbled,
Delicate with the infinite,
Which swells from the tallest branch

/

Having grown swollen
As low-hanging fruit, I tell Nadra,
I couldn't help it—

/

The fresh heave of new breast
Thick switch of hip: a group
Of unnamed gifts is called a steal

/

She says, fruit you can reach is still
Precious. Her name means *rare:* her lean
Thins towards the unusual.

/

In Lagos, we name our girls
Darling, Sincere, Precious, because
A name is a stake in the grave

/

Having grieved and taken and taken
On the way to Eros, Thanatos
Having arrived late to my own bloom:

Halve me like a walnut
Pry the part of me that is hollow
From the part that yields fruit.

To the Cherry Blossoms on 16th and Wharton

Poem by Kayleb Rae Candrilli

Art & Letters by Hazel Newlevant

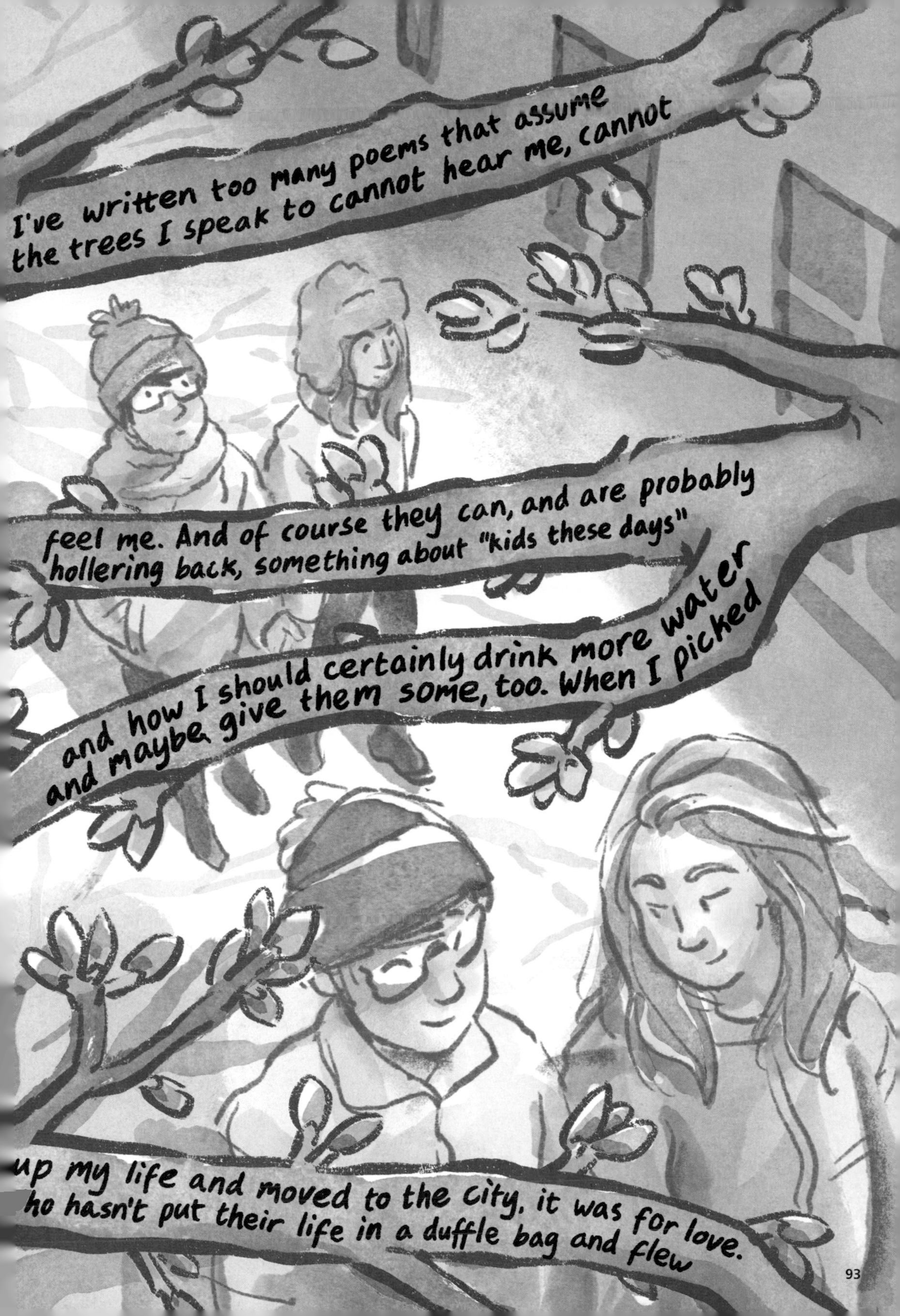
I've written too many poems that assume the trees I speak to cannot hear me, cannot
feel me. And of course they can, and are probably hollering back, something about "kids these days"
and how I should certainly drink more water and maybe give them some, too. When I picked
up my life and moved to the city, it was for love. ho hasn't put their life in a duffle bag and flew

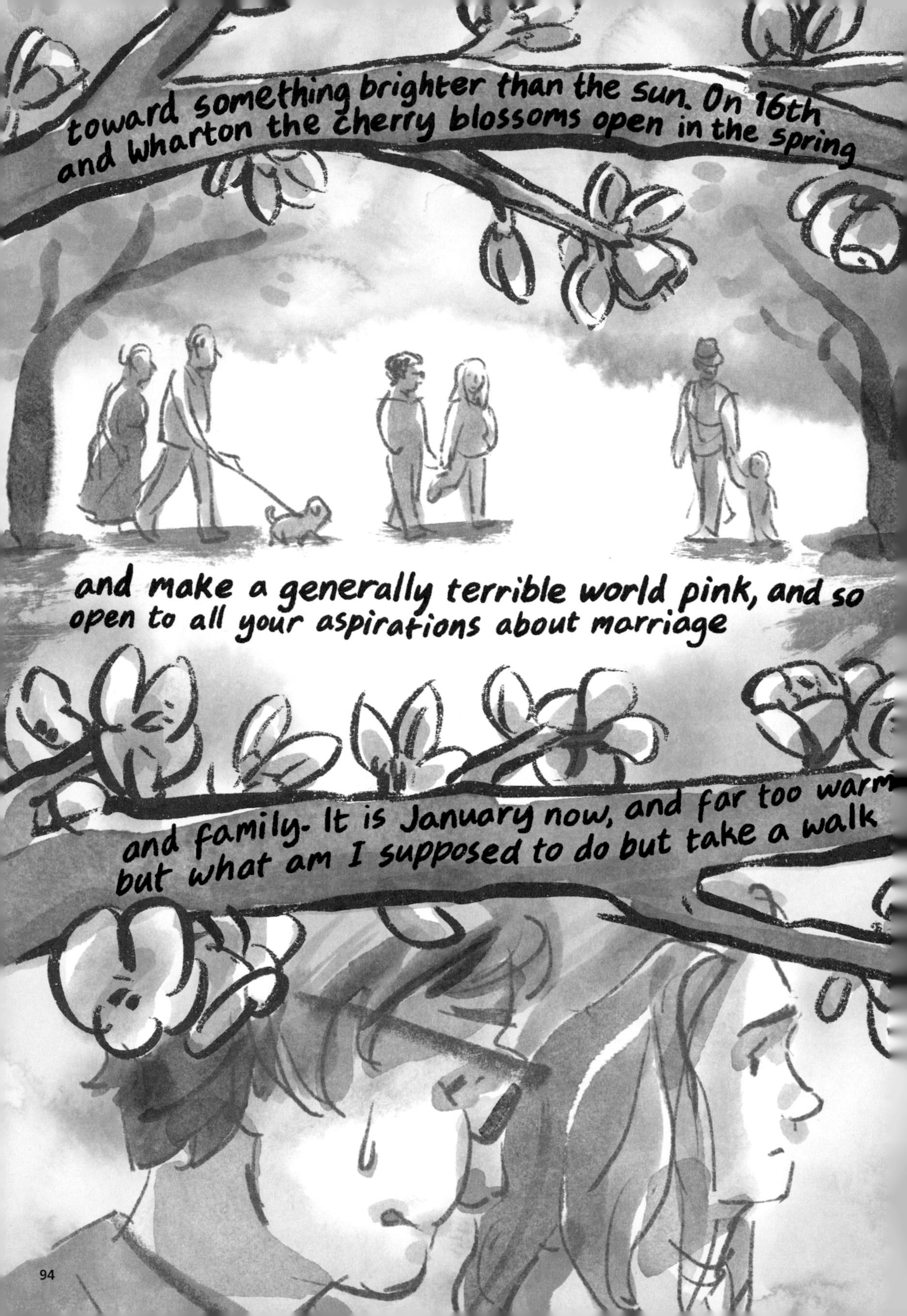

toward something brighter than the sun. On 16th and Wharton the cherry blossoms open in the spring
and make a generally terrible world pink, and so open to all your aspirations about marriage
and family. It is January now, and far too warm but what am I supposed to do but take a walk

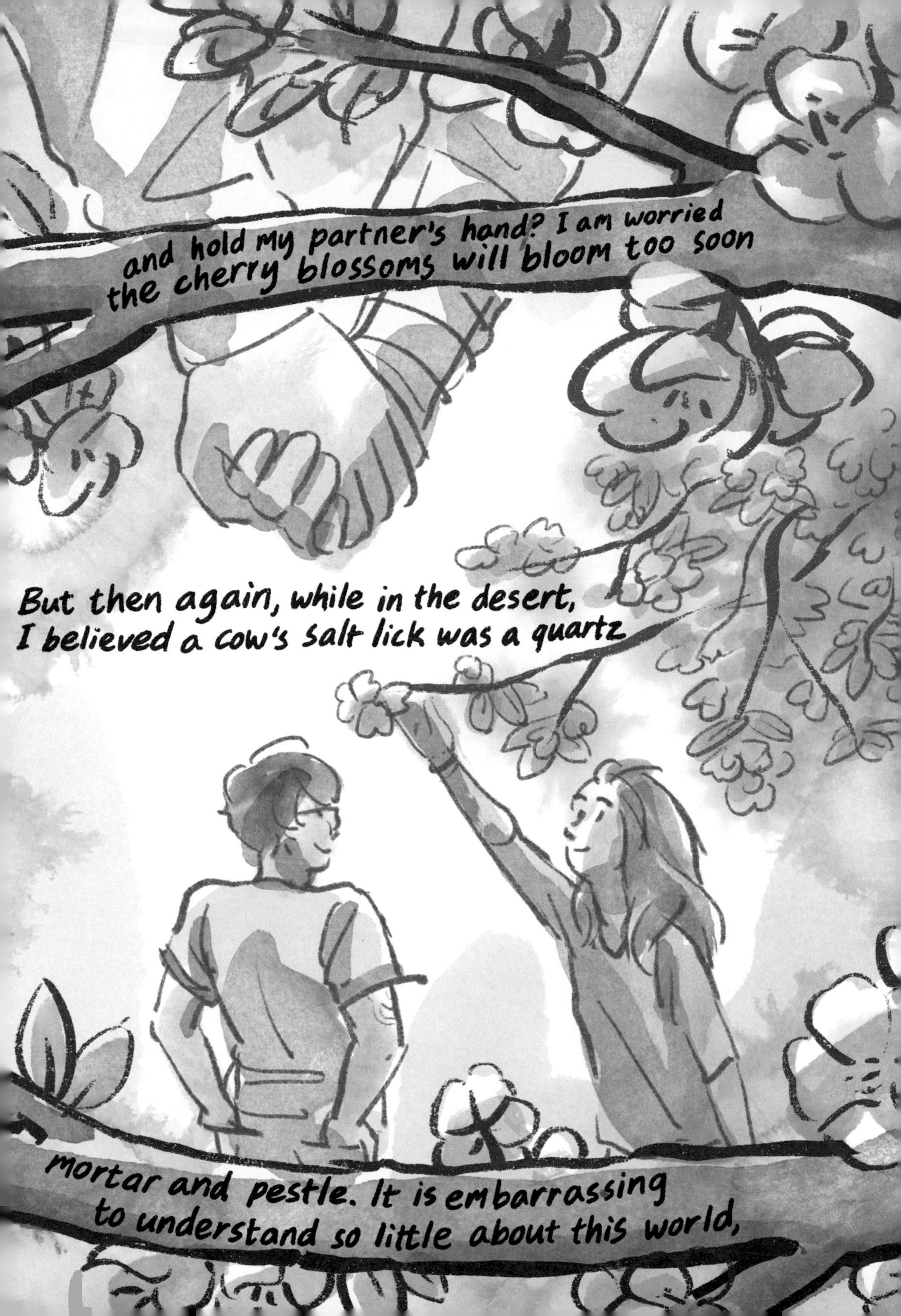

and hold my partner's hand? I am worried
the cherry blossoms will bloom too soon
But then again, while in the desert,
I believed a cow's salt lick was a quartz
mortar and pestle. It is embarrassing
to understand so little about this world,

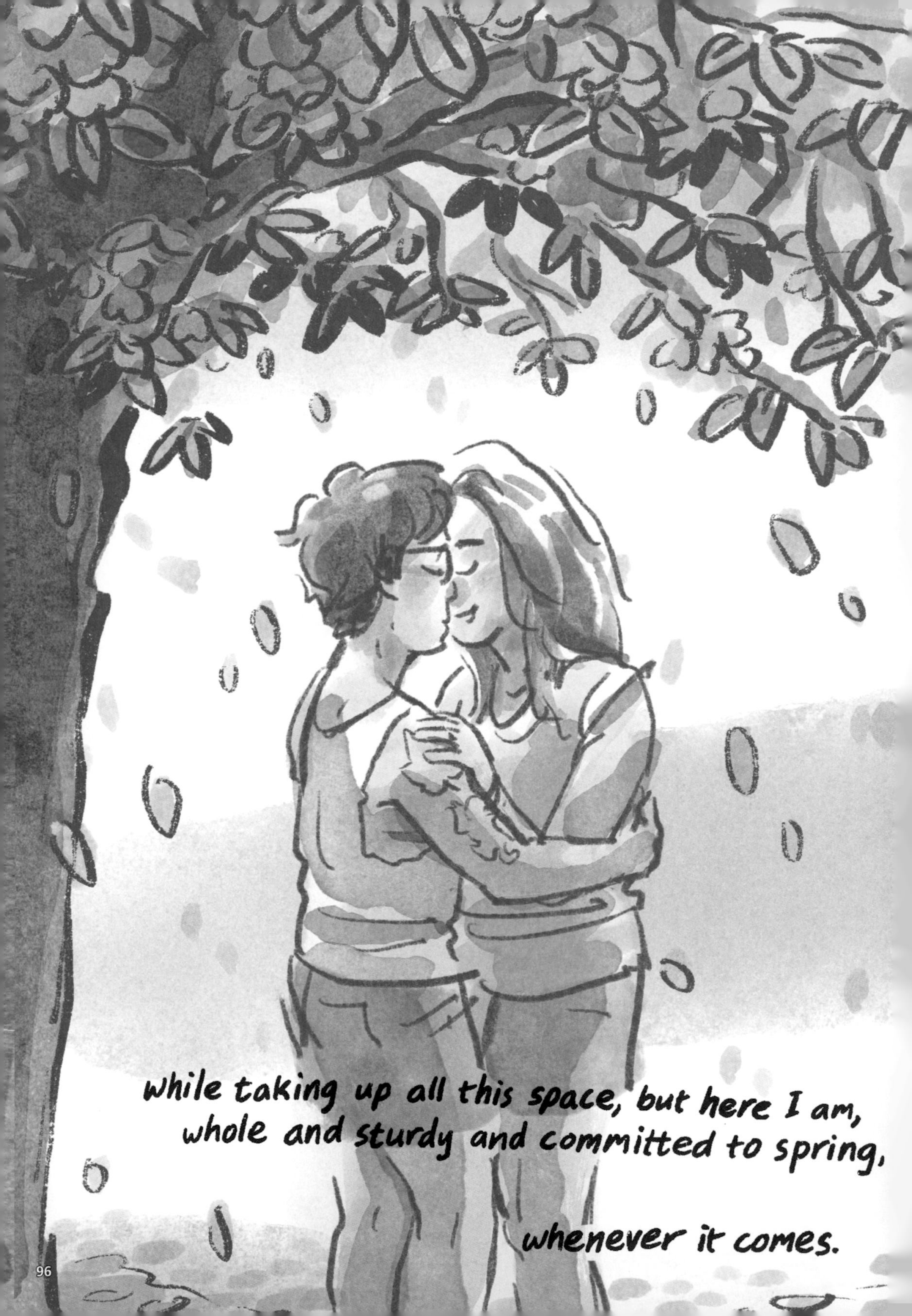
while taking up all this space, but here I am,
whole and sturdy and committed to spring,
whenever it comes.

TO THE CHERRY BLOSSOMS ON 16TH AND WHARTON
by Kayleb Rae Candrilli

after Ross Gay's "To the Fig Tree on 9th and Christian"

I've written too many poems that assume
the trees I speak to cannot hear me, cannot

feel me. And of course they can, and are probably
hollering back, something about "kids these days"

and how I should certainly drink more water
and maybe give them some, too. When I picked

up my life and moved it to the city, it was for love.
Who hasn't put their life in a duffle bag and flew

toward something brighter than the sun. On 16th
and Wharton the cherry blossoms open in spring

and make a generally terrible world pink, and so
open to all your aspirations about marriage

and family. It is January now, and far too warm,
but what am I supposed to do but take a walk

and hold my partner's hand? I am worried
the cherry blossoms will bloom too soon

but then again, once, while in the desert,
I believed a cow's salt lick was a quartz

mortar and pestle. It is embarrassing
to understand so little about the world,

while taking up all this space, but here I am,
whole and sturdy and committed to Spring,

whenever it comes.

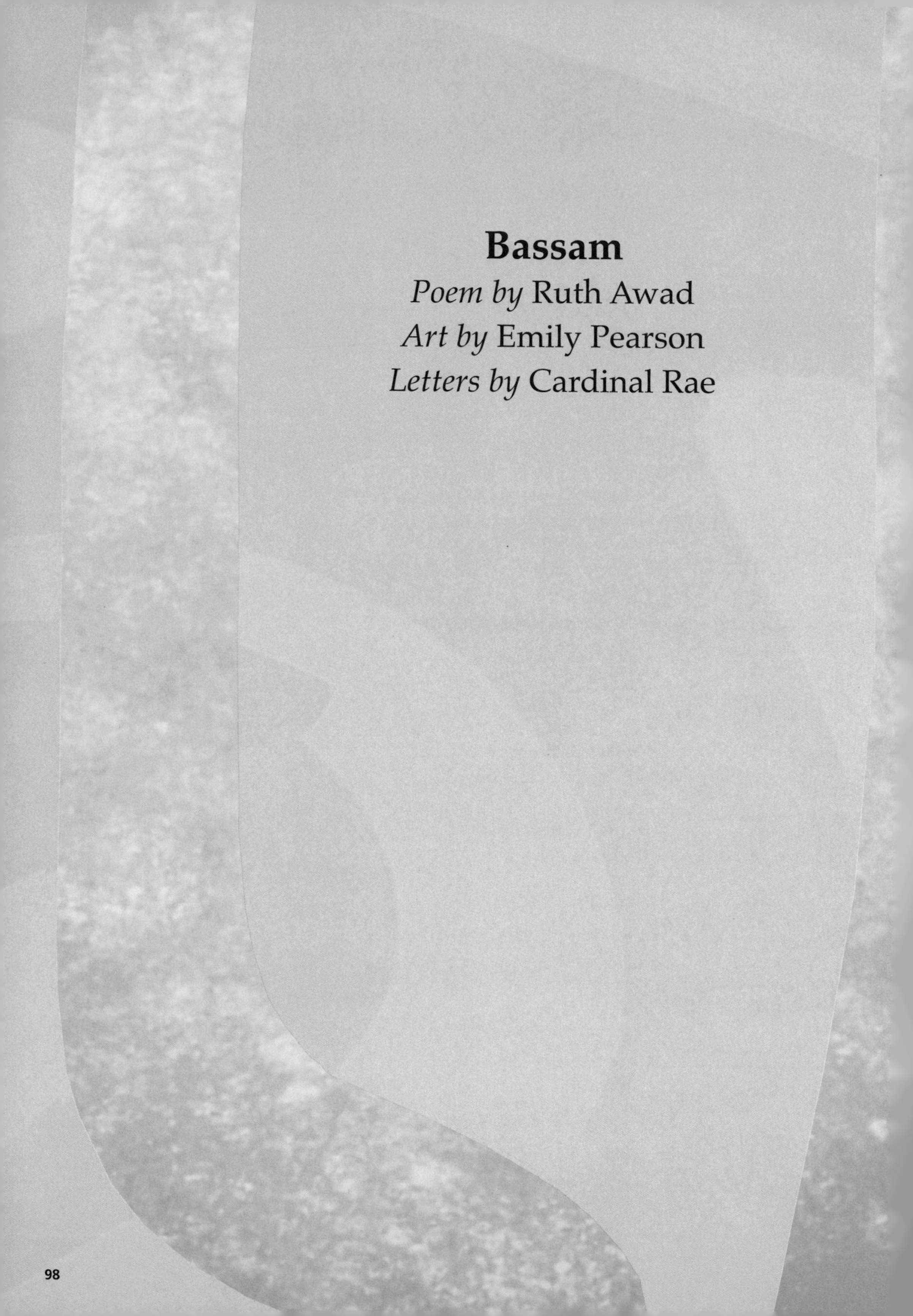

Bassam

Poem by Ruth Awad
Art by Emily Pearson
Letters by Cardinal Rae

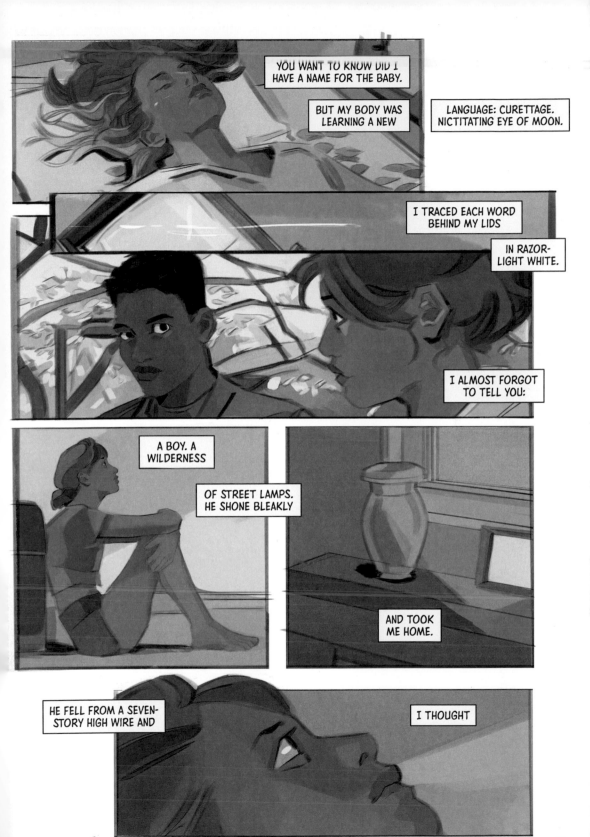

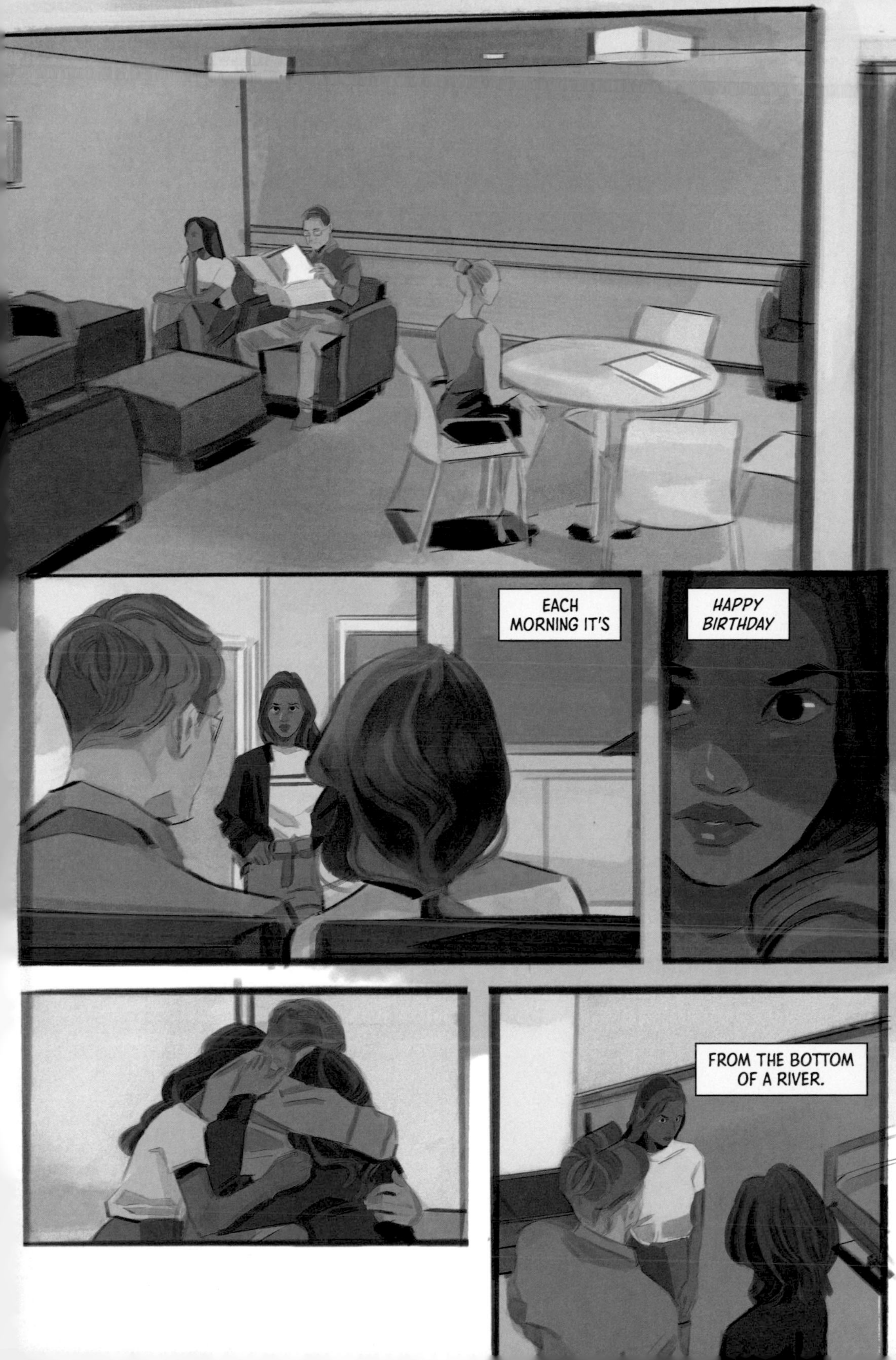
EACH
MORNING IT'S
*HAPPY
BIRTHDAY*
FROM THE BOTTOM
OF A RIVER.

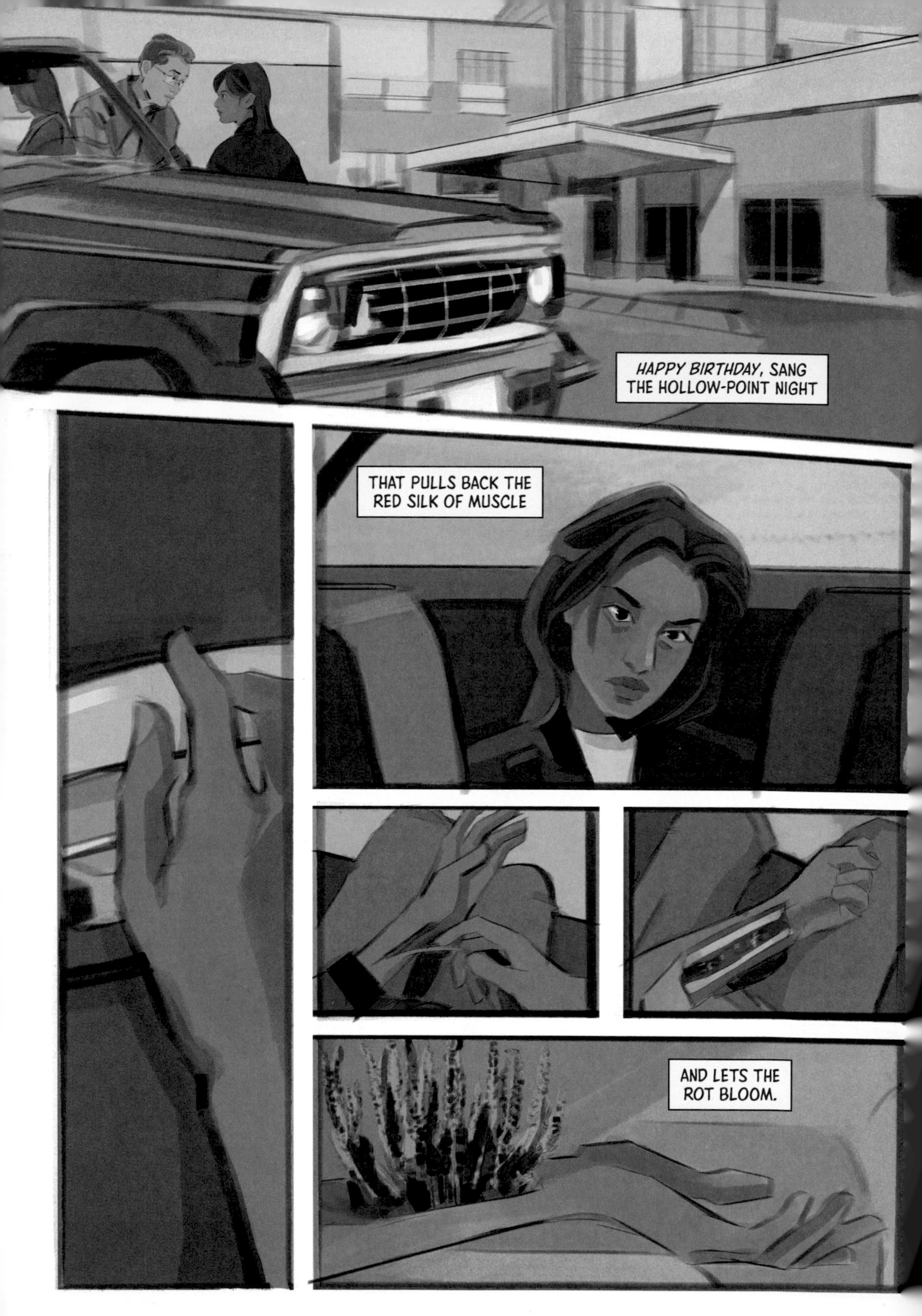
HAPPY BIRTHDAY, SANG
THE HOLLOW-POINT NIGHT
THAT PULLS BACK THE
RED SILK OF MUSCLE
AND LETS THE
ROT BLOOM.

Bassam
by Ruth Awad

You want to know did I have a name for the baby.
But my body was learning a new   language: curettage. Nictitating eye of moon.

I traced each word behind my lids

                in razor-light white.

I almost forgot to tell you: a boy. A wilderness
of street lamps. He shone bleakly   and took me home.

He fell from a seven-story high wire and   I thought   *it had to be a dream,*
I thought   *I'm so happy you're*

      not

   dead.

Each morning I wake up a little crueler. Each morning my heart is

    a vulture beating its wings for scraps.

Each morning it's   *happy birthday*
from the bottom of a river.   *Happy birthday,* sang the hollow-point night

that pulls back the red silk of muscle

      and lets the rot bloom.

Speak-House

Poem by Carolina Ebeid
Art by Marika Cresta
Colors by Gab Contreras
Letters by Cardinal Rae

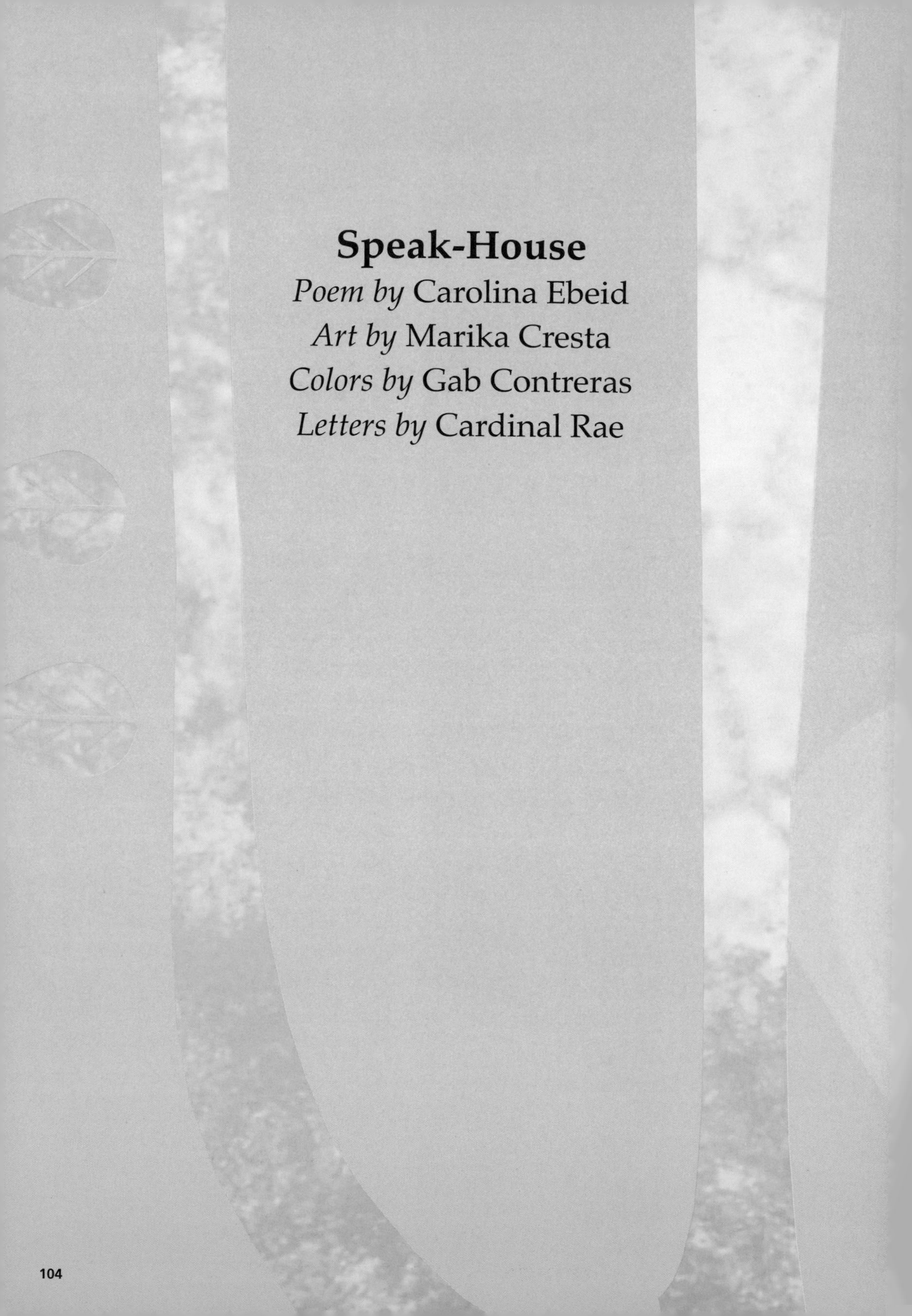

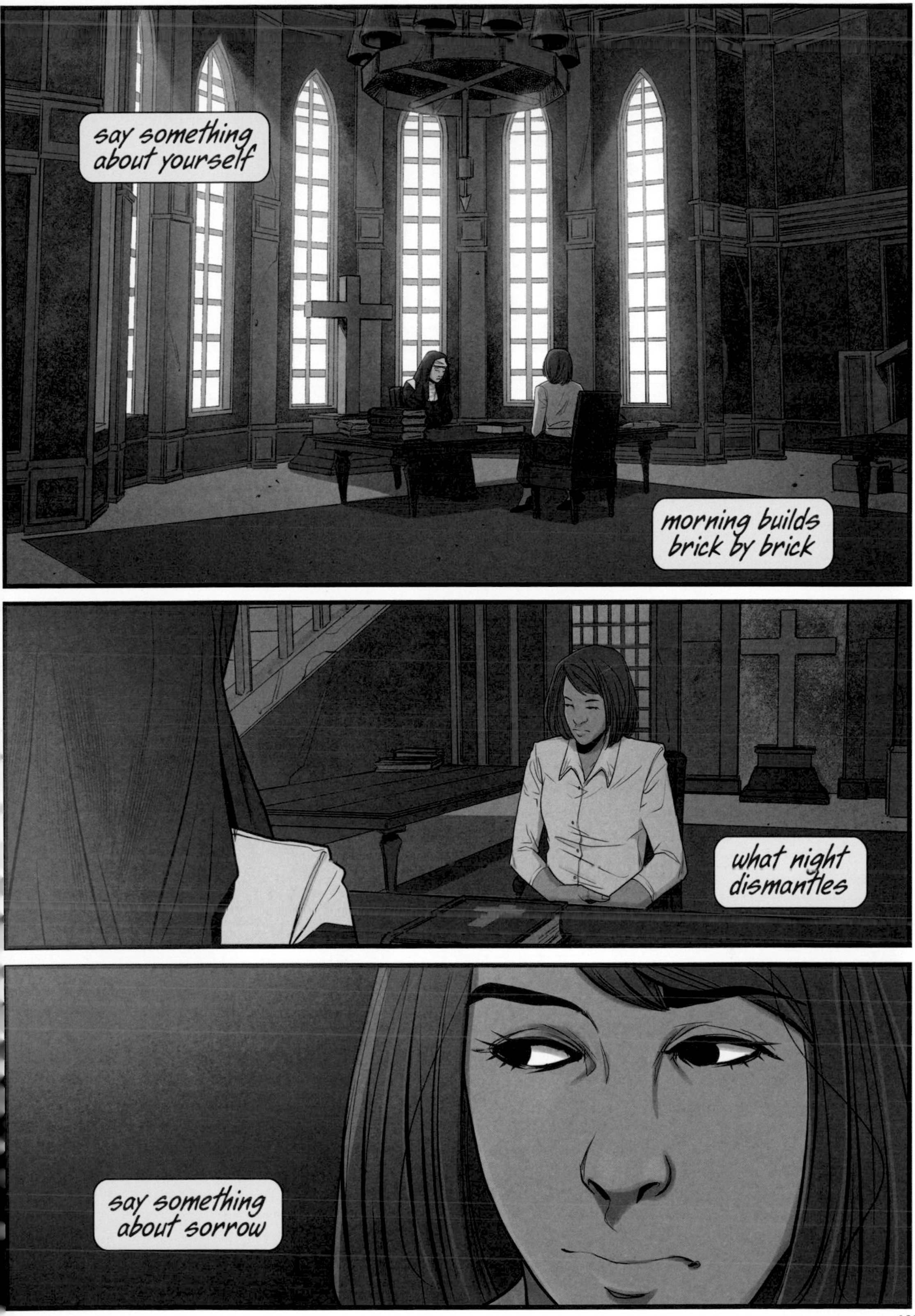
say something about yourself
morning builds brick by brick
what night dismantles
say something about sorrow

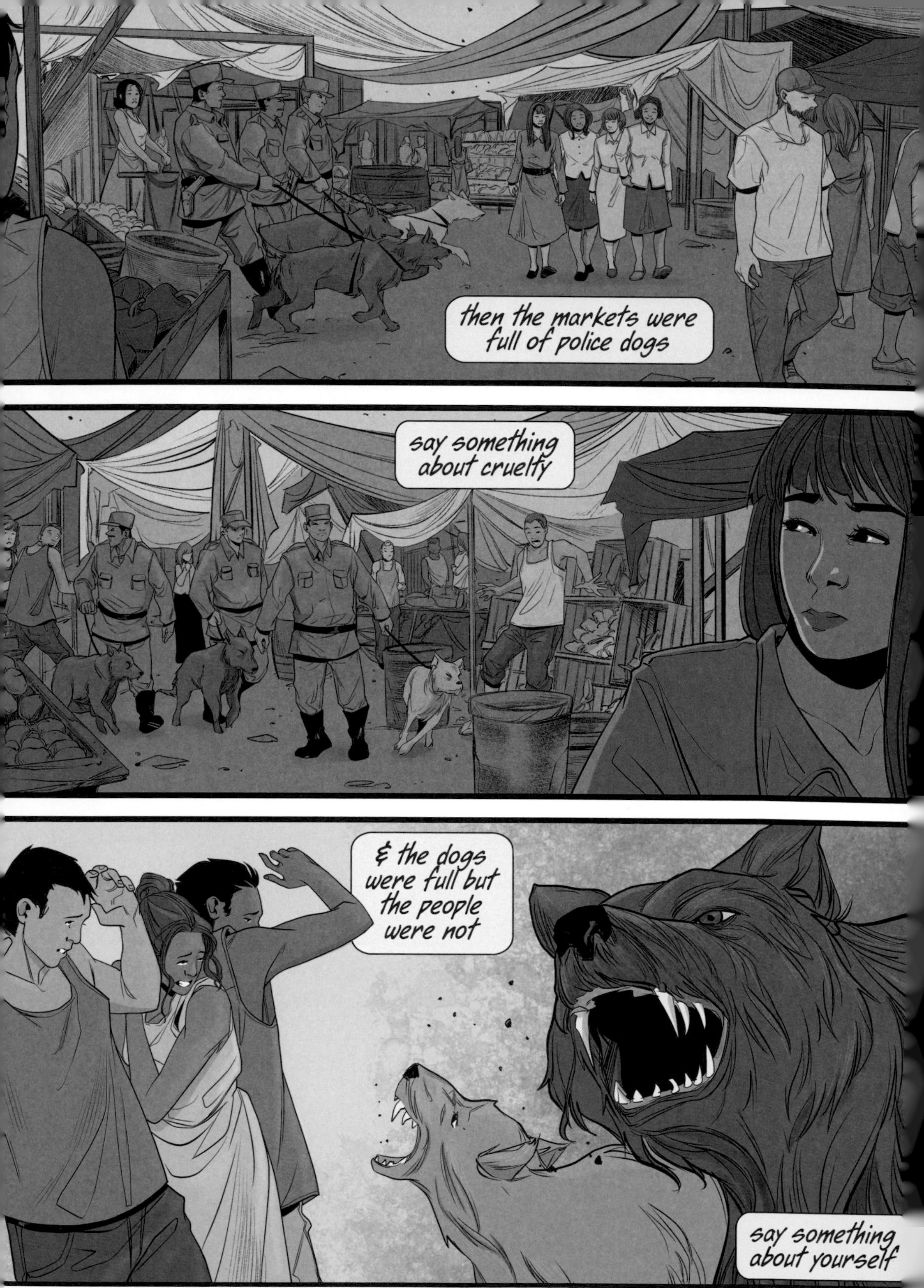
then the markets were full of police dogs
say something about cruelty
& the dogs were full but the people were not
say something about yourself

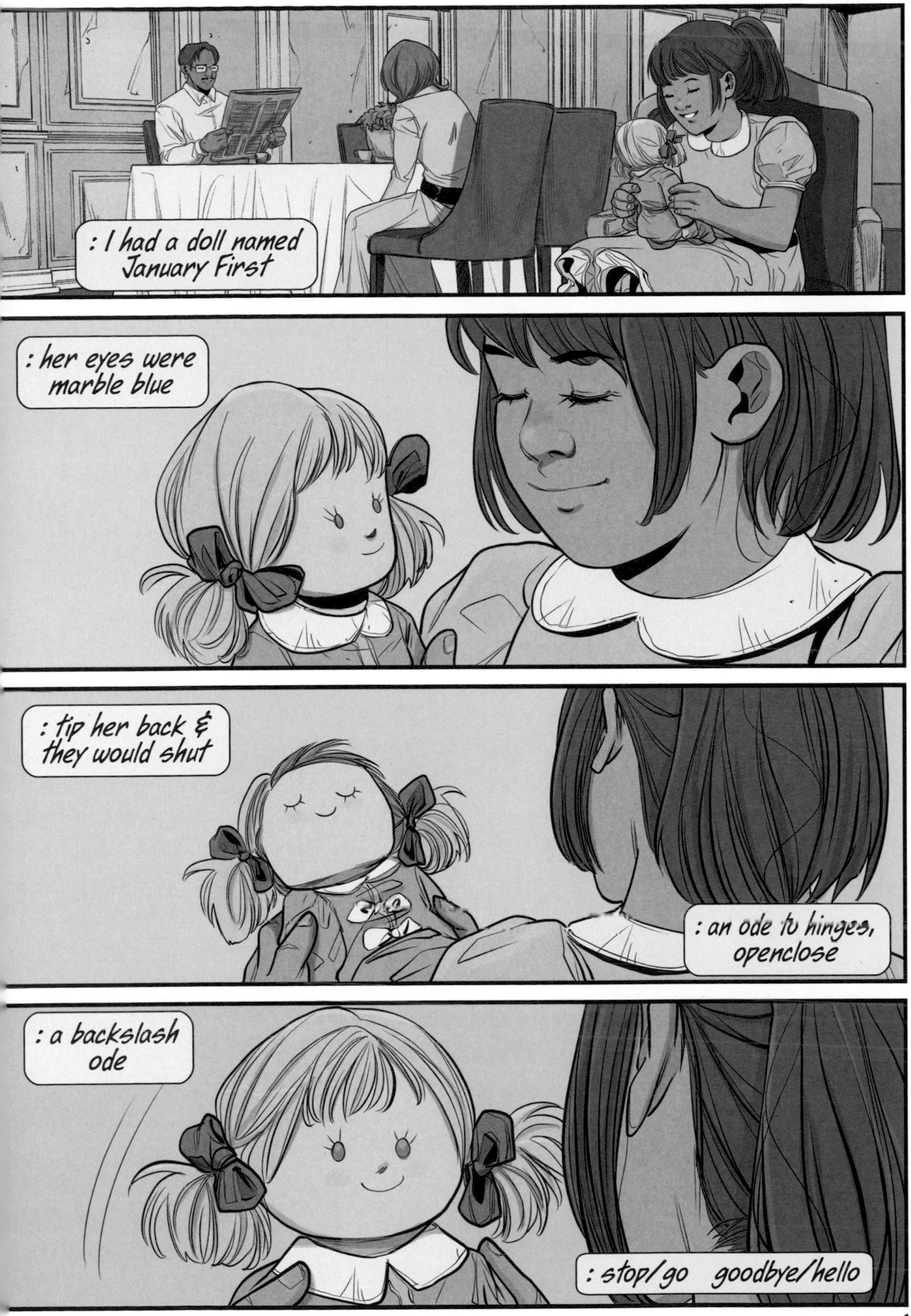
: I had a doll named January First
: her eyes were marble blue
: tip her back & they would shut
: an ode to hinges, openclose
: a backslash ode
: stop/go goodbye/hello

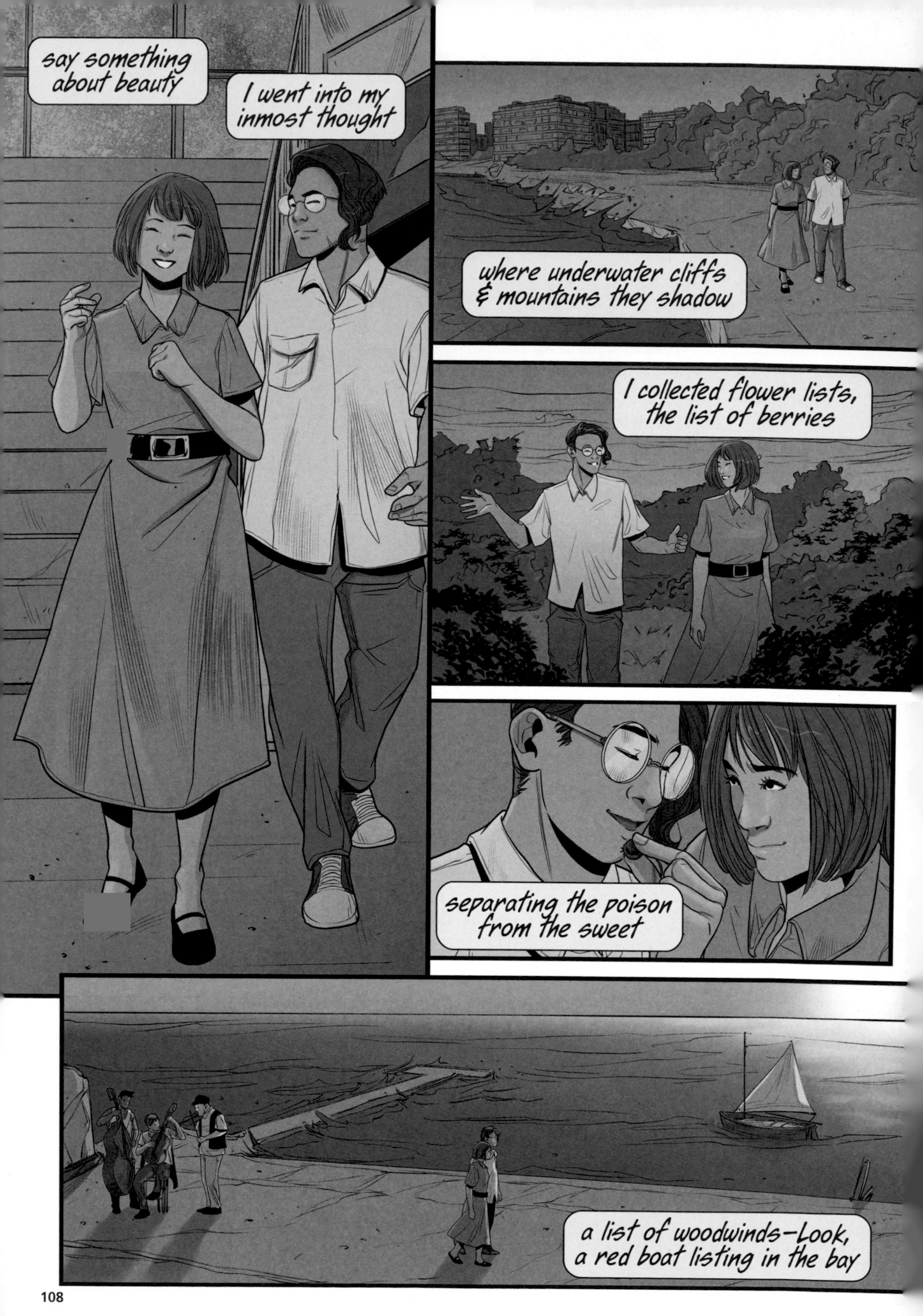
say something about beauty
I went into my inmost thought
where underwater cliffs & mountains they shadow
I collected flower lists, the list of berries
separating the poison from the sweet
a list of woodwinds—Look, a red boat listing in the bay

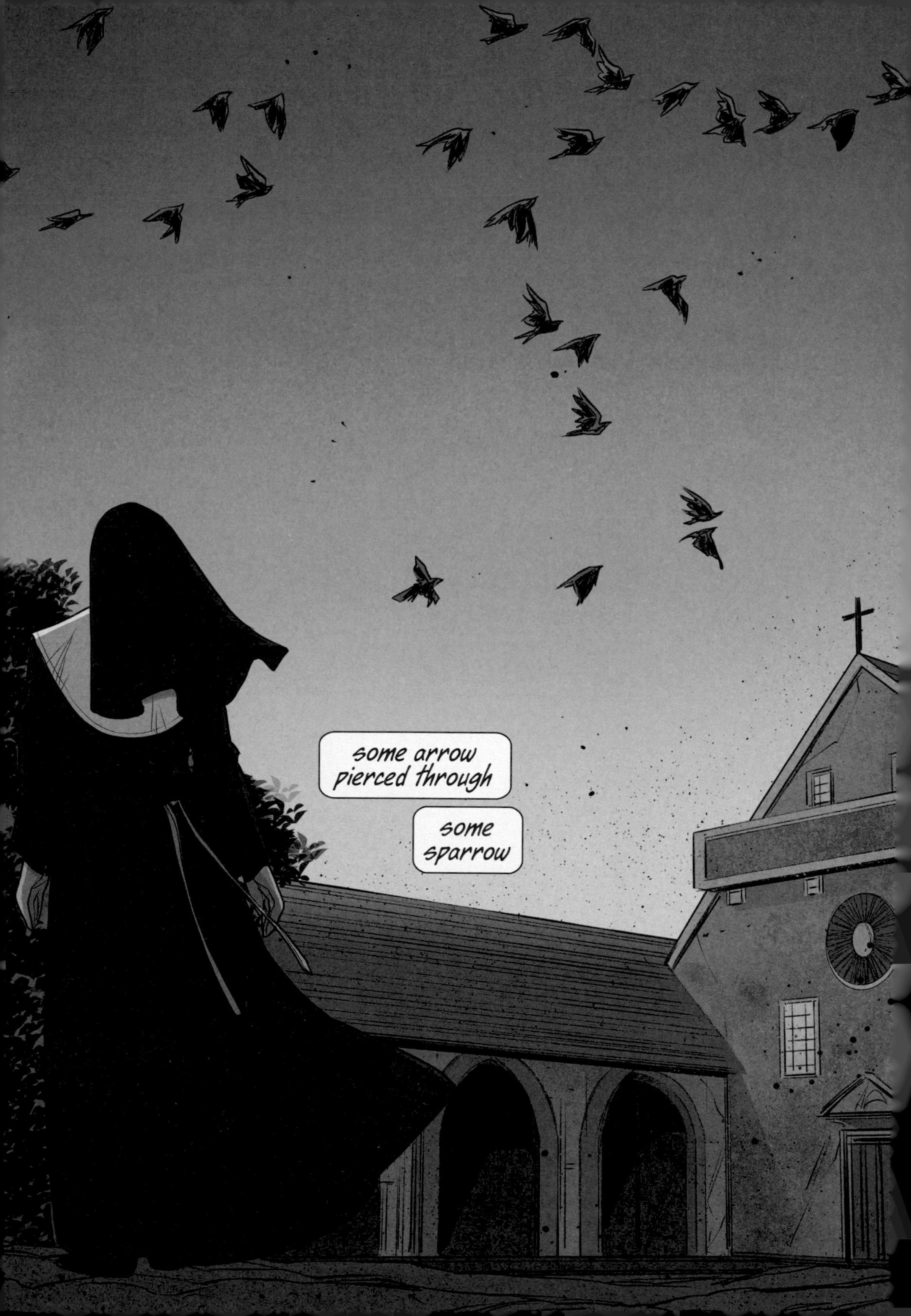
some arrow pierced through
some sparrow

Speak-House
by Carolina Ebeid

say something about yourself

morning builds brick by brick
what night dismantles

say something about sorrow

then the markets were full
of police dogs

say something about cruelty

& the dogs were full but the people
were not

say something about yourself

: I had a doll named January First
: her eyes were marble blue
: tip her back & they would shut
: an ode to hinges, openclose
: a backslash ode
: stop/go   goodbye/hello

say something about beauty

I went into my inmost thought
where underwater cliffs
& mountains they shadow

I collected flower lists, the list of berries
separating the poison from the sweet

a list of woodwinds—Look,
a red boat listing in the bay

say something about cruelty

no one cares whether or not you eat

say something about the voice-out-of-a-
whirlwind

yours is a mortuary art
heart gets atomized
to e-a-r-t-h
in your vernacular

say something about the bride

Then there will be pills for laughing
& for remembering
pills for staying awake
a bracelet that will track your sleep

say something about lovers

it's a feeling itn the torso
put your hand here—
some arrow pierced through
some sparrow

University Toxic

Poem by Laura Hinton

Art & Letters by Kaylee Rowena

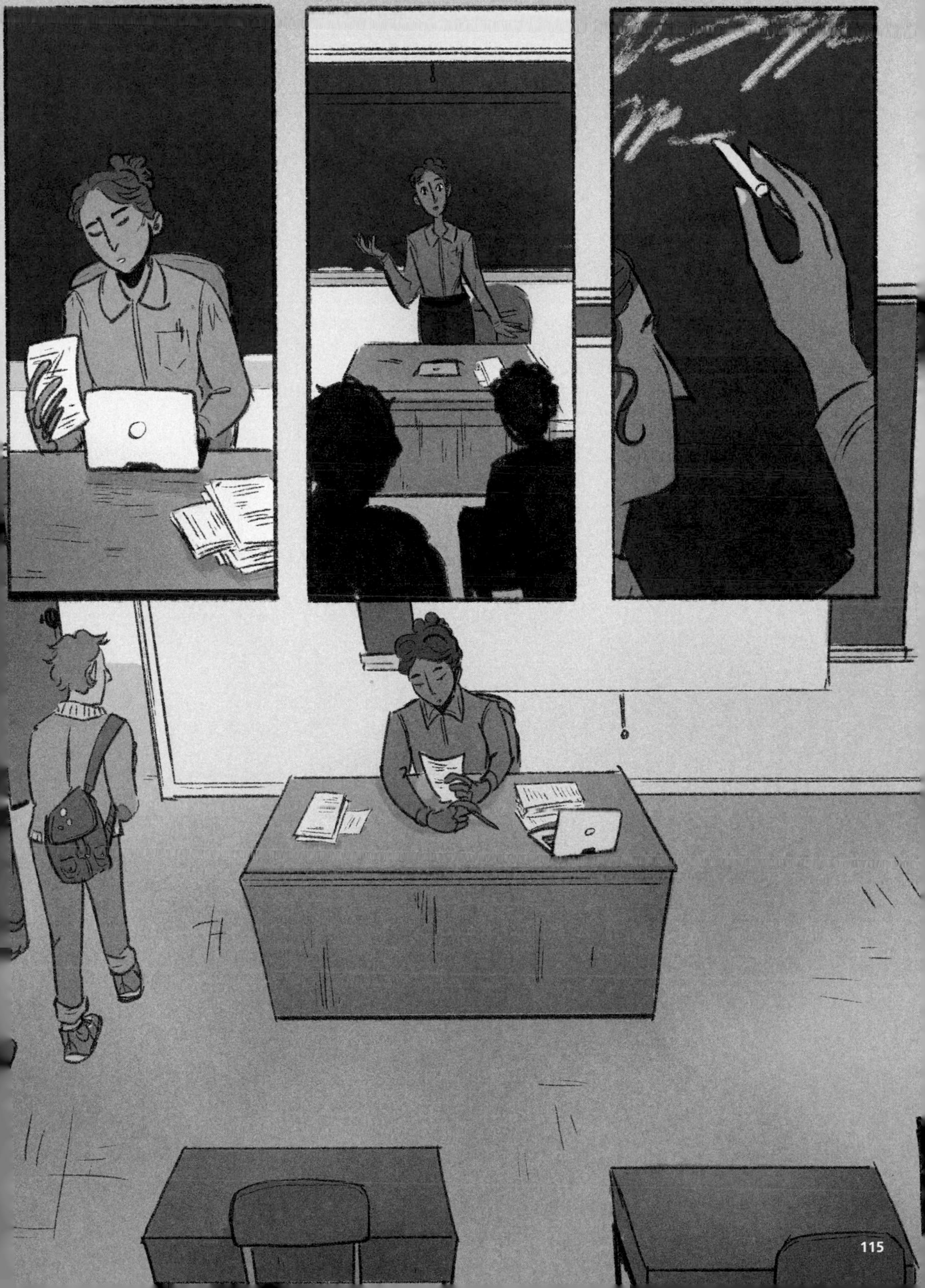

YOU THINK HE IS PLEASED TO SEE YOU.

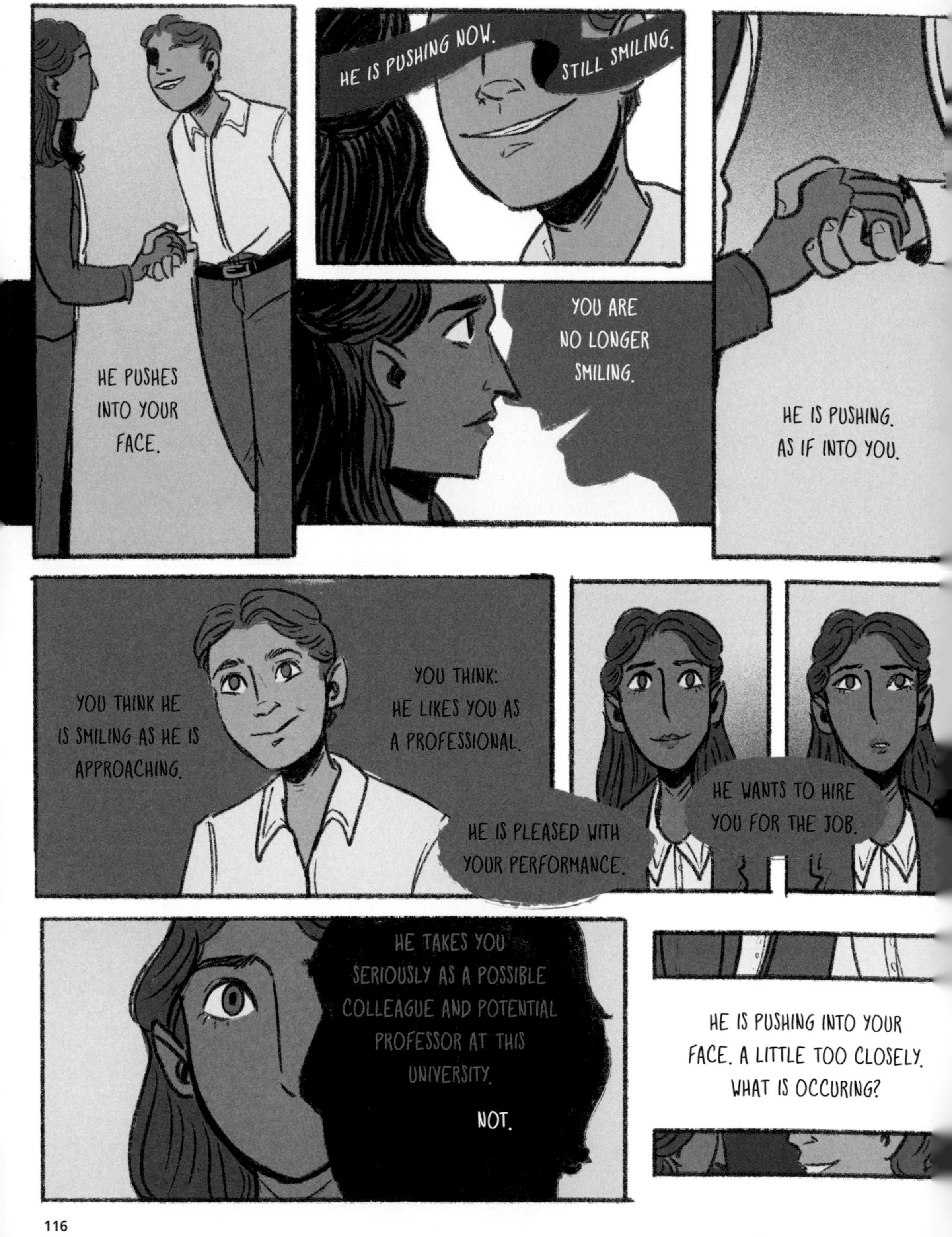
HE PUSHES INTO YOUR FACE.
HE IS PUSHING NOW.
STILL SMILING.
YOU ARE NO LONGER SMILING.
HE IS PUSHING. AS IF INTO YOU.
YOU THINK HE IS SMILING AS HE IS APPROACHING.
YOU THINK: HE LIKES YOU AS A PROFESSIONAL.
HE IS PLEASED WITH YOUR PERFORMANCE.
HE WANTS TO HIRE YOU FOR THE JOB.
HE TAKES YOU SERIOUSLY AS A POSSIBLE COLLEAGUE AND POTENTIAL PROFESSOR AT THIS UNIVERSITY.
NOT.
HE IS PUSHING INTO YOUR FACE. A LITTLE TOO CLOSELY. WHAT IS OCCURING?

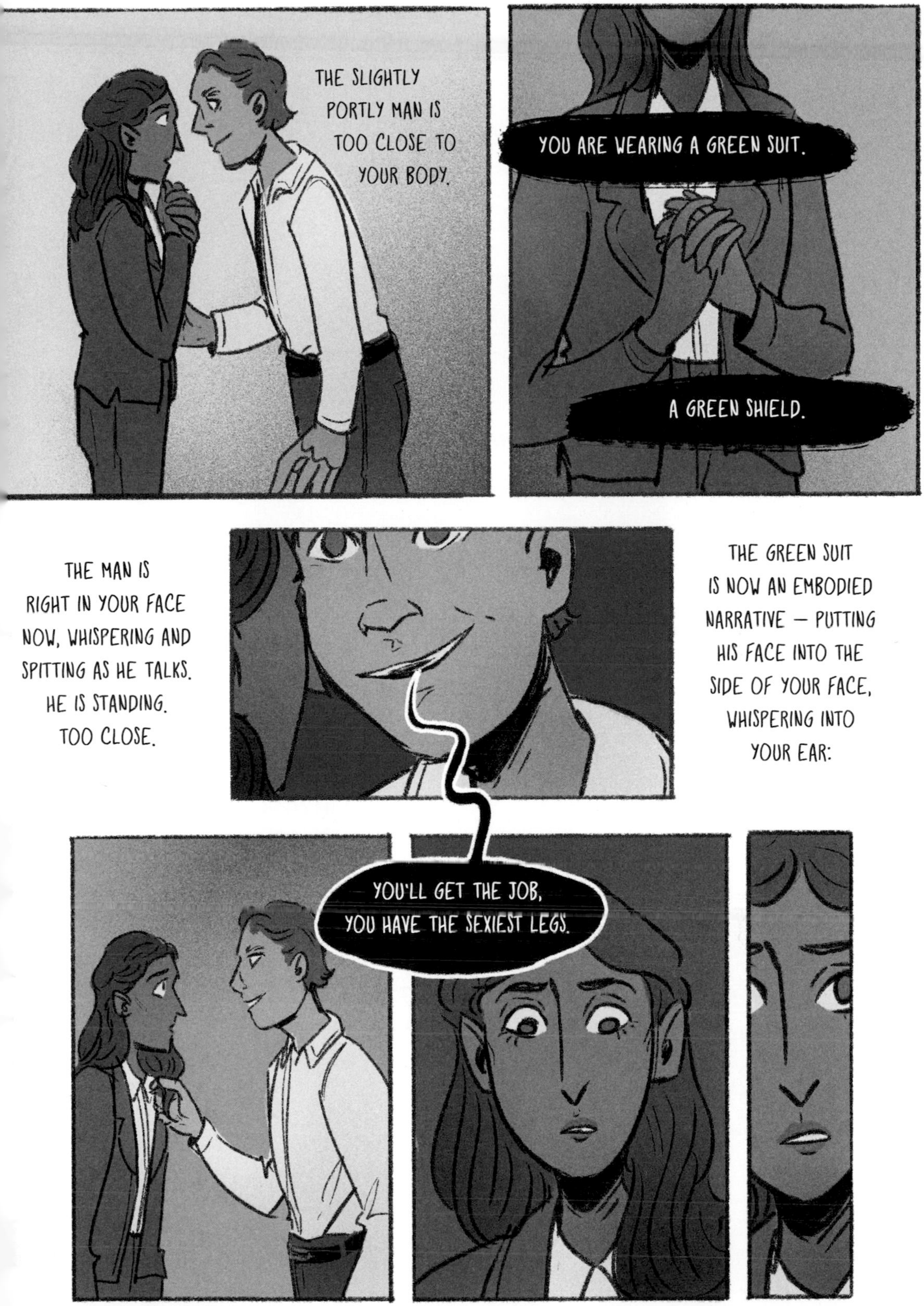
THE SLIGHTLY PORTLY MAN IS TOO CLOSE TO YOUR BODY.
YOU ARE WEARING A GREEN SUIT.
A GREEN SHIELD.
THE MAN IS RIGHT IN YOUR FACE NOW, WHISPERING AND SPITTING AS HE TALKS. HE IS STANDING. TOO CLOSE.
THE GREEN SUIT IS NOW AN EMBODIED NARRATIVE — PUTTING HIS FACE INTO THE SIDE OF YOUR FACE, WHISPERING INTO YOUR EAR:
YOU'LL GET THE JOB, YOU HAVE THE SEXIEST LEGS.

HE SAID IT.

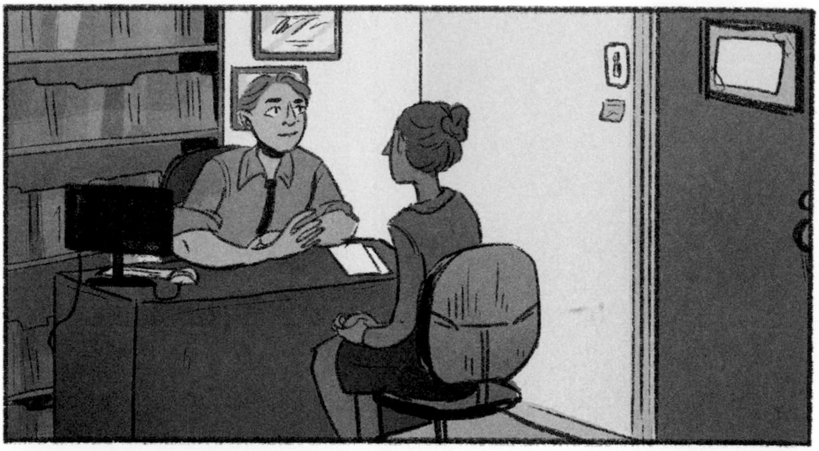

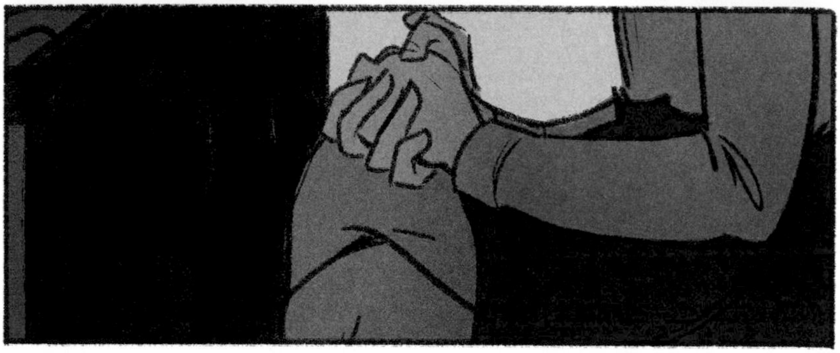

HE SAID THAT.

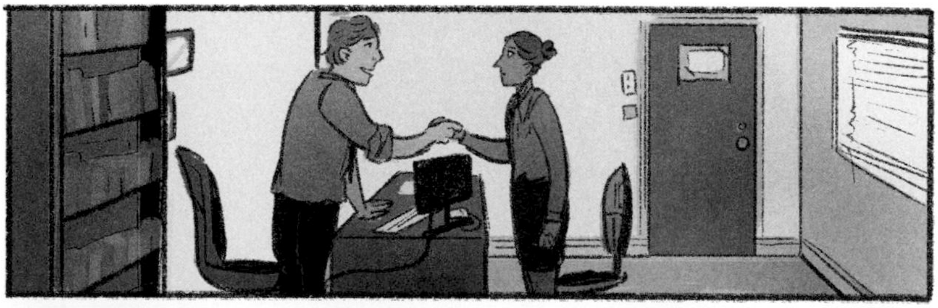

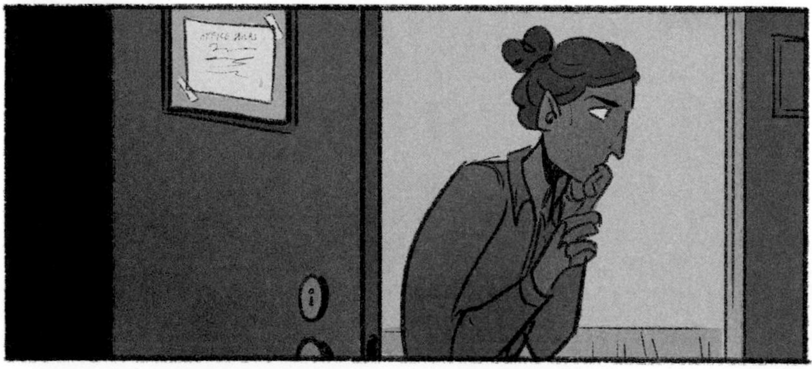

University Toxic
(excerpt)
by Laura Hinton

You think he is pleased to see you.

He pushes into your face. He is pushing now. Still smiling. You are no longer smiling.
He is pushing.
As if into you.

You think he is smiling as he is approaching. You think:

He likes you as a professional.

He is pleased with your performance.

He wants to hire you for the job.

He takes you seriously as a possible colleague and potential professor at this university.

Not. He is pushing into your face. A little too closely. What is occurring?

The slightly portly man is too close to your body. You are wearing a green suit.
A green shield.

The man is right in your face now whispering and spitting as he talks. He is standing.
Too close. The green suit is now an embodied narrative—

putting his face into the side of your face, whispering into your ear:

You'll get the job, you have the sexiest legs.

He said it. He said that.

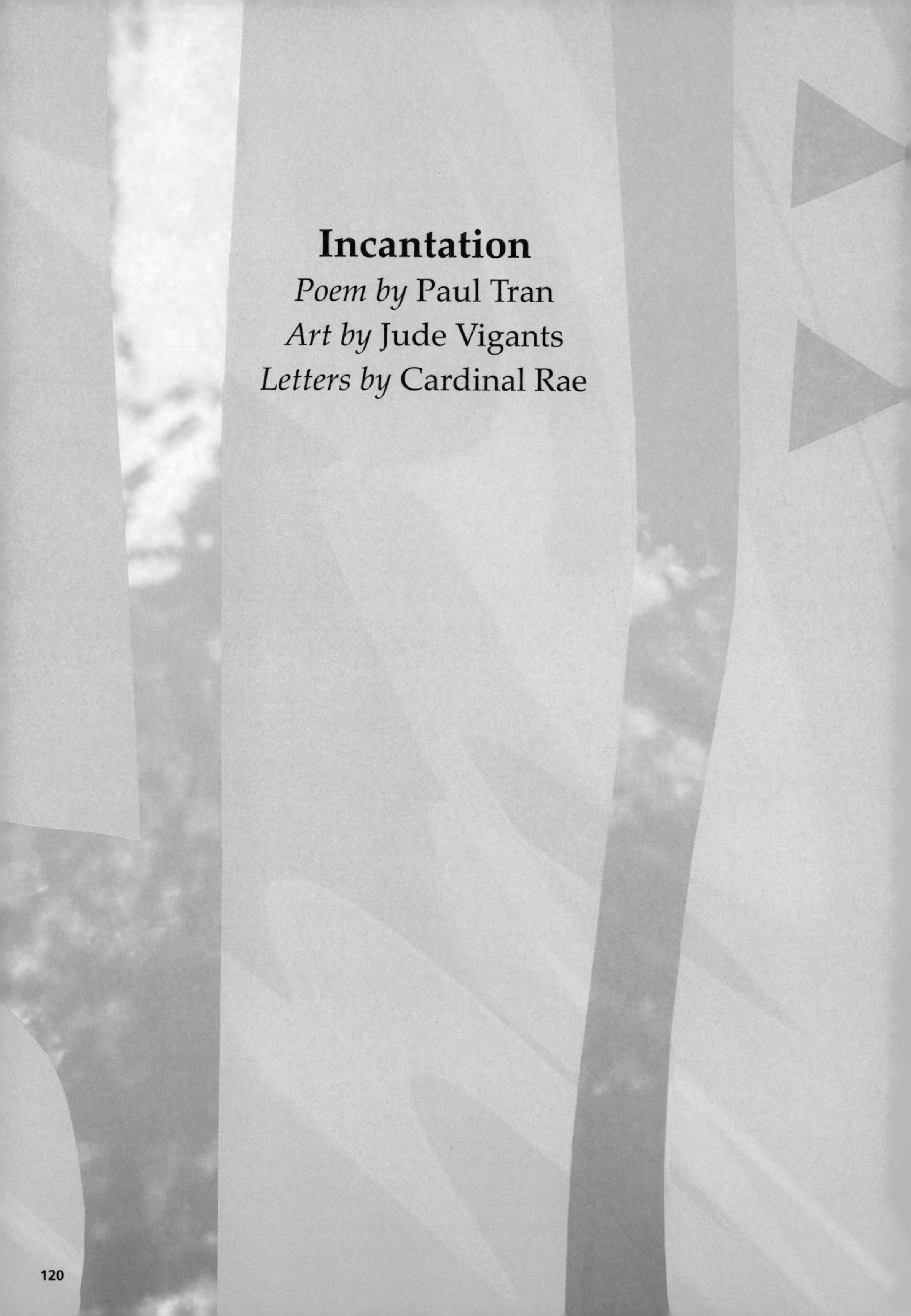

Incantation

Poem by Paul Tran

Art by Jude Vigants

Letters by Cardinal Rae

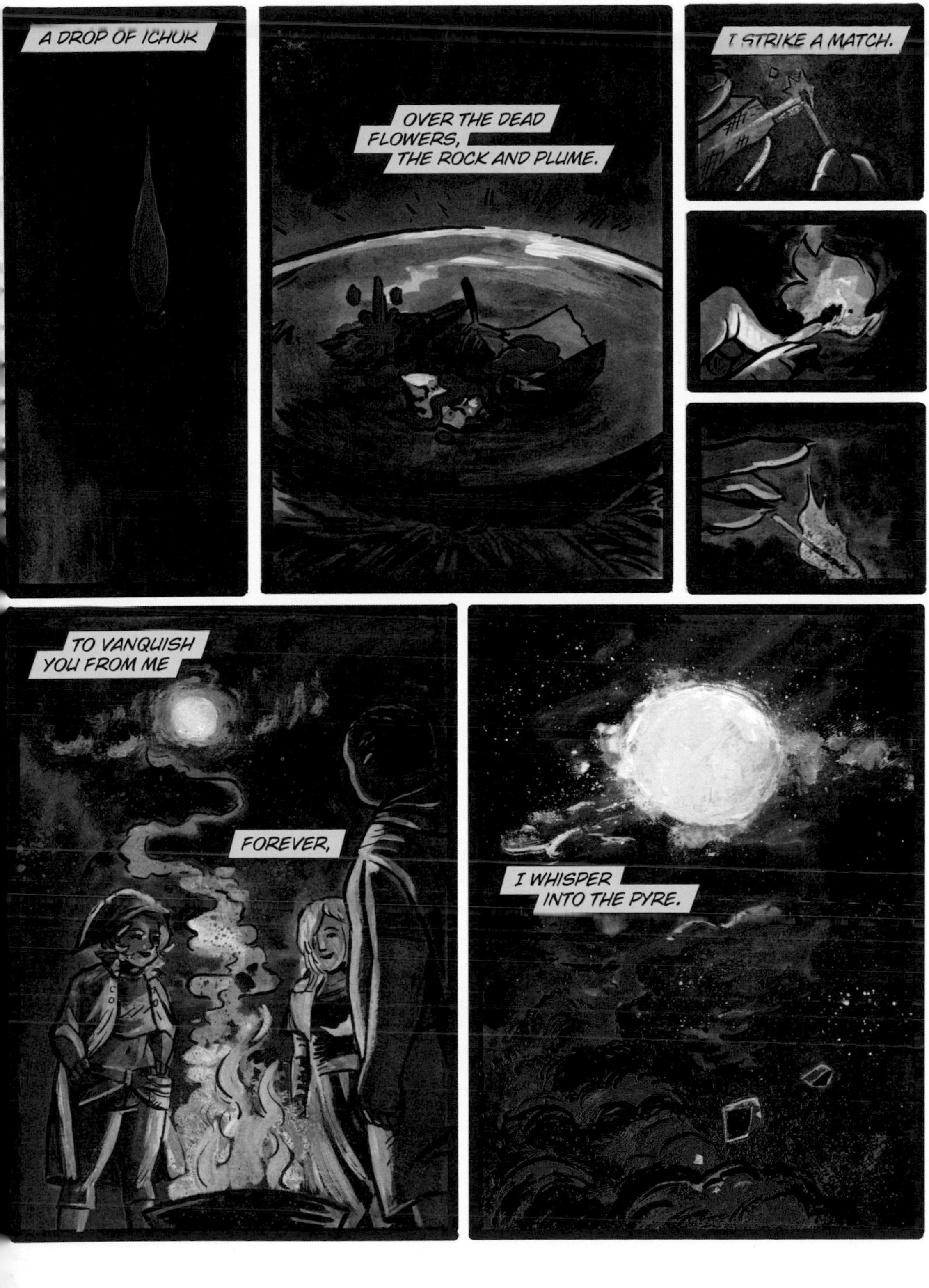
A DROP OF ICHOR
OVER THE DEAD FLOWERS, THE ROCK AND PLUME.
I STRIKE A MATCH.
TO VANQUISH YOU FROM ME
FOREVER,
I WHISPER INTO THE PYRE.

Incantation
by Paul Tran

I write your name
   on a sheet
of paper.
   I fold it
in half.

   In the center
of a bowl:
   Lavender.
Quartz.
   A feather.

With a kitchen knife
   I summon blood
to the surface
   of my left palm.
Love line.

   Life line.
Tell me
   what this means.
I clench my fist.
   I squeeze

a drop of ichor
   over the dead
flowers,
   the rock and plume.
I strike a match.

   To vanquish
you from me
   forever,
I whisper
   into the pyre.

Good-bye.
   I bury
your ash
   in the garden.
Good-bye.

   Winter
to spring.
   Good-bye.
Then summer.
   Nothing blooms

where I keep you.
   Not hoa lan
or birds of paradise
   choking
the encroaching fern.

Except me,
   you still kill
everything.

Capitalism Ruins Everything, Even Witch Craft

Poem by Kendra DeColo

Art by Ned Barnett

Colors by Lesley Atlansky

Letters by Cardinal Rae

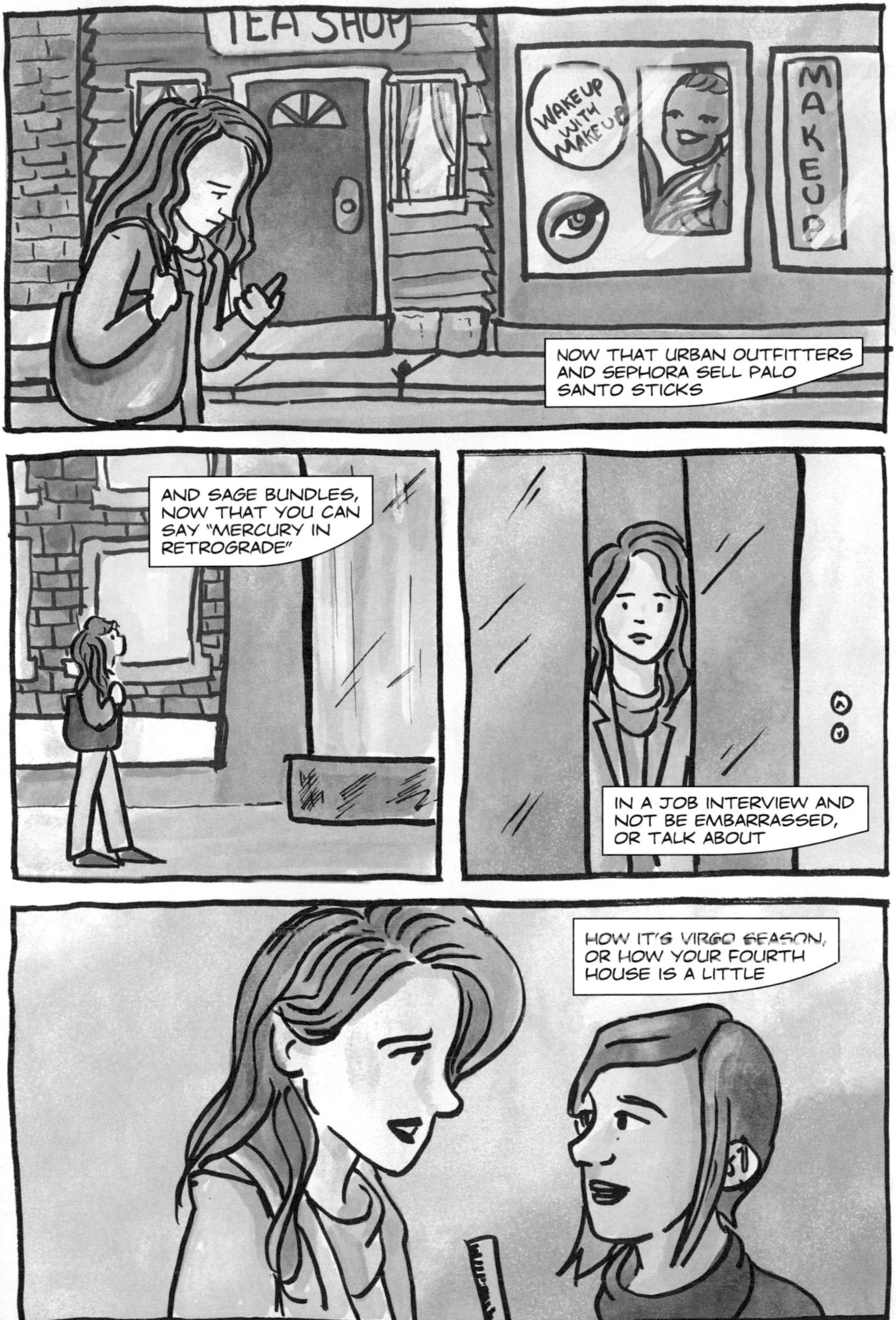
TEA SHOP
WAKE UP WITH MAKEUP
MAKEUP
NOW THAT URBAN OUTFITTERS AND SEPHORA SELL PALO SANTO STICKS
AND SAGE BUNDLES, NOW THAT YOU CAN SAY "MERCURY IN RETROGRADE"
IN A JOB INTERVIEW AND NOT BE EMBARRASSED, OR TALK ABOUT
HOW IT'S VIRGO SEASON, OR HOW YOUR FOURTH HOUSE IS A LITTLE

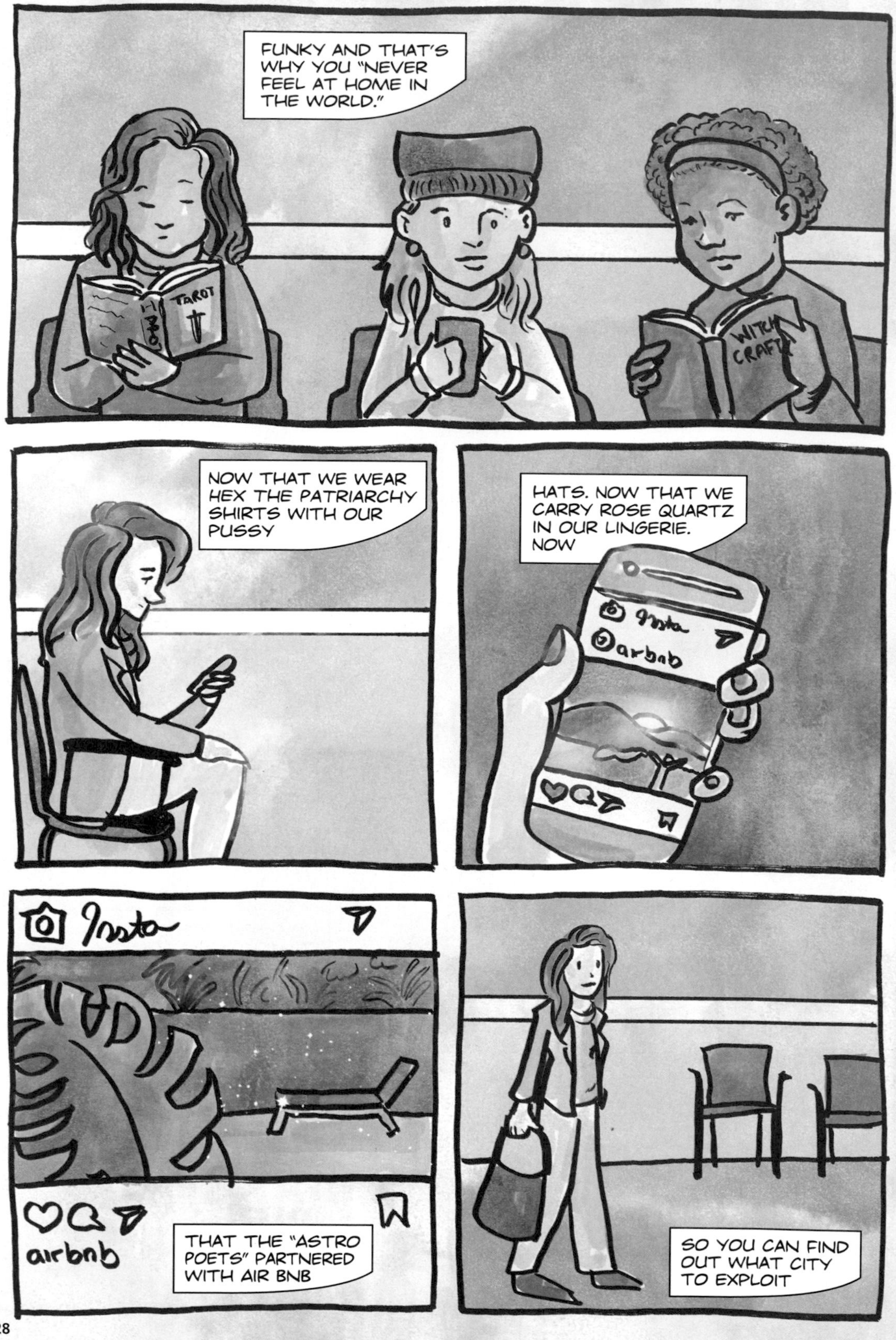
FUNKY AND THAT'S WHY YOU "NEVER FEEL AT HOME IN THE WORLD."
TAROT
WITCH CRAFT
NOW THAT WE WEAR HEX THE PATRIARCHY SHIRTS WITH OUR PUSSY
HATS. NOW THAT WE CARRY ROSE QUARTZ IN OUR LINGERIE. NOW
Insta
airbnb
Insta
airbnb
THAT THE "ASTRO POETS" PARTNERED WITH AIR BNB
SO YOU CAN FIND OUT WHAT CITY TO EXPLOIT

Capitalism Ruins Everything, Even Witch Craft
by Kendra DeColo

Now that Urban Outfitters and Sephora sell palo santo sticks
and sage bundles, now that you can say "mercury in retrograde"
in a job interview and not be embarrassed, or talk about
how it's Virgo season, or how your fourth house is a little

funky and that's why you "never feel at home in the world."
Now that we wear *Hex the Patriarchy* shirts with our pussy
hats. Now that we carry rose quartz in our lingerie. Now
that the "Astro Poets" partnered with Air BnB

so you can find out what city to exploit
based on your sun sign. Or rising. You can read your
star chart like a Cheesecake Factory menu.
You can cast a circle in four directions. You can go

to the crystal store where a sales clerk tells you
that the stone you're holding is the soul
of the baby you couldn't carry to term
and you will want to slap her

and weep
and you buy the fucking crystal
and hold it each morning
before you lay it back down

by the plant whose leaves
look like hands almost
reaching to touch your face.

Drown

Poem by Venus Thrash
Art by Y Sanders
Letters by Cardinal Rae

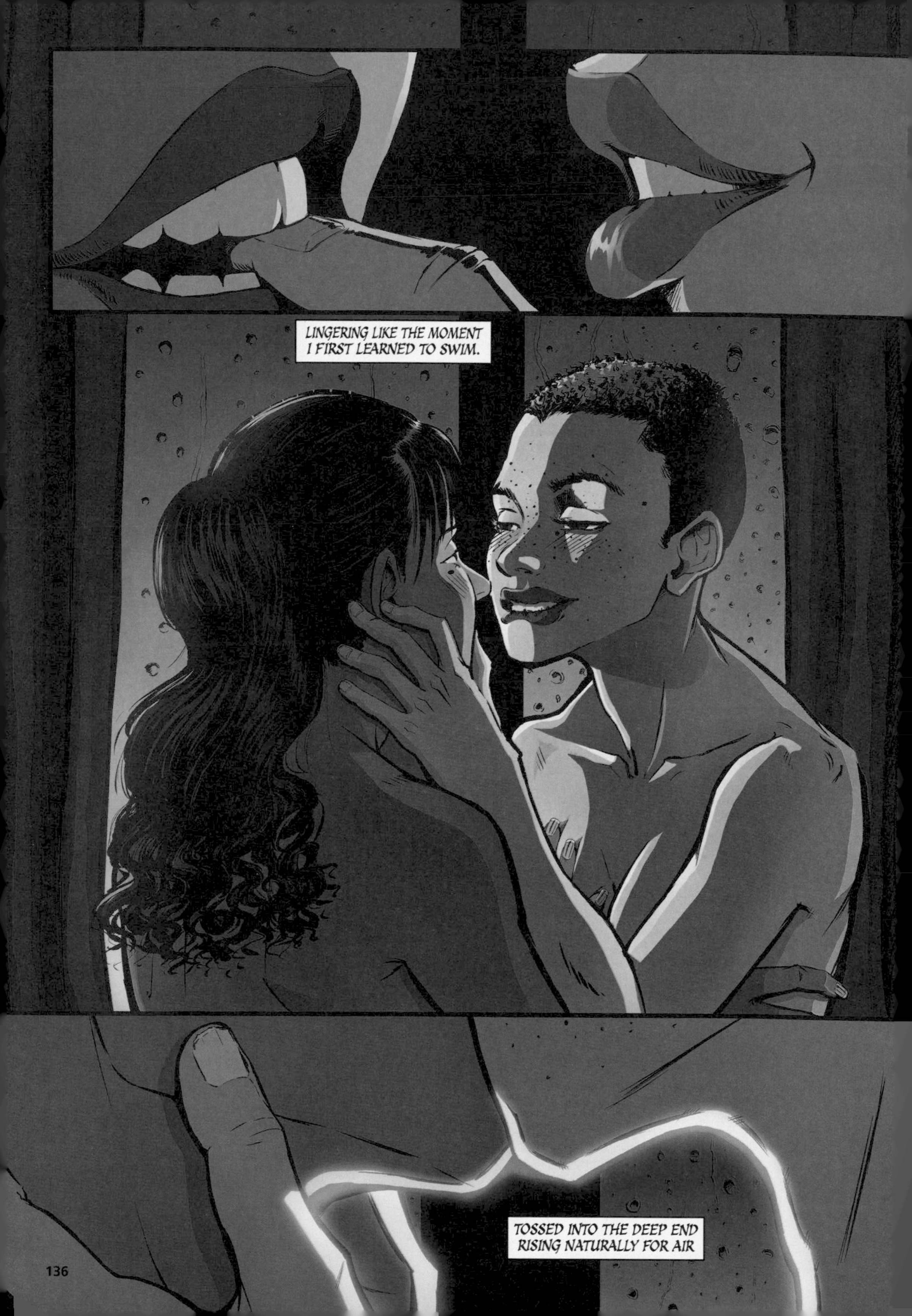
LINGERING LIKE THE MOMENT
I FIRST LEARNED TO SWIM.
TOSSED INTO THE DEEP END
RISING NATURALLY FOR AIR

Drown
by Venus Thrash

Ten summers gone since we made love non-stop
in a shady hotel while Chelsea New York vibed
below us. Me with pinkeye and you still wanting
to kiss my devoted mouth. Your plump lips on mine
lingering like the moment I first learned to swim.
Tossed into the deep end rising naturally for air
knowing then no rushing waters can ever claim
me nor empty promises we dared not make as we
returned to regimented lives never again to touch
to palm your ample breasts in my hands caress
curves enough to match my own   Mercy.
To nibble the tender nipple. To flick the jewel between
my teeth. You in a downpour. And I catching rain
on my tongue.

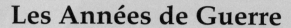

Les Années de Guerre

Poem by Virginia Konchan
Art by Takeia Marie
Colors by Gab Contreras
Letters by Cardinal Rae

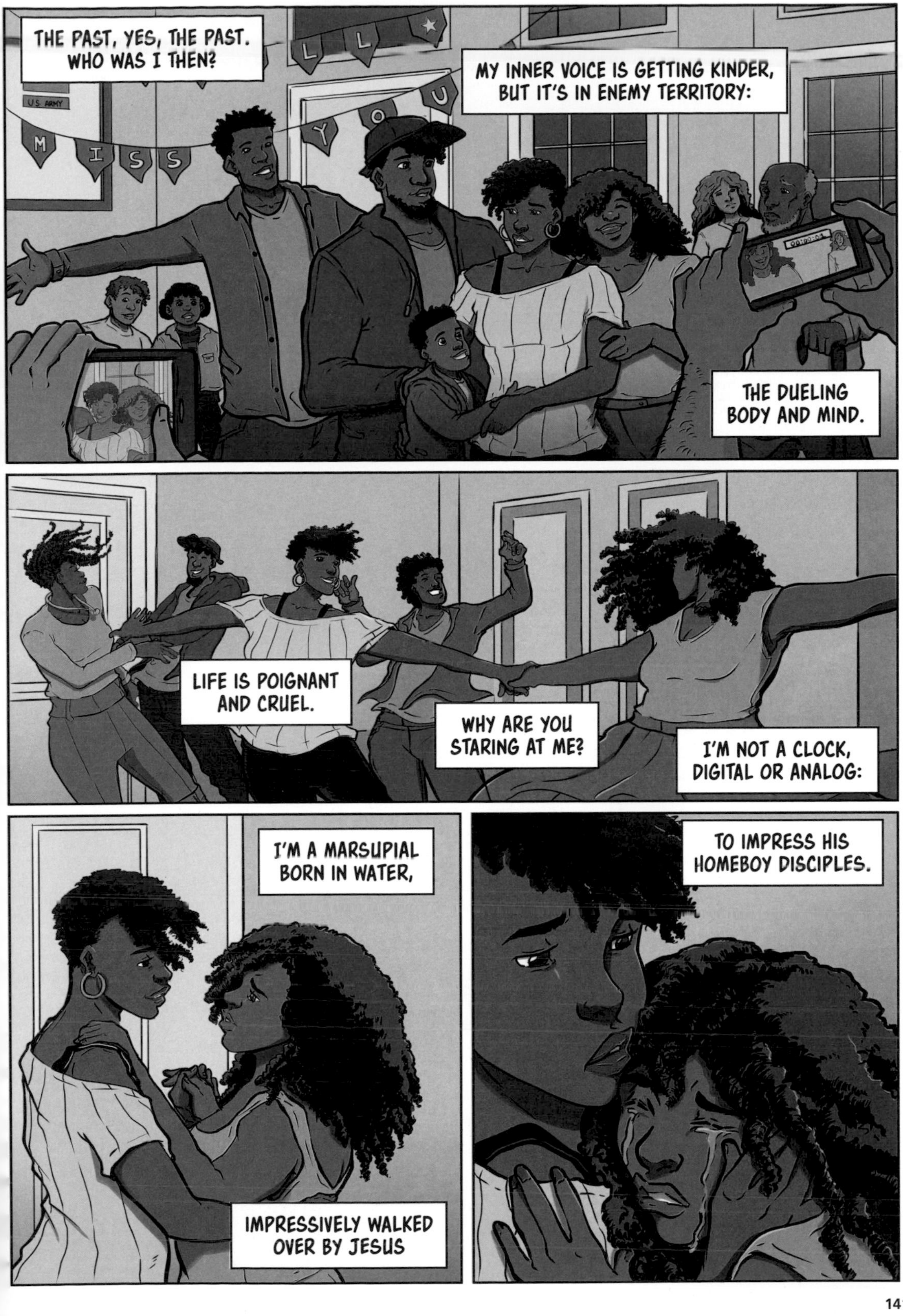
THE PAST, YES, THE PAST. WHO WAS I THEN?
MY INNER VOICE IS GETTING KINDER, BUT IT'S IN ENEMY TERRITORY:
THE DUELING BODY AND MIND.
MISS YOU
U.S. ARMY
LIFE IS POIGNANT AND CRUEL.
WHY ARE YOU STARING AT ME?
I'M NOT A CLOCK, DIGITAL OR ANALOG:
I'M A MARSUPIAL BORN IN WATER,
IMPRESSIVELY WALKED OVER BY JESUS
TO IMPRESS HIS HOMEBOY DISCIPLES.

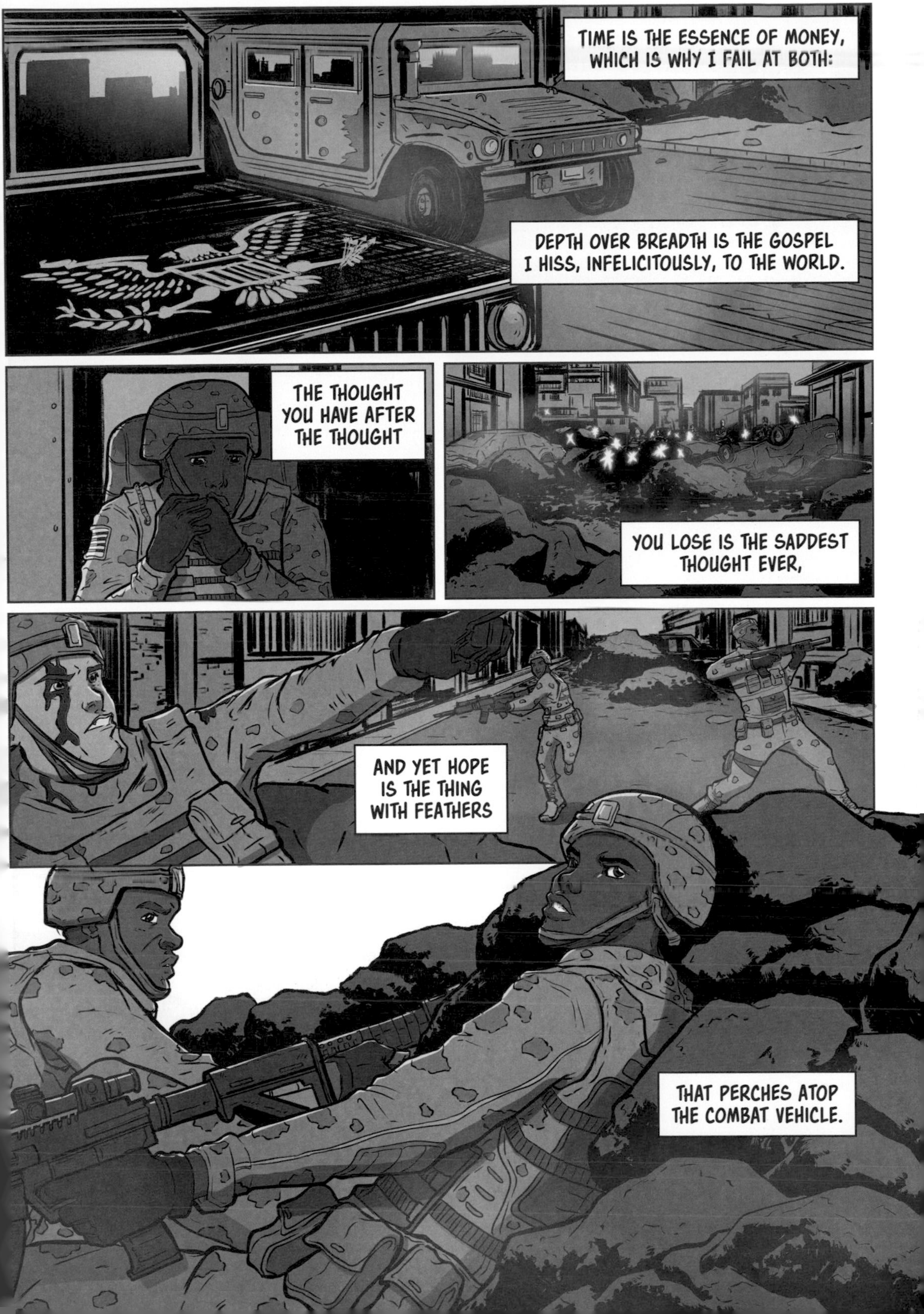
TIME IS THE ESSENCE OF MONEY, WHICH IS WHY I FAIL AT BOTH:
DEPTH OVER BREADTH IS THE GOSPEL I HISS, INFELICITOUSLY, TO THE WORLD.
THE THOUGHT YOU HAVE AFTER THE THOUGHT
YOU LOSE IS THE SADDEST THOUGHT EVER,
AND YET HOPE IS THE THING WITH FEATHERS
THAT PERCHES ATOP THE COMBAT VEHICLE.

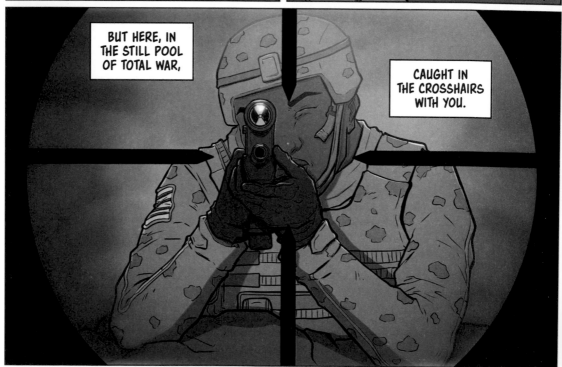

Les Années de Guerre
by Viginia Konchan

The past, yes, the past. Who was I then?
My inner voice is getting kinder,
but it's in enemy territory:
the dueling body and mind.

Life is poignant and cruel.
Why are you staring at me?

I'm not a clock, digital or analog:
I'm a marsupial born in water,
impressively walked over by Jesus
to impress his homeboy disciples.

But who's counting his awesome miracles?
I was happy peeling potatoes in the army:
happy with my ration of butter and bread.

Dramatis personae, all rise.
Court is now in session,
presided over by Your Honor
in deed and name.

Time is the essence of money,
which is why I fail at both:

depth over breadth is the gospel
I hiss, infelicitously, to the world.

The thought you have after the thought
you lose is the saddest thought ever,

and yet hope is the thing with feathers
that perches atop the combat vehicle.

Who reminds repetition of repetition?
What is the antidote to territorialism,
binding men to evil like Elmer's glue?

Me? I reject all domestic certainties.
I've never wanted to be anywhere

but here, in the still pool of total war,
caught in the crosshairs with you.

Settlement

Poem by Vanessa Angélica Villarreal
Art by Ronnie Garcia
Letters by Cardinal Rae

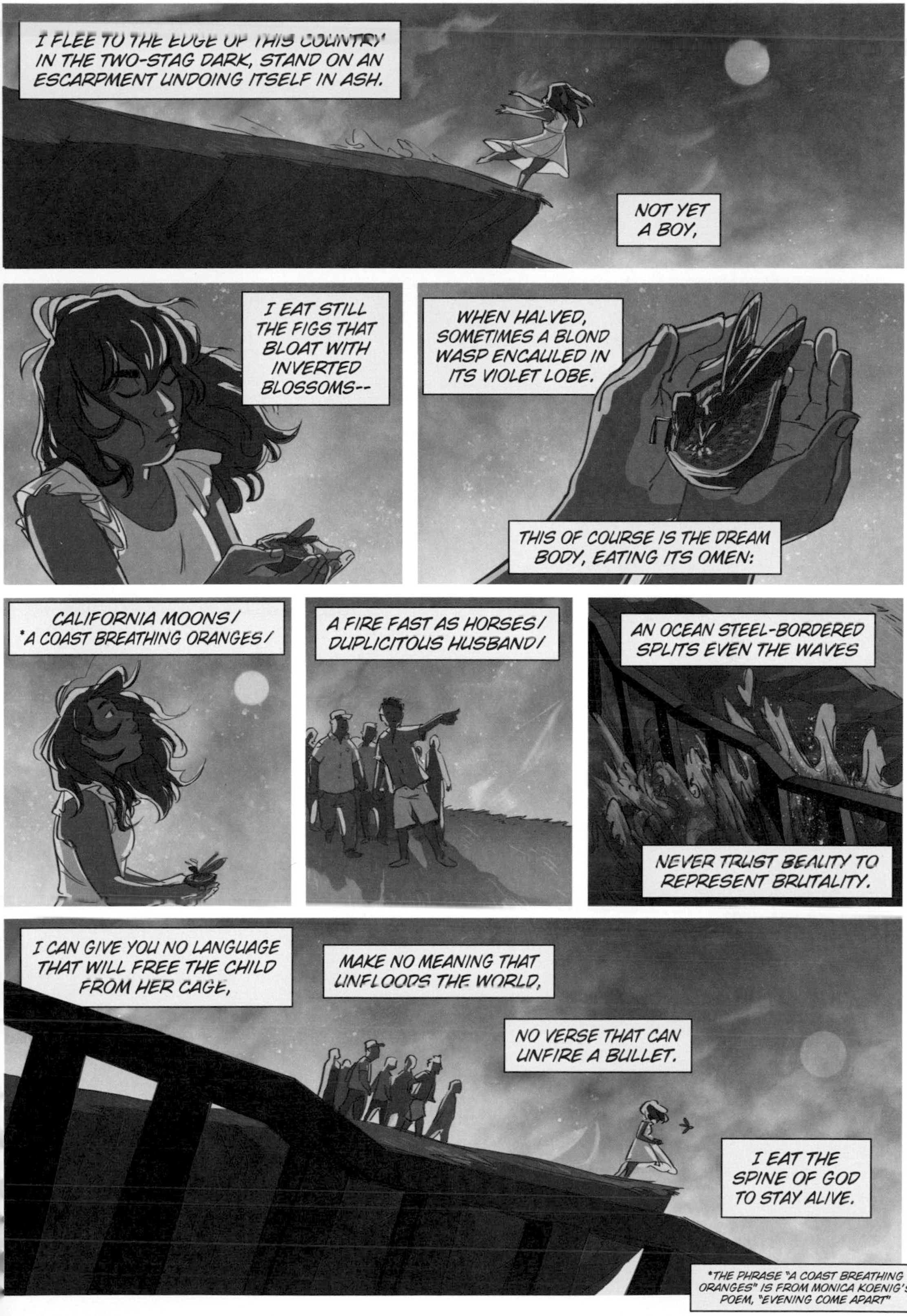
I FLEE TO THE EDGE OF THIS COUNTRY IN THE TWO-STAG DARK, STAND ON AN ESCARPMENT UNDOING ITSELF IN ASH.
NOT YET A BOY,
I EAT STILL THE FIGS THAT BLOAT WITH INVERTED BLOSSOMS--
WHEN HALVED, SOMETIMES A BLOND WASP ENCAULED IN ITS VIOLET LOBE.
THIS OF COURSE IS THE DREAM BODY, EATING ITS OMEN:
CALIFORNIA MOONS/ *A COAST BREATHING ORANGES/
A FIRE FAST AS HORSES/ DUPLICITOUS HUSBAND/
AN OCEAN STEEL-BORDERED SPLITS EVEN THE WAVES
NEVER TRUST BEAUTY TO REPRESENT BRUTALITY.
I CAN GIVE YOU NO LANGUAGE THAT WILL FREE THE CHILD FROM HER CAGE,
MAKE NO MEANING THAT UNFLOODS THE WORLD,
NO VERSE THAT CAN UNFIRE A BULLET.
I EAT THE SPINE OF GOD TO STAY ALIVE.

*THE PHRASE "A COAST BREATHING ORANGES" IS FROM MONICA KOENIG'S POEM, "EVENING COME APART"

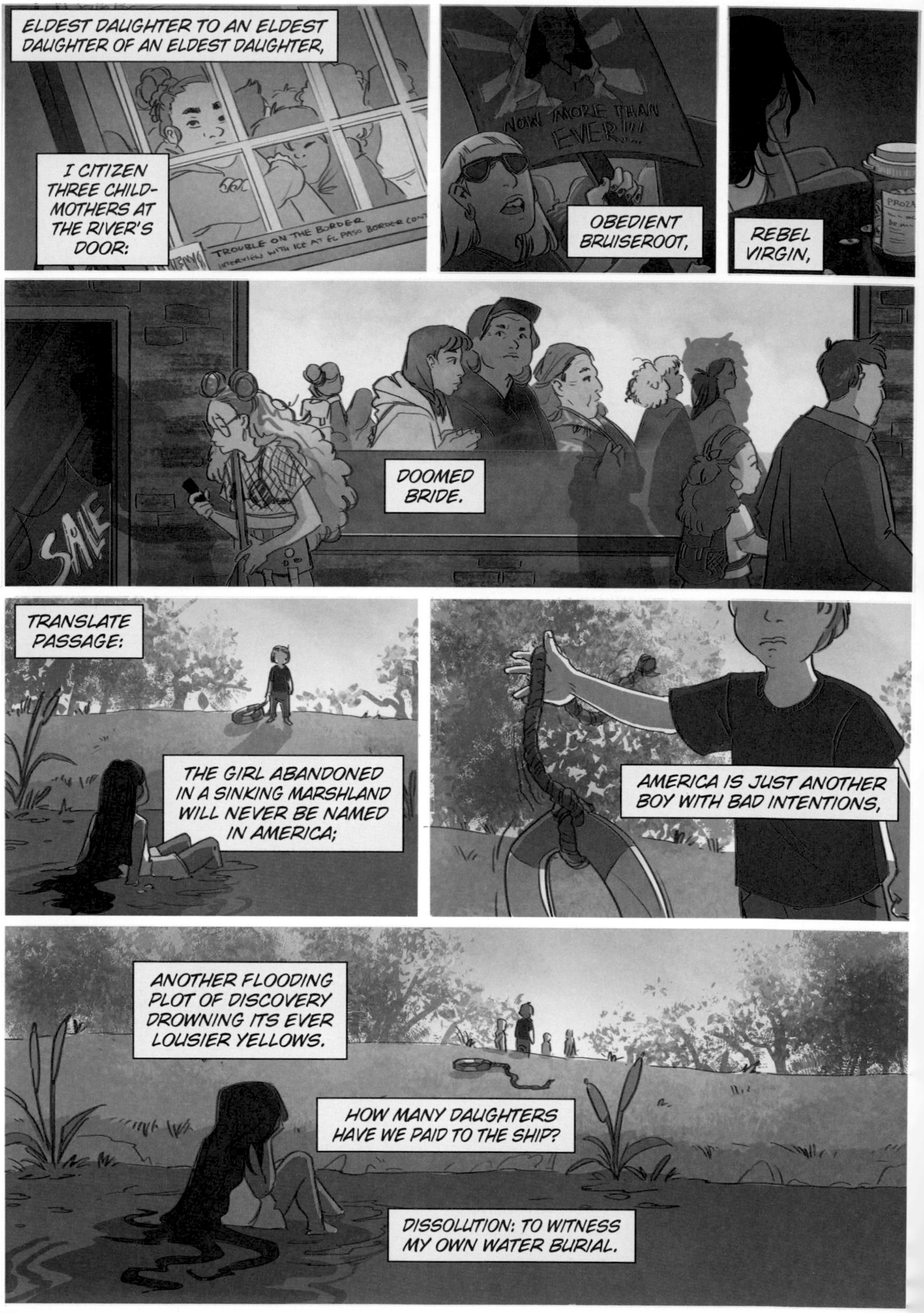
ELDEST DAUGHTER TO AN ELDEST DAUGHTER OF AN ELDEST DAUGHTER,
I CITIZEN THREE CHILD-MOTHERS AT THE RIVER'S DOOR:
TROUBLE ON THE BORDER
NOW MORE THAN EVER!!!
OBEDIENT BRUISEROOT,
REBEL VIRGIN,
SALE
DOOMED BRIDE.
TRANSLATE PASSAGE:
THE GIRL ABANDONED IN A SINKING MARSHLAND WILL NEVER BE NAMED IN AMERICA;
AMERICA IS JUST ANOTHER BOY WITH BAD INTENTIONS,
ANOTHER FLOODING PLOT OF DISCOVERY DROWNING ITS EVER LOUSIER YELLOWS.
HOW MANY DAUGHTERS HAVE WE PAID TO THE SHIP?
DISSOLUTION: TO WITNESS MY OWN WATER BURIAL.

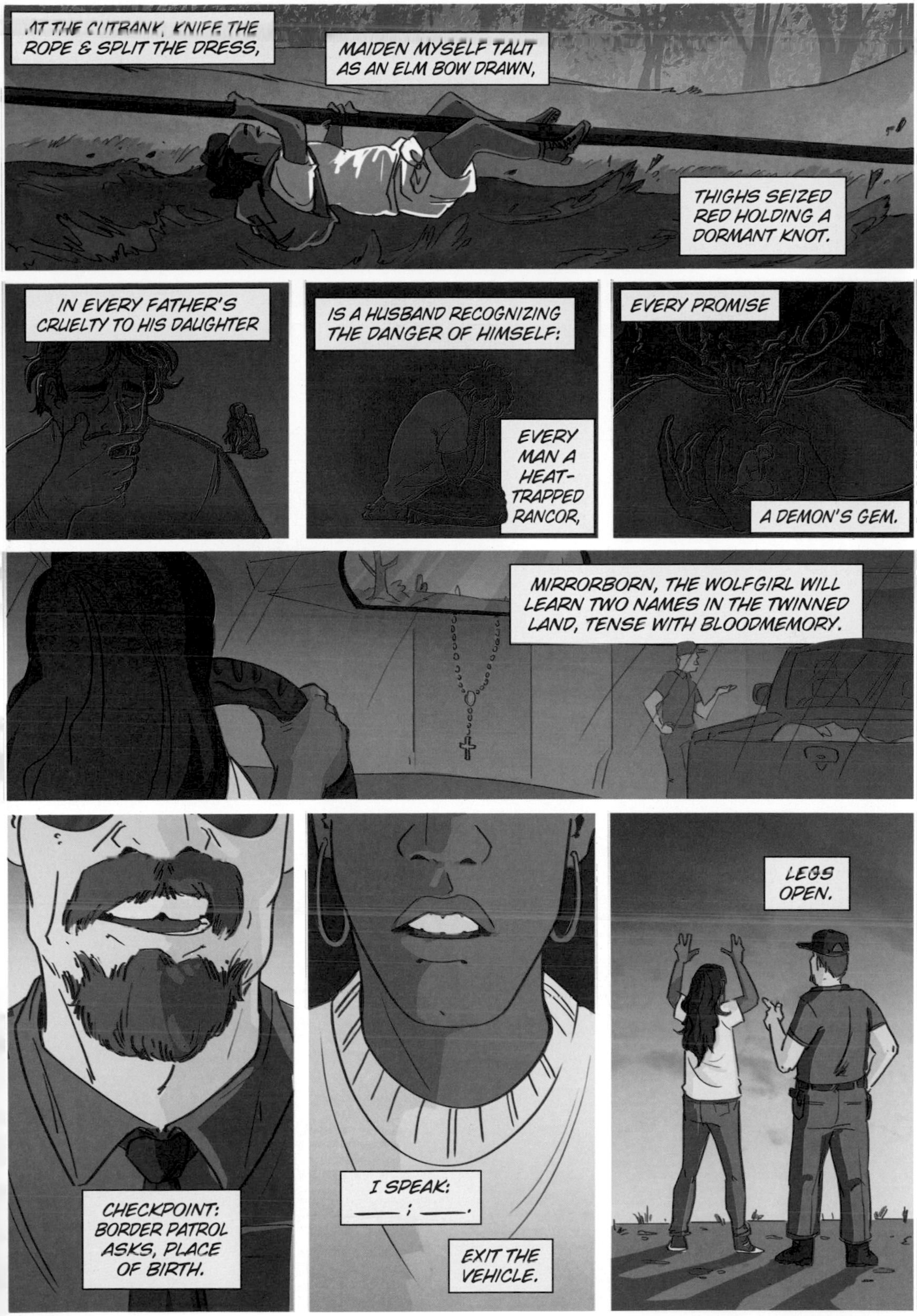
AT THE CUTBANK, KNIFE THE ROPE & SPLIT THE DRESS,
MAIDEN MYSELF TAUT AS AN ELM BOW DRAWN,
THIGHS SEIZED RED HOLDING A DORMANT KNOT.
IN EVERY FATHER'S CRUELTY TO HIS DAUGHTER
IS A HUSBAND RECOGNIZING THE DANGER OF HIMSELF:
EVERY MAN A HEAT-TRAPPED RANCOR,
EVERY PROMISE
A DEMON'S GEM.
MIRRORBORN, THE WOLFGIRL WILL LEARN TWO NAMES IN THE TWINNED LAND, TENSE WITH BLOODMEMORY.
CHECKPOINT: BORDER PATROL ASKS, PLACE OF BIRTH.
I SPEAK: ____ ; ____.
EXIT THE VEHICLE.
LEGS OPEN.

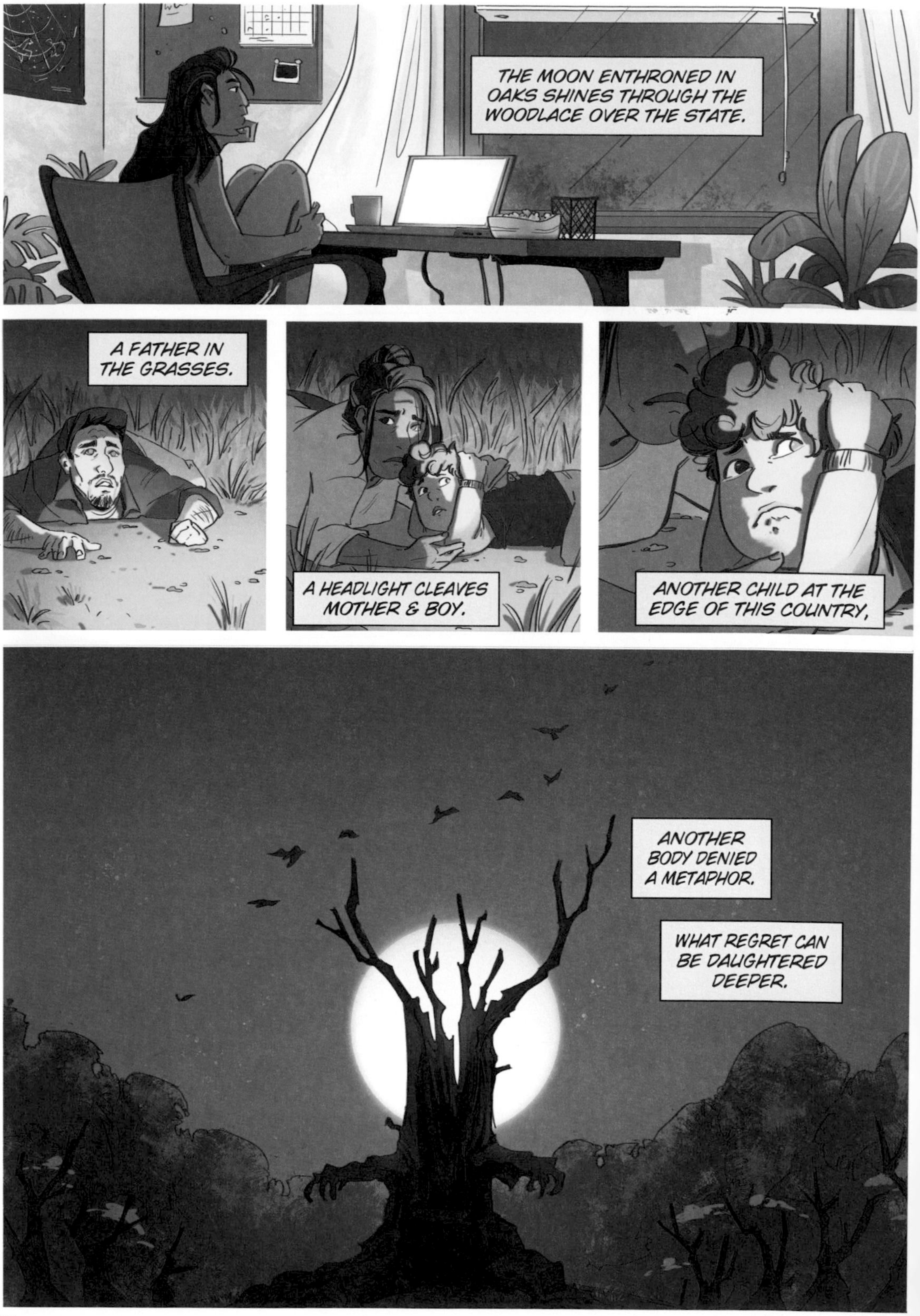

THE MOON ENTHRONED IN OAKS SHINES THROUGH THE WOODLACE OVER THE STATE.
A FATHER IN THE GRASSES.
A HEADLIGHT CLEAVES MOTHER & BOY.
ANOTHER CHILD AT THE EDGE OF THIS COUNTRY,
ANOTHER BODY DENIED A METAPHOR.
WHAT REGRET CAN BE DAUGHTERED DEEPER.

Settlement

by Vanessa Angélica Villarreal

I flee to the edge of this country in the two-stag dark, stand on an escarpment undoing itself in ash. Not yet a boy, I eat still the figs that bloat with inverted blossoms—when halved, sometimes a blond wasp encauled in its violet lobe. This of course is the dream body, eating its omen:

California moons / a coast breathing oranges / a fire fast as horses / duplicitous husband / an ocean steel-bordered splits even the waves

Never trust beauty to represent brutality.

:

I can give you no language that will free the child from her cage, make no meaning that unfloods the world, no verse that can unfire a bullet.

I eat the spine of god to stay alive.

::

Eldest daughter to an eldest daughter of an eldest daughter, I citizen three childmothers at the river's door: obedient bruiseroot, rebel virgin, doomed bride.

:

Translate passage: the girl abandoned in a sinking marshland will never be named in America; America is just another boy with bad intentions, another flooding plot of discovery drowning its ever lousier yellows. How many daughters have we paid to the ship? Dissolution: to witness my own water burial.

::

At the cutbank, knife the rope & split the dress, maiden myself taut as an elm bow drawn, thighs seized red holding a dormant knot. In every father's cruelty to his daughter is a husband recognizing the danger of himself: every man a heat-trapped rancor, every promise a demon's gem.

:

Mirrorborn, the wolfgirl will learn two names in the twinned land, tense with bloodmemory. Checkpoint: border patrol asks, place of birth. I speak: ____;____. Exit the vehicle. Legs open.

::

The moon enthroned in oaks shines through the woodlace over the state. A father in the grasses. A headlight cleaves mother & boy. Another child at the edge of this country, another body denied a metaphor. What regret can be daughtered deeper.

† The phrase "a coast breathing oranges" is from Monica Koenig's poem, "Evening Come Apart"

Dancing with Kiko on the Moon

Poem by Rosebud Ben-Oni

Art by Rio Burton

Letters by Saida Temofonte

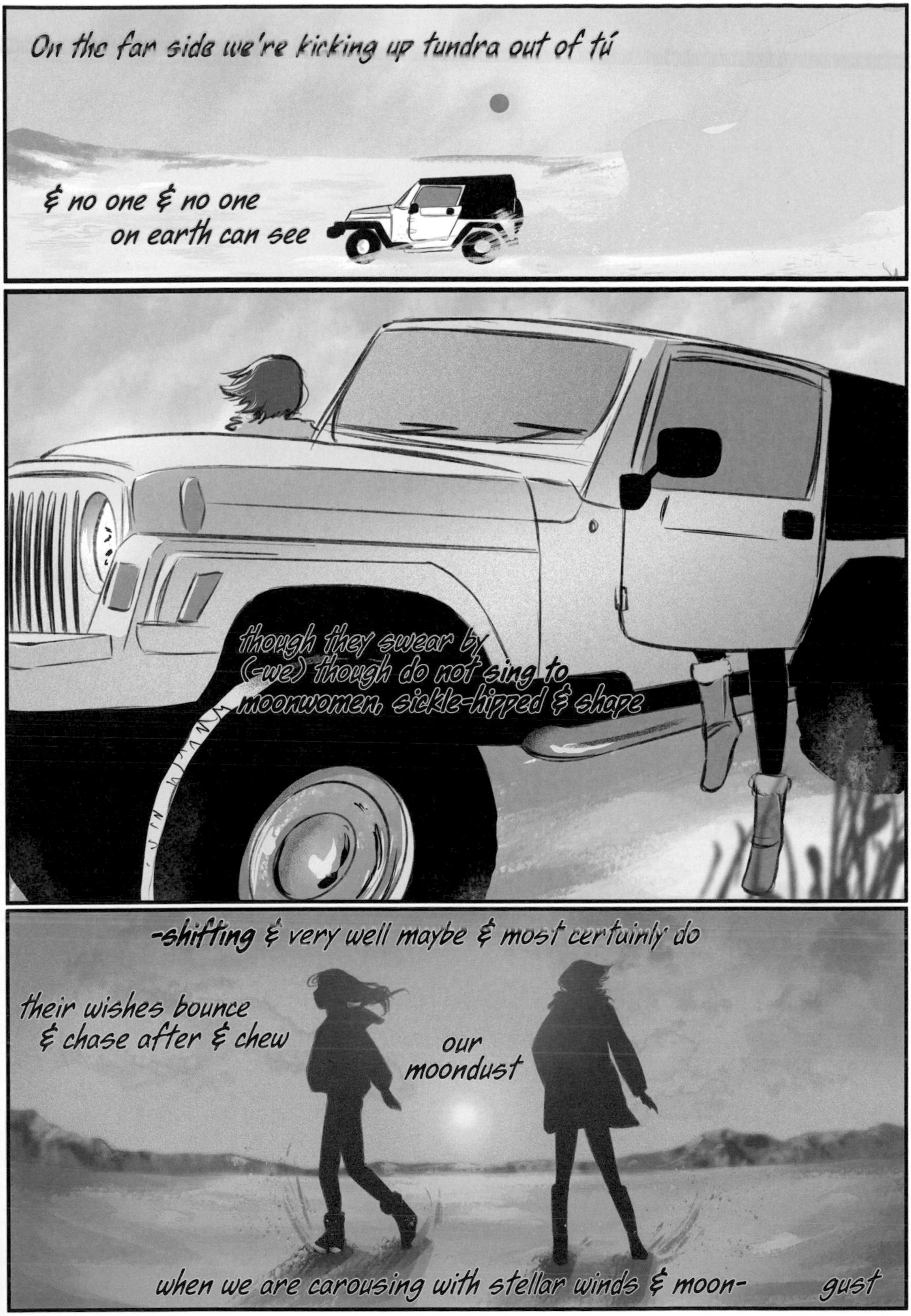
On the far side we're kicking up tundra out of tú
& no one & no one
on earth can see
though they swear by
(-we) though do not sing to
moonwomen, sickle-hipped & shape
-shifting & very well maybe & most certainly do
their wishes bounce
& chase after & chew
our
moondust
when we are carousing with stellar winds & moon-
gust

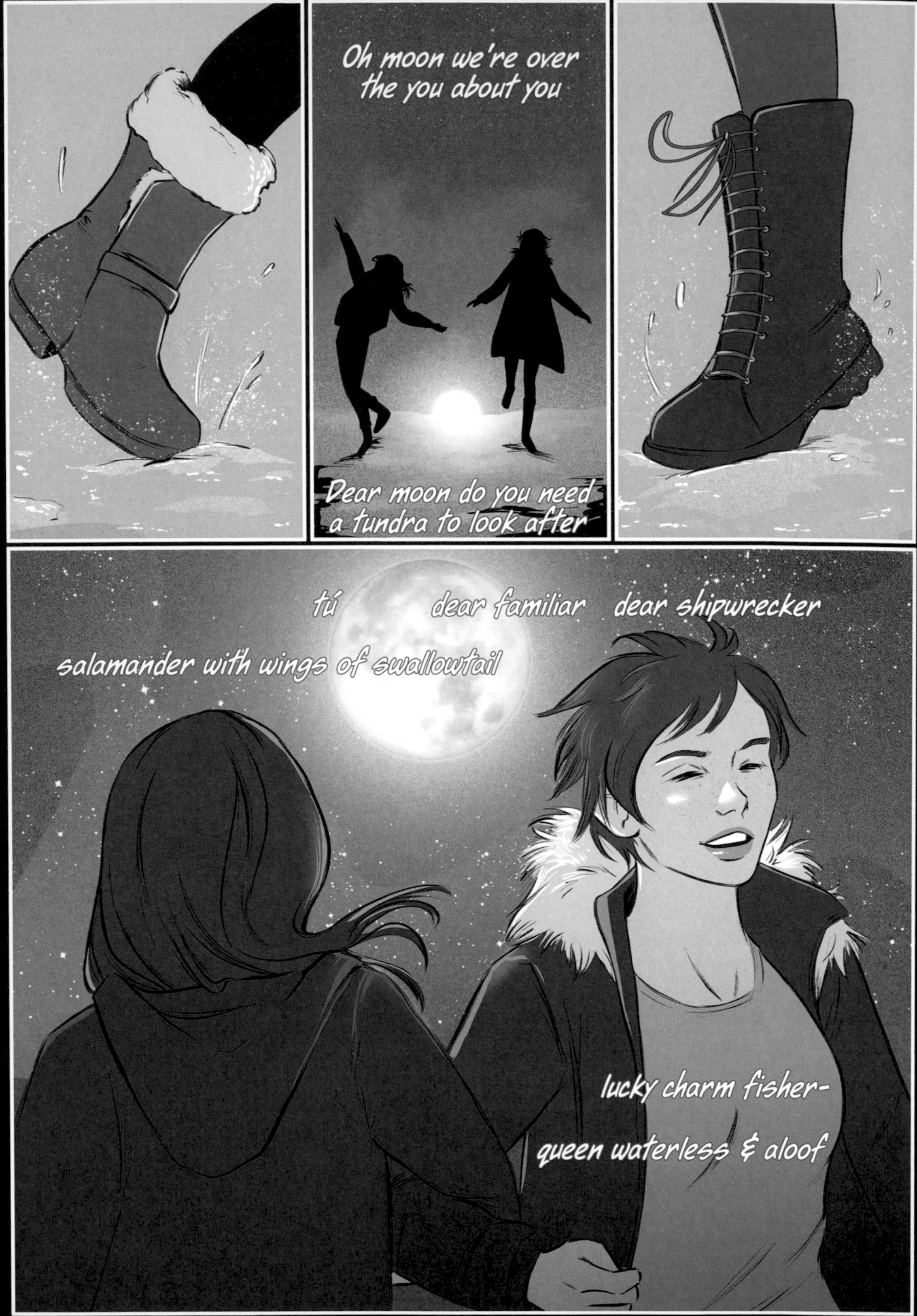
Oh moon we're over
the you about you
Dear moon do you need
a tundra to look after
tú
dear familiar
dear shipwrecker
salamander with wings of swallowtail
lucky charm fisher-
queen waterless & aloof

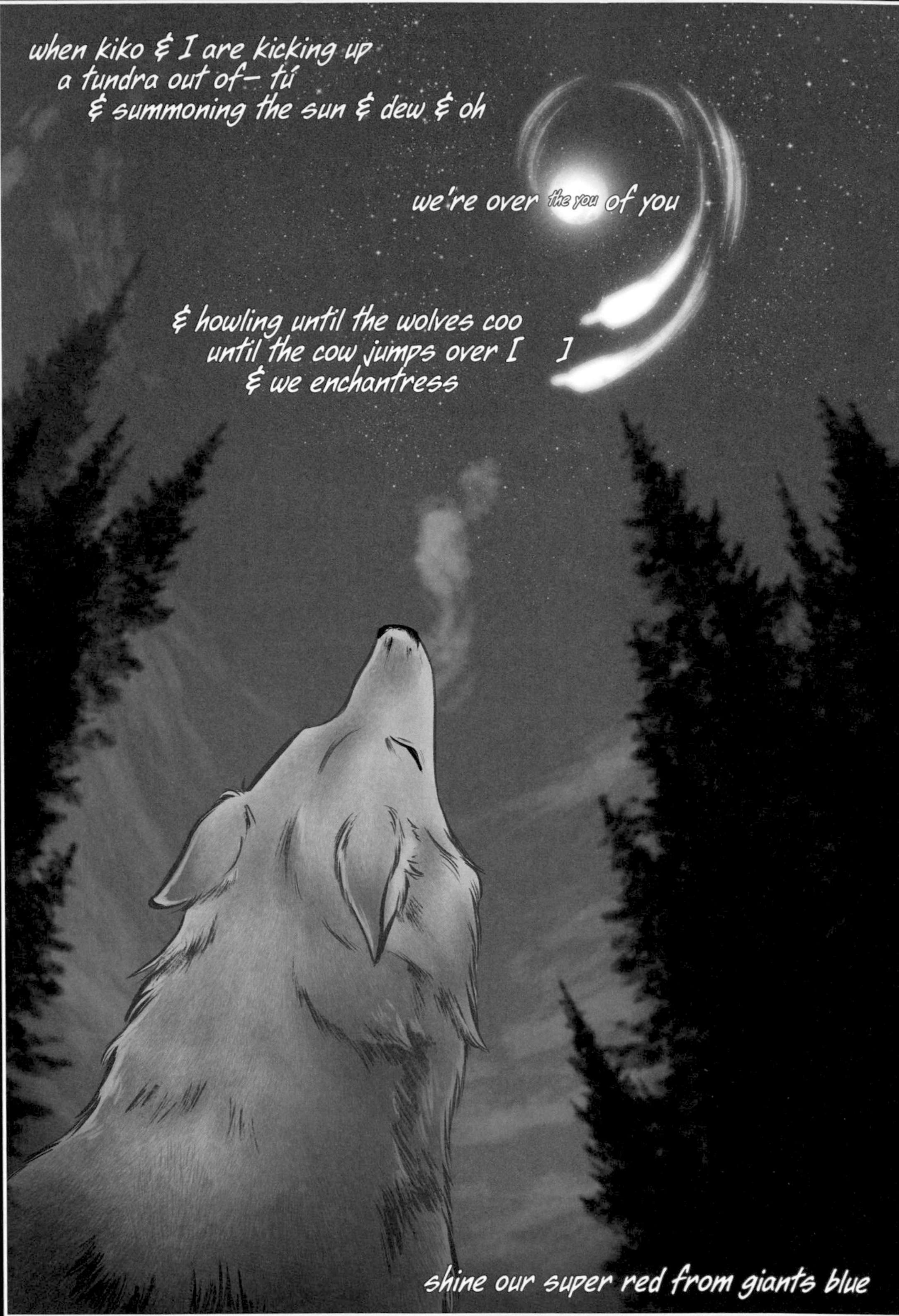
when kiko & I are kicking up
a tundra out of– tú
& summoning the sun & dew & oh
we're over the you of you
& howling until the wolves coo
until the cow jumps over [ ]
& we enchantress
shine our super red from giants blue

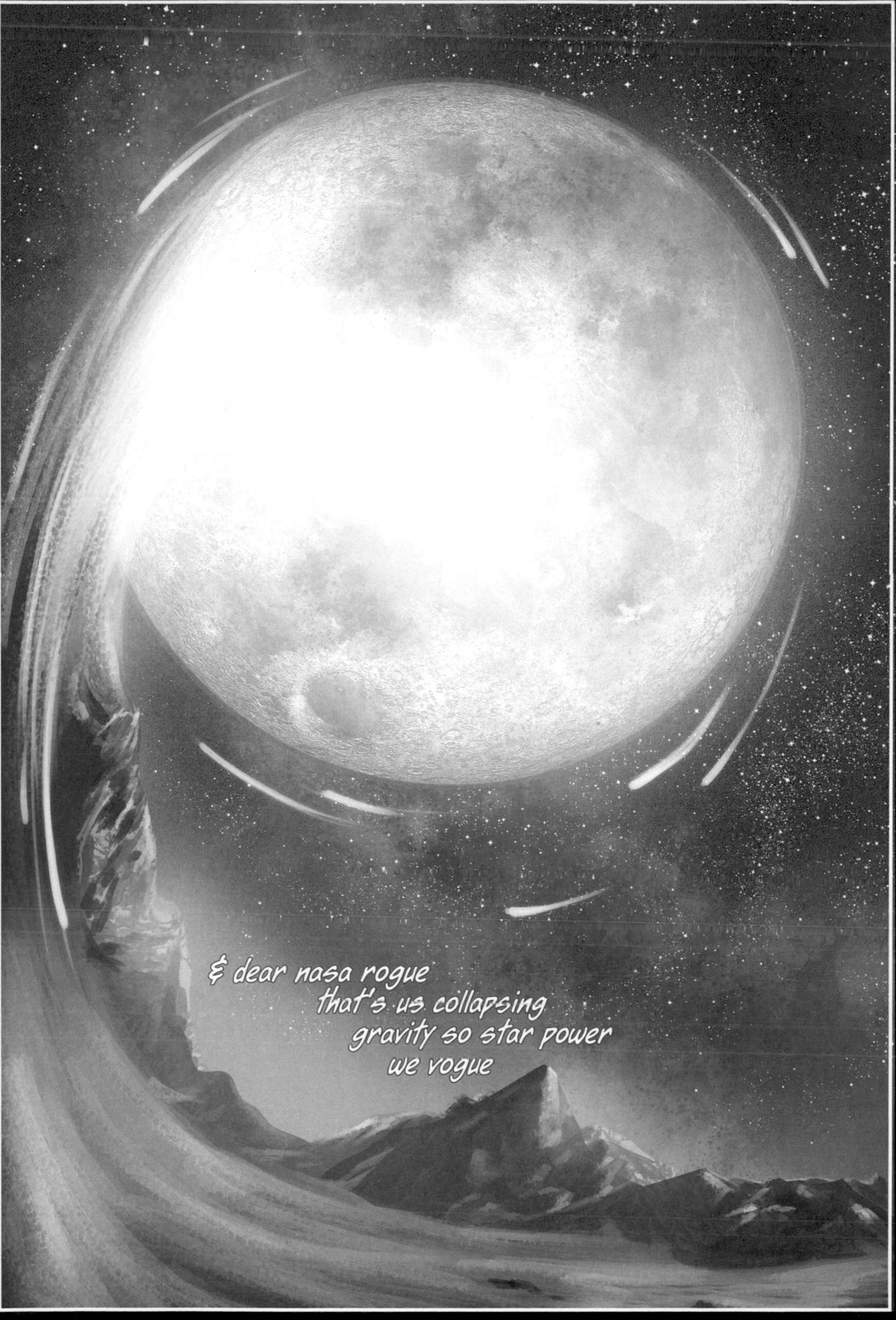
& dear nasa rogue
that's us collapsing
gravity so star power
we vogue

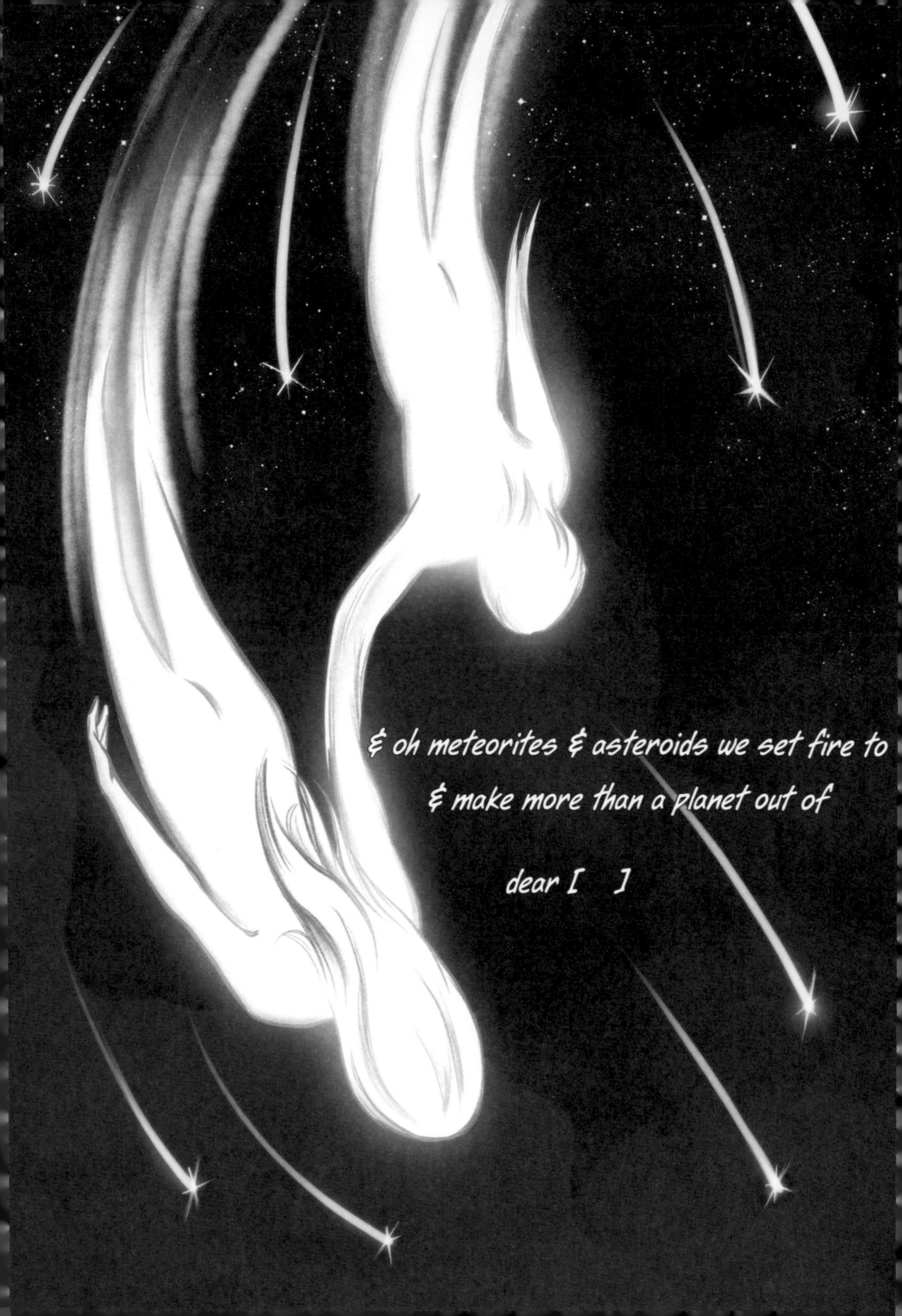
& oh meteorites & asteroids we set fire to
& make more than a planet out of
dear [ ]

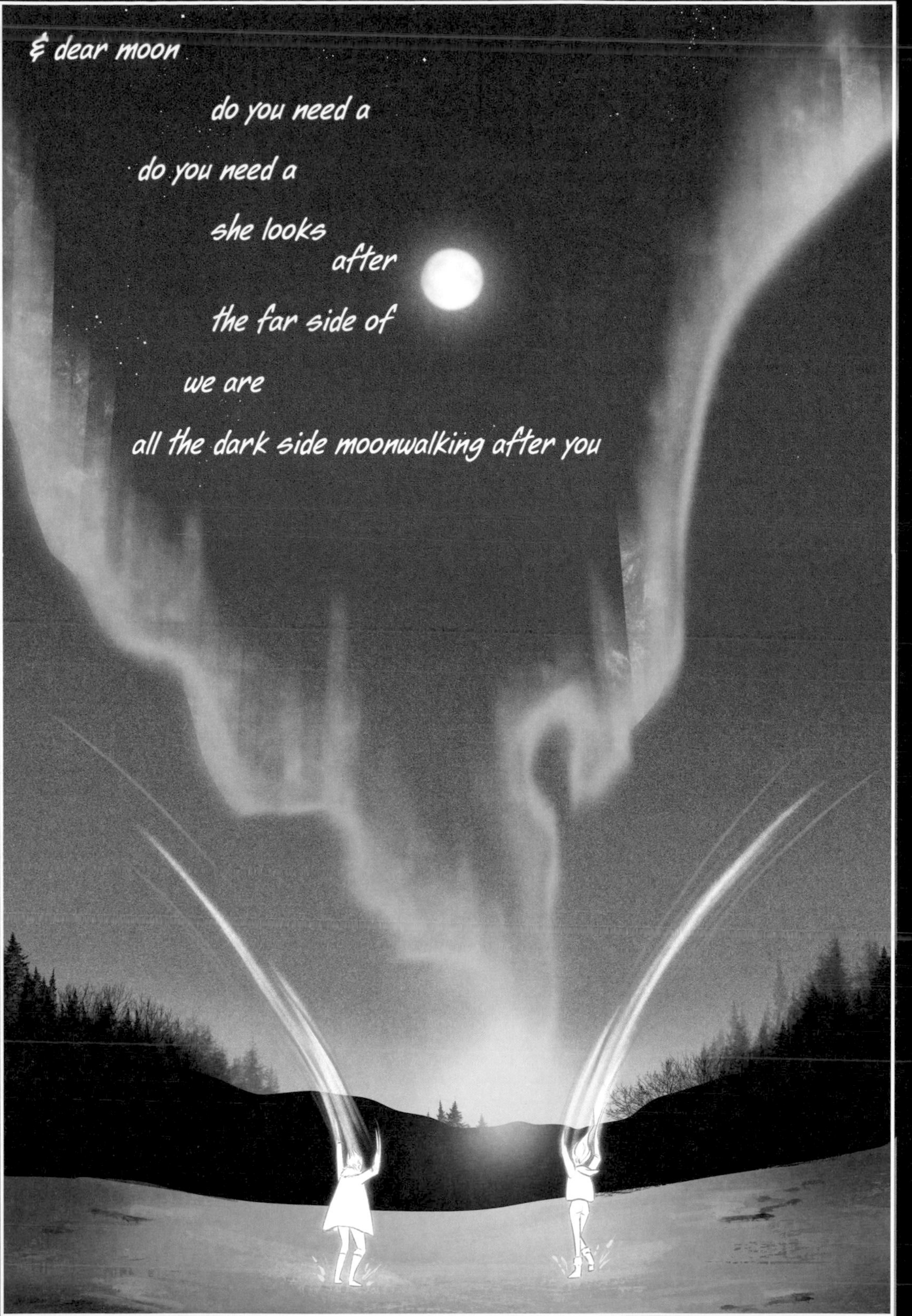
& dear moon
do you need a
do you need a
she looks
after
the far side of
we are
all the dark side moonwalking after you

Dancing with Kiko on the Moon
by Rosebud Ben-Oni

On the far side we're kicking up tundra out of tú

& no one & no one

   on earth can see

     though they swear by
     (-we) though *do not sing to*
     moonwomen, sickle-hipped & shape

       -shifting & very well maybe & most certainly do

         their wishes bounce

      & chase after & chew

    our moondust

   when we are carousing with stellar winds & moon-
             gust

Oh moon we're over the you about you

Dear moon do you need a tundra to look after

    tú   dear familiar dear shipwrecker

   salamander with wings of swallowtail

      lucky charm fisher-

   queen waterless & aloof

It's just us two & we are twisters
that don't leave the ground to [   ]

Welcome to our moonhaus
& we don't have to ghost

shout— we're all the worlds living between tú

which is why the moon

        wears her sunglasses at night
        where exploding stars fall
        shock breakout bright

when kiko & I are kicking up
a tundra out of— tú
& summoning the sun & dew & oh

      we're over ^{the you} of you

         & howling until the wolves coo
         until the cow jumps over [   ]
         & we enchantress

    shine our super red from giants blue

  & dear nasa rogue
     that's us collapsing
       gravity so star power
        we vogue

& oh meteorites & asteroids we set fire to

& make more than a planet out of

   dear [   ]

    & dear moon

      do you need a

  do you need a

       she looks
          after

    the far side of

  we are

all the dark side moonwalking after you

Birth

Poem by Wendy Chin-Tanner
Art by Miss Lasko-Gross
Letters by Cardinal Rae

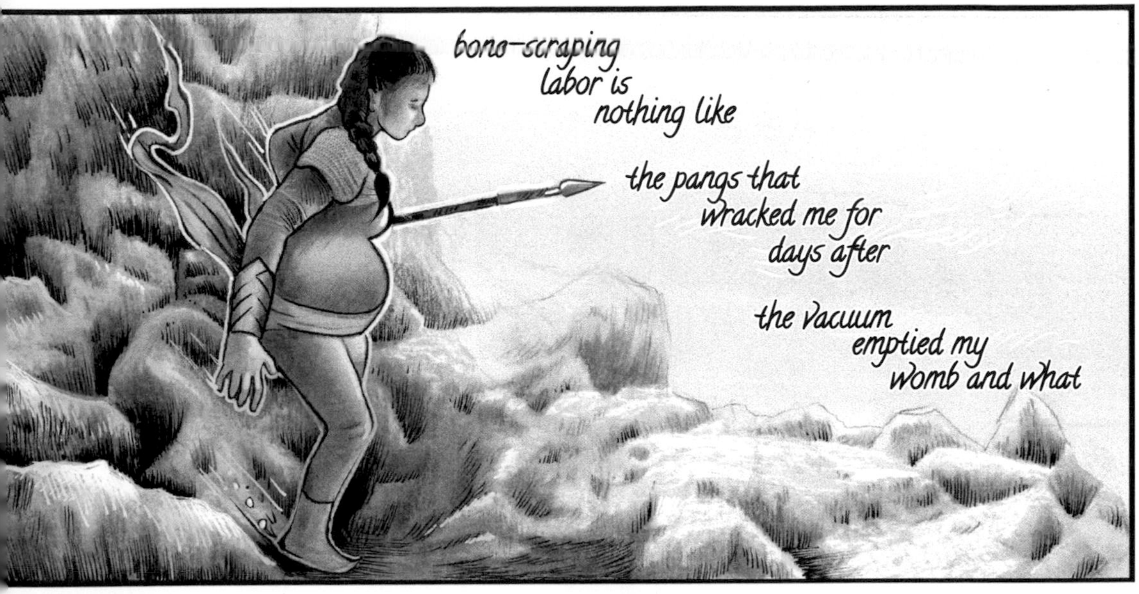
bono-scraping labor is nothing like
the pangs that wracked me for days after
the vacuum emptied my womb and what

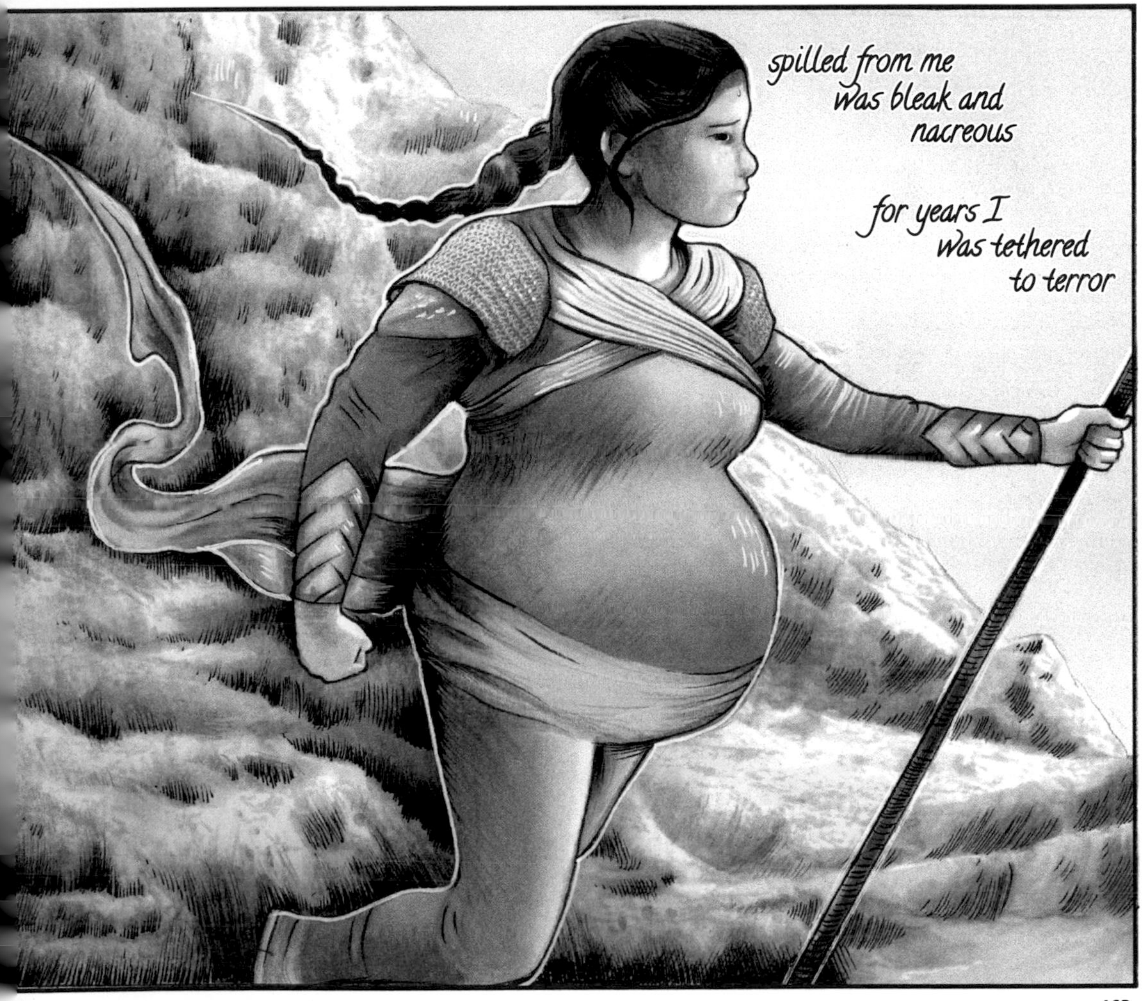
spilled from me was bleak and nacreous
for years I was tethered to terror

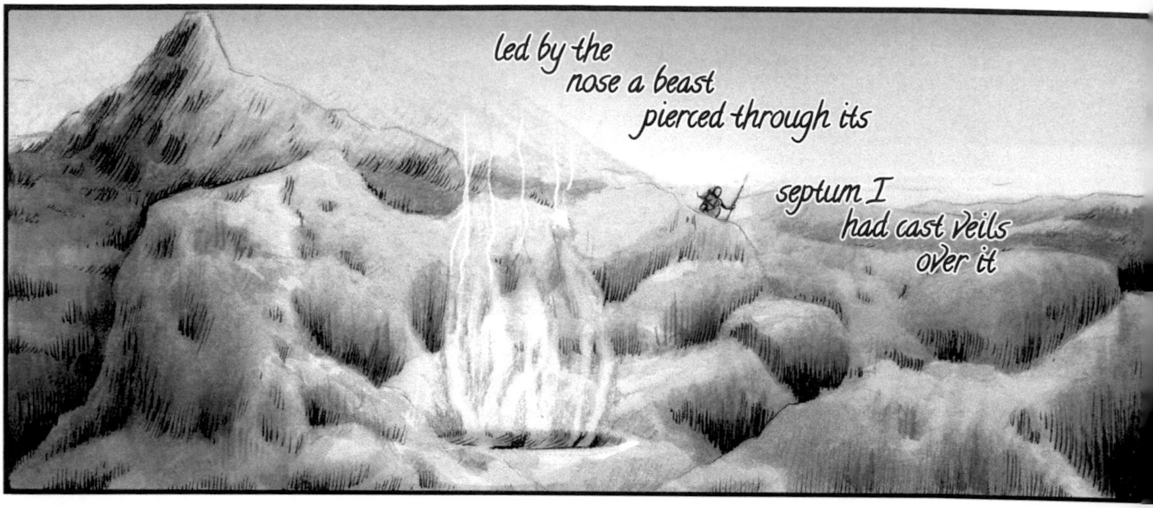
led by the
nose a beast
pierced through its
septum I
had cast veils
over it

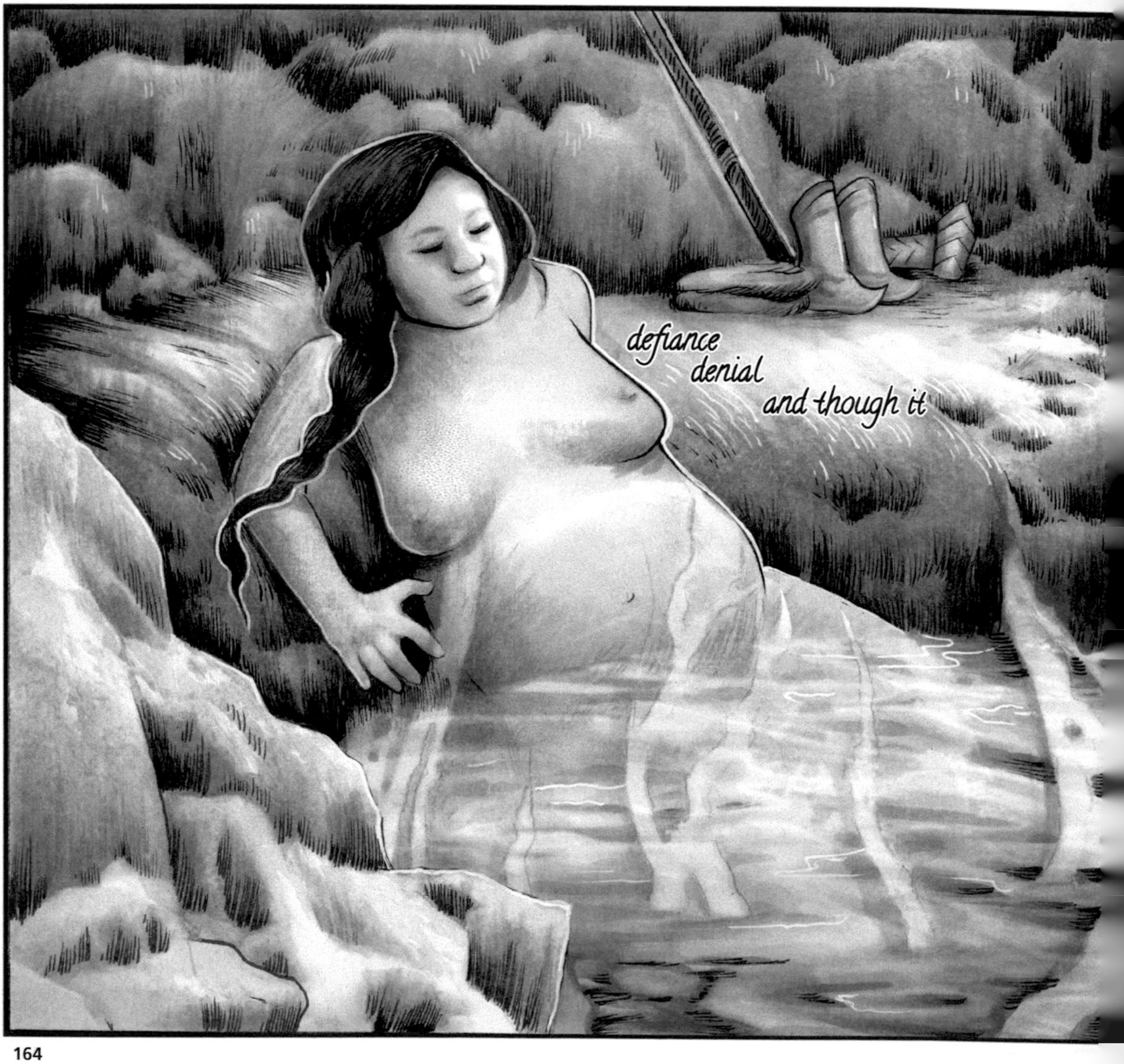
defiance
denial
and though it

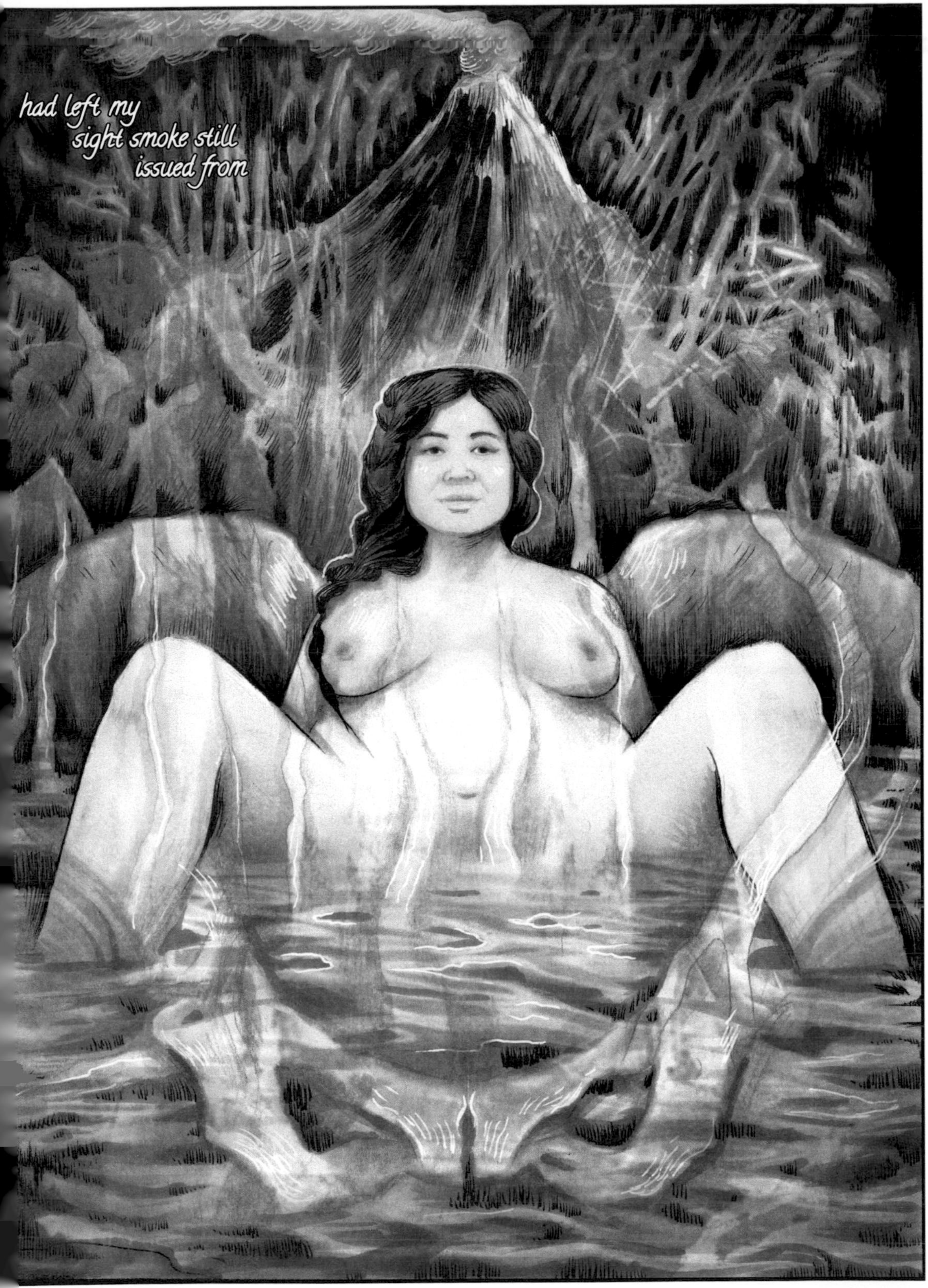
had left my sight smoke still issued from

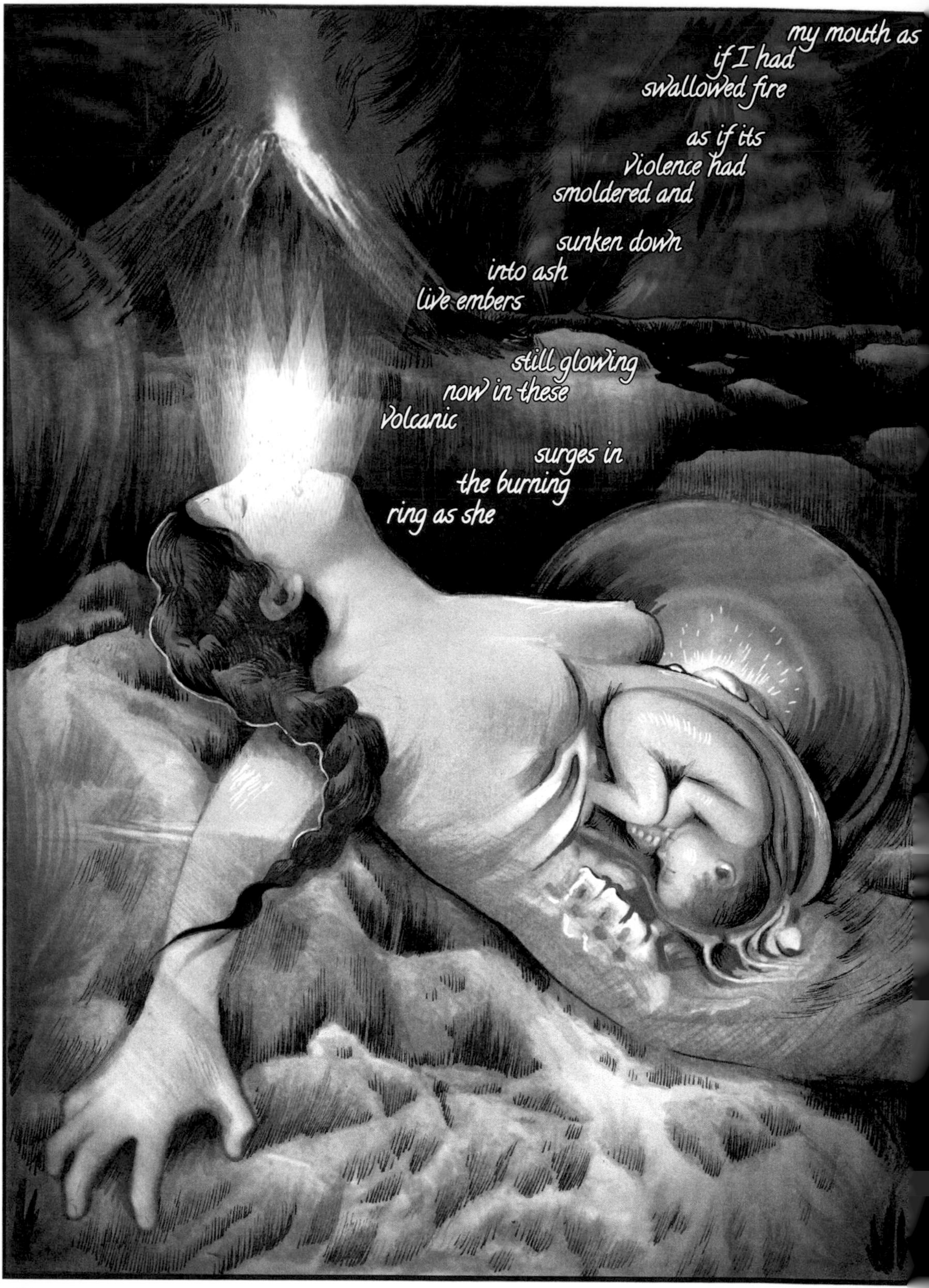
my mouth as
if I had
swallowed fire
as if its
violence had
smoldered and
sunken down
into ash
live embers
still glowing
now in these
volcanic
surges in
the burning
ring as she

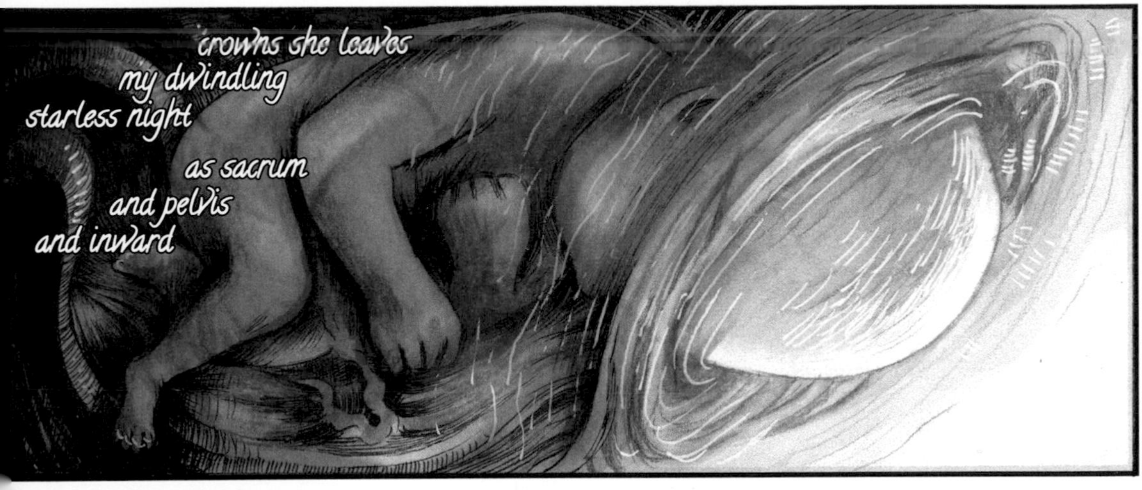
crowns she leaves
my dwindling
starless night
as sacrum
and pelvis
and inward

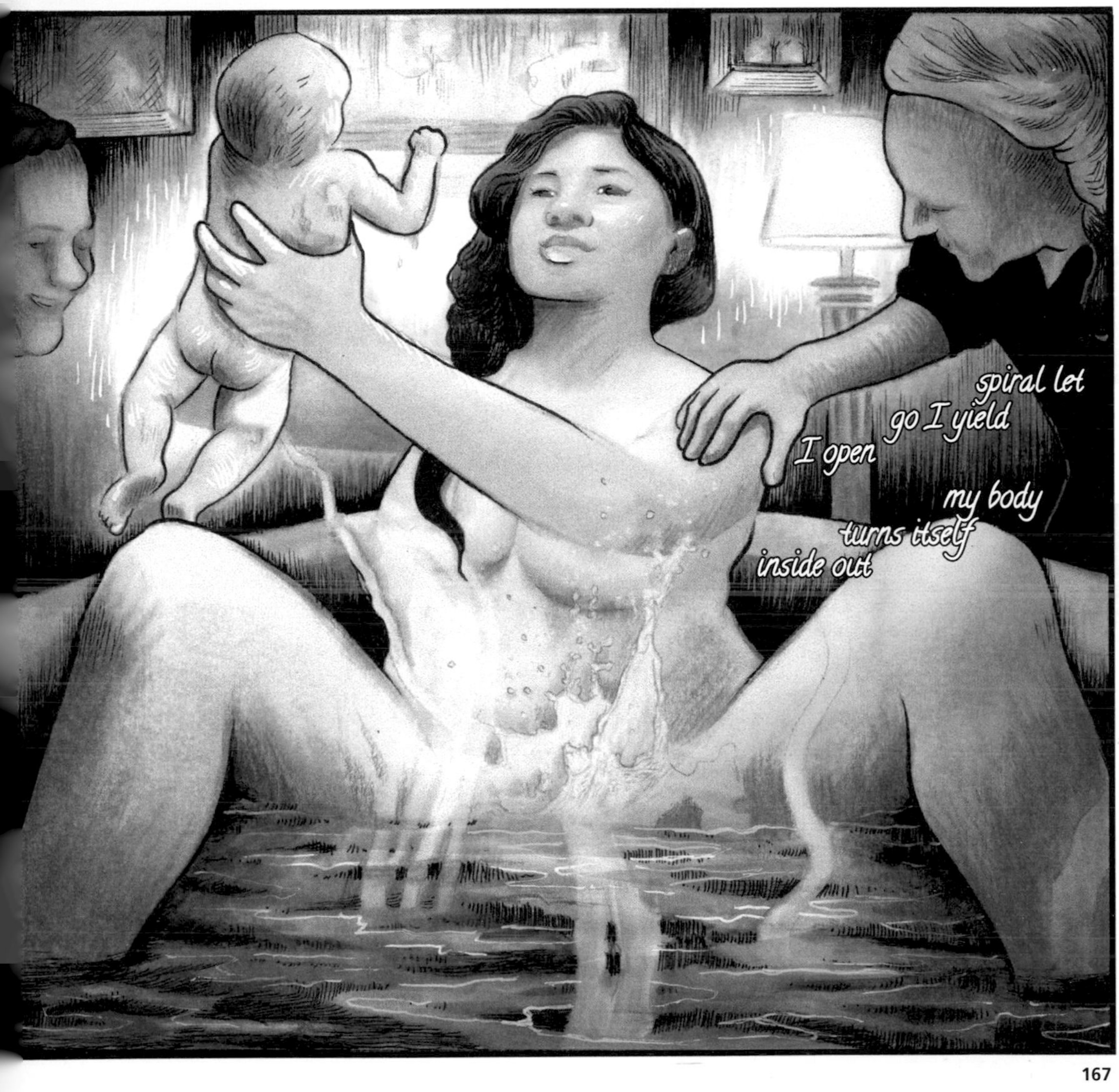
spiral let
go I yield
I open
my body
turns itself
inside out

BIRTH
by Wendy Chin-Tanner

bone-scraping
    labor is
        nothing like

    the pangs that
        wracked me for
            days after

      the vacuum
        emptied my
            womb and what

       spilled from me
         was bleak and
            nacreous

        for years I
           was tethered
             to terror

         led by the
           nose a beast
             pierced through its

         septum I
           had cast veils
             over it

         defiance
           denial
             and through it

         had left my
           sight smoke still
             issued from

                                        my mouth as
                                if I had
                        swallowed fire

                                as if its
                        violence had
                smoldered and

                        sunken down
                into ash
        live embers

                        still glowing
                now in these
        volcanic

                        surges in
                the burning
        ring as she

                crowns she leaves
        my dwindling
    starless night

                as sacrum
        and pelvis
    and inward

            spiral let
    go I yield
I open

        my body
    turns itself
inside out

ACKNOWLEDGMENTS

Grateful acknowledgment is made to the following publications where these poems or earlier versions first appeared:

Voyages, Miller Oberman
"The Unstill Ones," (Princeton University Press, 2017)

[You Know What Living Means? Tits Out, Tits in the Rain. Tits], Diane Seuss
Gulf Coast, Spring/Fall 2019 issue
"frank: sonnets," (Graywolf Press, 2021)

Good Bones, Maggie Smith
Waxwing, Issue 9 Summer 2016 issue
"Good Bones," (Tupelo Press, 2017)

Soft Landing, Sokunthary Svay & Annie Heath
The Margins, August 20, 2019

Rubble Girl, Jenn Givhan
HEArt online (Human Equity through Art), August 2017

Gender Studies, Caroline Hagood
"Lunatic Speaks," (Future Cycle Press, 2012)

A Love Letter to the Decades I have Kissed or Notes on Turning 50, JP Howard
"Reading Queer: Poetry in a Time of Chaos," (Anhinga Press, 2017)

Units & Increments, Shira Dentz
Drunken Boat, Issue 14, 2011
"SISYPHUSINA," (PANK Books, 2020)

X, Khadijah Queen
"Anodyne," (Tin House Books, 2020)

Tapestry, Khaty Xiong
The Spectacle, Issue 6, 2018

Half Girl, Then Elegy, Omotara James
Poem-a-Day, Academy of American Poets, January 23, 2019

Bassam, Ruth Awad
BOAAT Journal September/October 2017 issue
"Set to Music a Wildfire,"
    (Southern Indiana Review Press, 2017)

Speak-House. Carolina Ebeid
Linebreak, October 7, 2015

Incantation, Paul Tran
The Margins, Sept 1, 2015

Drown, Venus Thrash
Beltway Poetry Quarterly, Spring 2017

Dancing with Kiko on the Moon, Rosebud Ben-Oni
"Turn Around BRXGHT XYXS," (Get Fresh Books, 2019)

Birth, Wendy Chin-Tanner
"Choice Words, Writers on Abortion,"
(Haymarket Books, 2020)

STUDY GUIDE

VOYAGES

1. "Voyages" borrows its title and epigraph from the Hart Crane poem of the same name. How does this poem work from its epigraph? Reading it, who do you think "they" are, why is it an "if" whether they can hear the speaker's words, and what is it the speaker wants to "tell them"? Why is it important to do this telling in the form of a poem? What can a poem do that an essay, email, or letter cannot?

2. Most readers would not know this from looking at it, but "Voyages" is a formal poem called a "Beautiful Outlaw," which takes as its subject something that cannot be named within the poem. In this form, sometimes called a "something is missing poem," each stanza uses every letter in the alphabet except for one, making the poem a kind of reverse acrostic, as the letters missing from each stanza spell a word. Keeping this in mind, how is the language in this poem shaped by absence? In what ways do form and content work together?

[YOU KNOW WHAT LIVING MEANS? TITS OUT, TITS IN THE RAIN. TITS]

1. Why did the author choose the word "tits" as opposed to "breasts" in this poem?

2. This is a 14-line poem, a kind of sonnet. What elements of the sonnet are here, and what are missing? Why use a sonnet form for a poem that is so raw?

GOOD BONES

1. "Good Bones" is written in one continuous stanza that functions like a monologue. To whom do you think the poet is speaking?

2. Two of the techniques that Smith uses in this poem are repetition—anaphora, specifically— and caesura. How does the meaning of the line "Life is short" shift from one repetition to the other? How do the instances of caesura as they break up the long lines inform the way we read and understand the monologue?

SOFT LANDING

1. For 10 minutes, find a quiet and private space and close your eyes. Allow for instinctual movement impulses to enter and guide your body parts throughout this practice (maybe it's a turn of the head or pacing back and forth). Settle here and imagine a small replica of your body is inside the largeness of your actual, physical body. What do you find inside? Do you hear anything or smell anything? What is the temperature? And how does your mini-self warm your larger cavity?

2. In what words or places in "Soft Landing" do you find your mind lingering? Is it a part of speech, a concrete image, a movement? What are the ways to love and lose your body?

RUBBLE GIRL

1. How can reclaiming language and experiences that have been used against us and our bodies actually serve to empower us, as "Rubble Girl" does by turning some of the more negative connotations of her past selves into an incantatory, rhythmic call to arms?

2. "Rubble Girl" shows us how healing the present (self) can also work as a time-traveling balm to heal the past (selves). "Rubble Girl" is an iteration of the past that comes to teach the speaker of the poem, who asks of her, "teach me again how to live that loose" so that she can "mother" both selves "whole." What can your past selves teach you about how to heal your present and all the manifestations of your selves through time?

STUDY GUIDE

RED WOMAN

1. Discuss the epidemic of Missing/Murdered Indigenous Women (and Two-Spirit People & Girls). What is the context, and what are the effects on multiple generations of women?

2. What strategies might the speaker employ toward survivance?

GENDER STUDIES

1. Why do you think the poem is entitled "Gender Studies"?

2. What ideas about gender does this poem explore?

A LOVE LETTER TO THE DECADES I HAVE KISSED OR NOTES ON TURNING 50

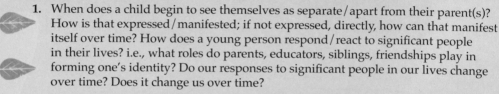

1. When does a child begin to see themselves as separate/apart from their parent(s)? How is that expressed/manifested; if not expressed, directly, how can that manifest itself over time? How does a young person respond/react to significant people in their lives? i.e., what roles do parents, educators, siblings, friendships play in forming one's identity? Do our responses to significant people in our lives change over time? Does it change us over time?

2. What's in a name? Our names carry power/herstory/history/past and future/connections/dis-connections/stories. What outside influences help or deter people from embracing their name(s)? Whether a given birth name or chosen name, embraced over time. Do childhood "nicknames" follow us into adulthood? Why or why not?

UNITS & INCREMENTS

1. "Units & Increments" is centered on gendered narratives of beauty and aging. How might the title of the poem relate to the ways in which women experience their bodies within our culture's beauty standards?

2. The word "sublime" in the poem becomes a point of departure for exploring notions of the Sublime as developed by Edmund Burke in the mid-eighteenth century, in the aesthetic movement of the same name. Burke defined sublime art as art that refers to a greatness beyond all possibility of calculation, measurement, or imitation. How does the protagonist of the story reckon with the conflict between this idea and the various constraints that are placed upon her as a woman?

X

1. What is the significance of the repetition of the letter X, once in the title and once again between the poem's two stanzas? What associations does the letter X evoke?

2. The only capitalized words in this poem are "Blombos" and "Blackest." What is the relationship between these two words and why do you think the poet might have highlighted them in this way?

TAPESTRY

1. What kind of tapestry is being woven here?

2. How does the poem's form inform the use of light and shadow?

HALF GIRL, THEN ELEGY

1. As the speaker of the poem goes about her daily business of being a woman, how does the world define her and how does she articulate her position of transitional and unfixed womanhood, and of the struggle between possession of and division from the self? How does the metaphorical conceit of a great fall relate to this?

2. As opposed to the confinement of the rabbit hole, how does the chosen image of the sky reflect the public nature of the pilgrimage of girlhood and in what ways does the poem challenge the idea that girlhood is finite? In what ways does the rhythm of the poem attempt to capture this slippage while turning on the homonymy of half and halve?

TO THE CHERRY BLOSSOMS ON 16TH AND WHARTON

1. In Candrilli's "To the Cherry Blossoms on 16th and Wharton," the poem balances the delight of love and chosen family with the fear of impending climate catastrophe. How, linguistically, and formally, is this balance managed?

2. Candrilli writes, "It is January now, and far too warm, / but what am I supposed to do but take a walk // and hold my partner's hand?" How is this rhetorical question working to push the poem forward? How can you employ the rhetorical question to move your poems forward?

BASSAM

1. How is the in-line open space functioning in this poem?

2. How does metaphor help create the emotional logic of this poem?

SPEAK-HOUSE

1. Knowing a speak-house is a space in a sanctuary for people who have taken a vow of silence to talk aloud openly, how would you characterize the dialogue in this poem?

2. The poem shifts swiftly from image to image, from bricks to police dogs to a doll named January. How would you describe this ever moving system of figures; how does the poem bring them into the same field of the page; what patterns emerge?

UNIVERSITY TOXIC

1. How does the speaker of this prose poem describe herself from the beginning as conflicted about her female looks and physicality — between the confidently embodied job candidate carefully groomed wearing a "green suit," and then suddenly the "ashamed" speaker after she is accosted by the man from the job committee? Why might she have felt physically vulnerable even before this man "pushes into your face" and makes objectifying comments to her about her "legs"?

2. If you were in her situation, would you have felt shame? Rage? A combination of the two? Do women in general tend to internalize comments about their sexuality by men in power? What is the alternative?

STUDY GUIDE

INCANTATION

1. An incantation is a series of words that are spoken, sung, or chanted as a magic spell, charm, or enchantment intended to trigger a magical effect in a person or objects. What is the incantation in this poem attempting to do?

2. Often poets from the margins are told to say more about this or that in a poem, in order to provide unfamiliar readers with historical, cultural, or autobiographical context. This poem tells you only what it wants you to know. How is emotional or psychological context just as, if not more important, than that of history, culture, or autobiography?

CAPITALISM RUINS EVERYTHING, EVEN WITCH CRAFT

1. How would you describe the emotional landscape of this poem and how does it evolve? How does the form echo or contrast with the emotion?

2. How does evasiveness show up on this poem? What does it looks like? What marks the moment when the speaker is finally able to name her loss?

Prompt: write about a difficult experience set against the backdrop of pop culture and/or consumerism, maybe something that you aren't quite ready to talk about yet but need to write about. Allow yourself to wander through different rooms/backdrops as you write about the difficult experience. Have three moments of evasiveness before you say directly what it is you are recovering from. End with an image.

DROWN

1. "Drown" is a poem about desire but not longing. It is a poem of fond memory and sensuality. It is about two black women who share a weekend of passionate lovemaking engrossed and entwined in each other's arms for a moment in time that could not last. Consider the placement of the word "Mercy." How does it interact with the preceding rhythm of the lines and why do you think it is standing alone to the right on the page?

2. "Drown" is a poem about sheer and utter ecstasy. It is a what-if poem: What if the two women in the poem had led the kind of lives that permitted them to have an ongoing sexual and romantic rendezvous each year?

LES ANNÉES DE GUERRE

1. The 1960s slogan (attributed to many) of feminism's second wave posited that "the personal is political." During COVID, I was appalled to see the rates of what researchers call "domestic" or "intimate" terrorism rise, with the lockdown, joblessness, and increased substance abuse occurring within private homes. This poem arose from that place, and my own abusive marriage (we're now divorced), but also seeks to go deeper, into a conflicted self and other historical binaries within patriarchal Western culture and civilization (Judeo-Christianity and philosophy). In writing your own poems, how far (or deep) a reach do you feel is appropriate or effective, macro- or microcosmically, in considering the themes, underpinnings, or "aboutness" of poems? Do you think it's your responsibility, or that of your readers, to determine what your poem or poems signify, and it is even a poem's work to "signify" (in the linguistic or structuralist sense)?

2. The title of this poem, "Les Années de Guerre," is borrowed from my friend Samuel Mercier's debut poetry collection (Les Éditions de l'Hexagone, 2014), which I translated into English (several sections appeared in The Brooklyn Rail). In four sections, this collection juxtaposes modern warfare (WWII, The War on Terror, the 2012 Quebec student protests, drone strikes) with the urgent need, now more than ever, for the continuation of the lyric project, on "lips the color/ of sand mixed with blood." In titling or writing your poems, to what degree do you invoke the words or work of other writers, past or present (overtly or covertly), the work of translation (literally or metaphorically), and the work of non-Anglophone writers? Is literary influence, for you, a question of "anxiety" (Harold Bloom), "ecstasy" (Jonathan Franzen), or something else entirely, and if so, what?

SETTLEMENT

1. From the legal settlement to the divorce settlement, to the settler colonial mappings of a burning and bordered land, pushed to the edge of the land during a wildfire, the speaker of this poem looks to the ocean, simultaneously processing the pain at end of her marriage through the pain of inherited and intimate colonial trauma, connecting it to climate violence, indigenous migrant violence, border violence, gender violence, all interconnected experiences stemming from the same colonial apparatus. How does "Settlement" examine the language of settler colonial violence, and its many manifestations—legal, intimate, political, spatial, ecological?

2. In the poet's interrogation of power and powerlessness, what strategies does she use to discuss the speaker's powerlessness throughout her life as well as the powerlessness of having to witness constant violence done to herself, her family, and people like her?

DANCING WITH KIKO ON THE MOON

1. How does the poet's experimentation with both form and sound in this poem shed light on its narrative of two women dancing on the moon? How does this experimentation also inform the speaker's relationship to the moon as "you/tú?"

2. Why do you think the poet chose to omit certain words, especially towards the end?

BIRTH

1. Although the title is "Birth," this poem opens with an image of an abortion before continuing to describe the experience of giving birth. What possible meanings does the juxtaposition between abortion and birth imply?

2. What do you notice about the form of this poem? In spite of its lack of punctuation and capitalization, how does the way the poem is constructed—both visually and rhythmically—signal the way it should be read?

CREATOR BIOS

Miller Oberman's collection of poems and translations, *The Unstill Ones*, was published in 2017 by Princeton University Press. He has received a number of awards for his poetry, including a Ruth Lilly Fellowship, a 92Y Discovery Prize, and *Poetry* magazine's John Frederick Nims Memorial Prize for Translation. His work has appeared in *Poetry, London Review of Books, The Nation, Boston Review, Tin House*, and *Harvard Review*. Miller is an editor at Broadsided Press, and directs the First-Year Writing program at Eugene Lang College and lives with his family in Queens, New York.

Jen Hickman is a visual storyteller from California. Past work includes *Lonely Receiver, TEST, Bezkamp, Moth & Whisper*, and more. They get really excited about dystopian fiction, good coffee, and drawing hands.

Cardinal Rae is a Ringo nominated comic book letterer and graphic designer working in the U.S. She letters the Eisner nominated series *Crowded* for Image Comics, the five-time Ringo nominated series *Forgotten Home* for comiXology Originals, as well as several other indie books for publishers big and small like Oneshi Press, A Wave Blue World, and Vices Press.

Diane Seuss's most recent collection, *Still Life with Two Dead Peacocks and a Girl*, (Graywolf Press 2018) was a finalist for the National Book Critics Circle Award and the *Los Angeles Times* Book Prize in Poetry. *Four-Legged Girl* (Graywolf Press 2015) was a finalist for the Pulitzer Prize. *frank: sonnets* is forthcoming from Graywolf in 2021. Seuss is a 2020 Guggenheim Fellow. She was raised by a single mother in rural Michigan, which she continues to call home.

Liana Kangas is a comic artist and creator best known for her work on *She Said Destroy* by Vault and other works with 2000AD, Black Mask Studios and Ringo and Eisner nominated anthologies with A Wave Blue World, Image and Comic Mix. Her clients include TKO, King Features, Legendary Pictures, Z2, Mad Cave, Vices Press and Scrappy Heart Productions. She has been featured on SYFY, Nerdist, Panel x Panel and more. She's a dog parent to two, and drums occasionally.

Maggie Smith is the author of three books of poetry: *Good Bones* (Tupelo Press, 2017); *The Well Speaks of Its Own Poison* (2015); and *Lamp of the Body* (Red Hen Press, 2005). Smith is also the author of three prizewinning chapbooks. Her poems are widely published and anthologized, appearing in *Best American Poetry, the New York Times, The New Yorker, Tin House, POETRY, The Paris Review, Ploughshares*, and elsewhere. In 2016 her poem "Good Bones" went viral internationally and has been translated into nearly a dozen languages. Public Radio International called it "the official poem of 2016." Her new book, *Keep Moving: Notes on Loss, Creativity, and Change*, a collection of essays and quotes, was released in October 2020 from One Signal/Simon & Schuster.

Carola Borelli was born and raised in southern Italy. She moved to Rome to attend the University of Architecture and the International School of Comics. She made her debut with *Yamazaki 18 Years Apocrypha* (Manfont Publishing) and subsequently worked with other Italian indie realities. In 2019, she begins her collaboration with Space Between Entertainment (Destiny NY vol.3) and also works as an assistant at IDW.

Sokunthary Svay is a Khmer writer from the Bronx. She is poetry editor for *Newtown Literary*, the only literary journal for the borough of Queens, and a founding member of the Cambodian American Literary Arts Association (CALAA), and an adjunct professor at Queens College. She has received fellowships from American Opera Projects, Poets House, Willow Books, and CUNY. Her first collection of poetry, *Apsara in New York*, is available from Willow Books. Her first opera, in collaboration with composer Liliya Ugay, premiered in January 2020 at the Kennedy Center Terrace Theater.

Annie Heath is a choreographer and dancer based in Brooklyn, NY. Her work has been presented at NYC venues including; New York Live Arts, New Dance Alliance, Issue Project Room, Movement Research at the Judson Church, Chen Dance Center, Access Theater, Center for Performance Research, Dixon Place, TADA! Youth Theater, Triskelion Arts, Brooklyn Arts Exchange, West End Theater, and Alchemical Laboratory. Outside of NYC, her work has been presented at Southern Vermont Dance Festival and Massachusetts Dance Festival. She has performed original works by RoseAnne Spradlin, Doug LeCours, Gabriella Carmichael, Pavel Machuca-Zavarzin, and Matthew Westerby Company. She was in residence at La Escuela Profesional de Danza de Mazatlán (Mazatlán, Mexico) and is currently a 2019-2021 Fresh Tracks resident artist at New York Live Arts.

Mia Casesa is a graphic designer by day and comic artist by night. She loves storytelling and world-building and thinks comic books are a perfect intersection of her hobbies and interests. When she's not doodling, she likes to go for walks, do yoga and play Minecraft.

Jennifer Givhan, a Mexican-American poet who has received NEA and PEN/Rosenthal Emerging Voices fellowships, is the author of two novels and four full-length collections of poetry, most recently *Rosa's Einstein* (University of Arizona Press), *Trinity Sight*, and *Jubilee* (Blackstone Publishing). Her work has appeared in *The Nation, The New Republic, Poetry, Salon,* and many other periodicals. She raises her two children in Albuquerque, New Mexico beside the Sleeping Sister volcanoes.

Sara Gómez Woolley is an award-winning illustrator, graphic novelist and educator living and working in Brooklyn, NY. She has had the pleasure of working on a variety of exciting projects for clients such as: *National Geographic,* DC Comics, Image Comics, and Scholastic. Sara's ongoing personal project, a fictionalized graphic memoir, *Los Pirineos: the Mostly True Memoirs of Esperancita Gómez*, was singled out for award by the National Association of Latino Arts and Culture. She teaches tomorrow's illustration professionals as faculty of the Communication Design Department at New York City College of Technology, CUNY

Kenzie Allen is a poet and multimodal artist. She is an Assistant Professor of English at York University, and her research centers on documentary and visual poetics, literary cartography, and the enactment of Indigenous sovereignties through creative works. She is a descendant of the Oneida Nation of Wisconsin. Kenzie's most recent project is a multimodal book of poetry which incorporates intergenerational histories and diasporic movements, Haudenosaunee traditions, and archival materials of the Carlisle Indian Boarding School. She received her PhD in English & Creative Writing from University of Wisconsin-Milwaukee, her MFA in Poetry from the Helen Zell Writers' Program at the University of Michigan, and her BA in Anthropology from Washington University in St. Louis. Her poems can be found in *Boston Review, Narrative Magazine, Best New Poets,* and other venues, and she is the founder and managing editor of the Anthropoid collective.

CREATOR BIOS

Weshoyot Alvitre is a female author and illustrator from the Tongva tribe of Southern California. She currently resides with her husband and two children on Ventureno Chumash Territory in Ventura, California. Her work focuses on an Indigenous lens and voice on projects from children's books to adult market graphic novels. She has recently been published as artist in *GHOSTRIVER: The Fall and Rise of the Conestoga* graphic novel from Red Planet Books, ABQ. in collaboration with the Library Company of Philadelphia; *At The Mountains Base* written by Traci Sorell, Kokila; and was Art Director on the video game *When Rivers Were Trails*. She enjoys spinning yarn and collecting antiques.

Caroline Hagood is an Assistant Professor of English and Director of First-Year Writing at St. Francis College. Her first book of poems, *Lunatic Speaks,* came out in 2012, her second poetry book, *Making Maxine's Baby,* came out in 2015 from Hanging Loose Press, her book-length essay, *Ways of Looking at a Woman,* came out in 2019 from Hanging Loose, and her forthcoming novel, *Ghosts of America*, will come out in 2021 from Hanging Loose.

Stelladia is a Spanish comic artist and colorist with a background in visual development for animation. Some of their titles include *The Wilds* #4 (Black Mask), *Submerged* (Vault Comics), *Metaphorical Her* (Webtoon) and *Teenage Wasteland* (ComiXology), and they are currently working for Mad Cave. When they are not making comics, you can probably find them somewhere drawing fantasy or sci-fi stuff, home-gardening, or studying philosophy and anthropology.

JP Howard is an author, educator, literary activist, curator and community builder. Her debut poetry collection, *SAY/MIRROR* (The Operating System), was a Lambda Literary Award finalist. She is also the author of *bury your love poems here* (Belladonna*) and co-editor of *Sinister Wisdom Journal Black Lesbians--We Are the Revolution!* JP is a featured author in Lambda Literary's LGBTQ Writers in Schools program and has received fellowships and grants from Cave Canem, VONA, Lambda, and Brooklyn Arts Council. She curates Women Writers in Bloom Poetry Salon, a NY based forum offering writers a monthly venue to collaborate. JP's poetry is widely anthologized.

Soo Lee is a comic artist and illustrator residing in NYC. She attended High School of Art & Design and the School of Visual Arts for cartooning. Soo has worked on various covers and sequential art published by Ahoy!, Oni Press, Valiant, Dynamite, Boom!, Action Lab and Image. She has also worked on editorial illustrations for *Analog Sci-Fi Magazine* and *Sierra Magazine*. Soo has also contributed the iconic cover art for the Ringo Award winning anthology, *Mine! By* ComicMix.

Shira Dentz is the author of five books including *SISYPHUSINA* (PANK, 2020), and two chapbooks. Her poetry, prose, visual and cross-genre writing appear widely in venues such as *Poetry, American Poetry Review, Cincinnati Review, Iowa Review, Academy of American Poets' Poem-a-Day series* (Poets.org), and *NPR*. She's a recipient of awards including an Academy of American Poets' Prize, Poetry Society of America's Lyric Poem Award, and Poetry Society of America's Cecil Hemley Memorial Award. A graduate of the Iowa Writer's Workshop, Shira holds a Ph.D. in Creative Writing and Literature from the University of Utah, and is Special Features Editor at *Tarpaulin Sky*.

Jessica Lynn was born in Paterson, NJ and has been drawing since she could hold a pencil. She currently lives in the Chicago area where she enjoys making her own comics and working on more art. She is inspired by Sailor Moon and Arthur Adams art. Her other influences include many manga artists such as Clamp and Yoshiyuki Sadamoto, fashion, nature, interior design, pastels, etc. She enjoys drawing busy scenes, women, foliage, and anything dark art related!

Kelly Fitzpatrick (she/her) is a Hugo-nominated comic book colorist and illustrator who has worked on over 400 comics since 2013. She emigrated to Calgary, AB with her Boston Terrier mix, Archie in 2019. In her free time, she creates illustrations, self-publishes books, and does aerial acrobatics and yoga. Kelly is also outspoken and committed to educating others on topics such as kink, fibromyalgia, asexuality, and anxiety/depression because they are often erased, misunderstood, overlooked, and disregarded in today's society and personally affect her.

Saida Temofonte was born in Italy but moved to Los Angeles, CA at a young age and now lives in Florida. She has been lettering and designing since 1997 and has worked for many of the major comic book publishers.

Khadijah Queen, PhD, is the author of six books, including *I'm So Fine: A List of Famous Men & What I Had On* (2017), praised in *O Magazine, The New Yorker, Rain Taxi, Los Angeles Review,* and elsewhere as "quietly devastating," and "a portrait of defiance that turns the male gaze inside out. Essays appear in *Harper's Magazine, The New York Times, North American Women Poets in the 21st Century* and *High Country News.* Her latest poetry collection, *Anodyne,* was published in August 2020 by Tin House.

Ashley A. Woods is a comic book artist, writer, & creator from Chicago known for her work on the *Niobe, Ladycastle,* and *Tomb Raider.* She got her start through self-publishing her action-fantasy comic series *Millennia War* which led to her career in comics and TV. After earning her degree in Film and Animation from IADT, she traveled to Kyoto, Japan where she presented her work in a gallery showcase called, "Out of Sequence". Recognized for her female illustrations and designs, her most prominent work is *Niobe: She is Life* with Stranger Comics. Ashley's latest work can be found in HBO's *Lovecraft Country* and *Heathen* from Vault Comics.

Khaty Xiong is a poet from Fresno, CA. She's the author of *Poor Anima* (Apogee Press, 2015), which holds the distinction of being the first full-length collection of poetry published by a Hmong American woman in the United States. In 2019, Xiong was awarded Best of the Net for her poem, "Year of the Cardinal's Song (VII)." Her recent honors include a 2020 Ruth Lilly and Dorothy Sargent Rosenberg Poetry Fellowship and a Vermont Studio Center Fellowship from the Ohio Arts Council.

Morgan Beem is a freelance artist who works predominantly with ink and watercolor. Her work includes *Swamp Thing: Twin Branches, The Family Trade, Adventure time, Planet of the Apes,* and a number of anthologies.

Omotara James is a writer, editor and visual artist. She is the author of the chapbook *Daughter Tongue* selected by African Poetry Book Fund, in collaboration with Akashic Books for the 2018 New Generation African Poets Box Set. Her work has been supported by the New York Foundation of the Arts, the Academy of American Poets, the 92Y Unterberg Poetry Center, Bread Loaf Writers' Conference, Cave Canem Foundation, Lambda Literary and other organizations. Her poems have appeared in *Poetry Magazine, The Paris Review,* the *Poem-a-Day series* for the *Academy of American Poets* and elsewhere. Born in Britain, she is the daughter of Nigerian and Trinidadian immigrants. Currently, she teaches and lives in New York City. Her debut poetry collection *Song of My Softening* is forthcoming from Alice James Books.

CREATOR BIOS

Ayşegül Sınav is a comic book artist and an illustrator currently located in Turkey, İstanbul. She attended The Joe Kubert School of Cartooning and Graphic Art. Since graduating in 2015 she has worked with A Wave Blue World on several anthologies such as *Dead Beats* and *Broken Frontier*. She has also been working at Sinegraf Movie Production company doing storyboards, character designs, poster designs and many more as an in-house illustrator since 2012.

She likes to dabble in all aspects of the arts whether it's oils, watercolors or digital. She enjoys telling stories and making things with her hands. Her biggest hope is that something she's made with her hand will make someone she's never met very happy. #istanbulconventionsaveslives

Kayleb Rae Candrilli is a 2019 Whiting Award Winner in Poetry and the author of *Water I Won't Touch* (Copper Canyon Press, 2021), *All the Gay Saints* (Saturnalia, 2020) and *What Runs Over* (YesYes Books, 2017). Their work is published or forthcoming in *Poetry, American Poetry Review, Boston Review* and many other periodicals.

Hazel Newlevant is a Portland-raised, Queens-residing cartoonist whose comics include *No Ivy League, Sugar Town, Tender-Hearted,* and *If This Be Sin*. They have edited and published the comics anthologies *Chainmail Bikini: The Anthology of Women Gamers* and *Comics for Choice*. Their work has been published by *Buzzfeed, The Nib*, Abrams ComicArts, IDW, Lion Forge Comics, and now A Wave Blue World! Hazel's work as an editor and cartoonist has been honored with the Ignatz Award, the Eisner Award, the Xeric Grant, and the Prism Comics Queer Press Grant.

Ruth Awad is the Lebanese-American author of *Set to Music a Wildfire* (Southern Indiana Review Press, 2017), winner of the 2016 Michael Waters Poetry Prize and the 2018 Ohioana Book Award for Poetry. Alongside Rachel Mennies, she is the co-editor of *The Familiar Wild: On Dogs and Poetry* (Sundress Publications, 2020). She is the recipient of a 2020 and 2016 Ohio Arts Council Individual Excellence Award, and she won the 2013 and 2012 Dorothy Sargent Rosenberg Poetry Prize and the 2011 Copper Nickel Poetry Contest. Her work appears in *Poetry, Poem-a-Day, The Believer, The New Republic, Pleiades, The Missouri Review, The Rumpus,* and elsewhere. She lives and writes in Columbus, Ohio, with her Pomeranians.

Emily Pearson is a comic book artist from California. Previously known for her art on *The Wilds* and *Snap Flash Hustle* from Black Mask Studios, she also has upcoming books *The Vain* from Oni Press and *Bonding* from Vault comics.

Carolina Ebeid is a multimedia poet. Her first book *You Ask Me to Talk About the Interior* was published by Noemi Press as part of the Akrilica Series, and selected as one of ten best debuts of 2016 by *Poets & Writers*. Her work has been supported by the Stadler Center for Poetry at Bucknell University, Bread Loaf, CantoMundo, the NEA, as well as a residency fellowship from the Lannan Foundation. She is on faculty at the Mile-High MFA at Regis University, the bilingual MFA at the University of Texas El Paso, and Lighthouse Writer's Workshop in Denver. A longtime editor, she currently edits poetry at *The Rumpus*, as well as the multimedia zine Visible Binary.

Marika Cresta is an Italian artist born in Terni in 1988. She enrolled at Sapienza Università di Roma and graduated with a degree in architecture in 2015. An avid learner, Marika is also a graduate of the Scuola Internazionale Comics di Roma where she stayed on for post-graduate work after receiving her diploma. Her first published work was in 2016, a well-received short story in the book *Yamazaki 18 Years Apocrypha* (Manfont Publishing). That same year, she debuted on the foreign market scene with a story in *Grimm Tales of Terror Holiday Special* for Zenescope Entertainment. Then she worked for Lion Forge on *Summit* for the Catalyst Prime universe. Scouted by Marvel's talent crew at Lucca Comics & Games, an annual convention in Lucca, Italy, Marika was brought on as a new artist to work on such iconic titles as *Power Pack*, *X-Men*, and *Dr Aphra*.

Gab Contreras is a comic book colorist, illustrator, and graphic designer from Lima, Peru. She has worked on books for various publishers, most notably *All We Ever Wanted: Stories of a Better World* and *Dead Beats* (A Wave Blue World), *2000 AD Summer Special 2018* (2000 AD), and others.

Laura Hinton is the author of *The Perverse Gaze of Sympathy: Sadomasochistic Sentiments from Clarissa to Rescue 911* (SUNY Press), and co-editor of *We Who Love to Be Astonished: Experimental Women's Writing and Performance Poetics* (University of Alabama Press). Her critical essays, poet interviews, and reviews have appeared in books and journals including *Contemporary Literature, Jacket2, Postmodern Culture, Textual Practice, Women's Studies, Rain Taxi, Jacket, Poetry Project Newsletter, The Journal of the Academy of American Poets*, among others. She is also a poet, and published the poetry book, *Sisyphus My Love (To Record a Dream in a Bathtub)*, with BlazeVox Books. She edits a chapbook series of performance poetry for Mermaid Tenement Press, and publishes a blog about multimedia poetry, Chant de la Sirene at chantdelasire.com.

Kaylee Rowena is a Baltimore-born, NYC-based comic creator and illustrator. She recently graduated from SVA with a Bachelor's in cartooning, and can now be found scouring the city (and the internet) for ghost stories of all varieties.

Paul Tran is the recipient of the Ruth Lilly & Dorothy Sargent Rosenberg Fellowship from the Poetry Foundation and the Discovery/*Boston Review* Poetry Prize. Their work appears in *The New Yorker, Poetry Magazine*, and elsewhere. They are the Poetry Editor at *The Offing Magazine* and a Wallace Stegner Fellow in Poetry at Stanford University.

Jude Vigants is a trans male Cartoonist and Illustrator living in Albany, NY. Not long after graduating from the School of Visual Arts in 2014, he went through some personal trauma that took his stories and art to a more spiritual and self fulfilling path. He loves stories of grotesque monsters doing good, unconventional romance, and lost people finding new strange families. Today, comics and sequential imagery are part of his way of practicing Witchcraft and Sex Magic on the regular.

Kendra DeColo is the author of *I am Not Trying to Hide My Hungers from the World* (BOA Editions, 2021), *My Dinner with Ron Jeremy* (Third Man Books, 2016) and *Thieves in the Afterlife* (Saturnalia Books, 2014), selected by Yusef Komunyakaa for the 2013 Saturnalia Books Poetry Prize. She has received awards and fellowships from the National Endowment for the Arts, the MacDowell Colony, the Bread Loaf Writers' Conference, the Millay Colony, Split this Rock, and the Tennessee Arts Commission. Her poems and essays have appeared in *American Poetry Review, Tin House Magazine, Bitch Magazine*, and elsewhere. She teaches at The Hugo House and lives in Nashville, Tennessee.

CREATOR BIOS

Ned Barnett makes comics about heroes, health and history. He's usually found in Cambridge, MA, where he lives with his husband. Ned delights in making history accessible through comics, especially the First World War. His work includes the full-length, self-published graphic novel, *Dreamers of the Day*, which follows his 2019 research trip to Oxford University to consult TE Lawrence (of Arabia)'s archives. Ned's comics have appeared in literary magazines and anthologies, including *Dead Beats* (A Wave Blue World 2019) and the PRISM-nominated *Being True* (Boston Comics Roundtable 2018). His favorite dinosaur is the compsognathus.

Lesley Atlansky is a comic colorist and visual artist living in a multi-generational household in beautiful Portland, Oregon. As a painter and former graphic designer, she bring a unique style and sense of color to comics. She enjoys working across many different art styles, as it allows her to learn and grow with each new project. There hasn't been a genre that she hasn't loved to tackle, because each new setting brings with it exciting problems to solve and techniques to explore.

Venus Thrash is the author of the *Fateful Apple* (Urban Poets, 2014), nominated for the 2015 PEN Open Book Award. Her work is forthcoming in the *100 Year House Anthology*, (Cherry Castle, 2021) and *This is What America Looks Like Poetry Anthology* (Washington Writers Publishing House, 2021).

Born from the cradles of Queens, NY, **Y. Sanders** was seven when her mother introduced her to the world of comics. Having found her life's purpose as a comic artist, her path led her to attend LaGuardia High School of the Arts and The School of Visual Arts. Currently, she continues to improve her talents at The Art Students League of New York. One of her many achievements included winning the Blue Dot Award for her short comic *Possessed*. Sanders has worked with UNESCO's Women in African History series and contributed to anthologies from Red Stylo Media and A Wave Blue World. She is currently working on the release of the upcoming series *Laughter* with writer Gavin Dillinger.

Virginia Konchan is the author of two poetry collections, *Any God Will Do* and *The End of Spectacle* (Carnegie Mellon, 2018 and 2020); a collection of short stories, *Anatomical Gift* (Noctuary Press, 2017); and four chapbooks, as well as coeditor (with Sarah Giragosian) of *Marbles on the Floor: How to Assemble a Book of Poems* (University of Akron Press, 2022). Her creative and critical work has appeared in *The New Yorker, The New Republic, The Believer, Boston Review,* and elsewhere. She lives in Halifax, Nova Scotia.

Takeia Marie is an illustrator from New York, comic book nerd, lover of food, and self-proclaimed hip hop enthusiast. She enjoys working with small businesses and individuals with big ideas, having worked with clients such as New Profit, The Mill, Action Lab, Brooklyn College Community Partnership, and more. Her work has been published in the Glyph Pioneer Award-winning anthology, *Artists Against Police Brutality,* and has been featured in *Black Comix Returns: African-American Comic Art & Culture.* She believes that great stories have the power to change people, change minds, and change the world.

Vanessa Angélica Villarreal was born in the Rio Grande Valley to Mexican immigrants. She is the author of the 2019 Whiting Award winning collection *Beast Meridian* (Noemi Press, Akrilica Series, 2017), a 2019 Kate Tufts Discovery Award finalist, and winner of the John A. Robertson Award for Best First Book of Poetry from the Texas Institute of Letters. Her work has appeared in *The New York Times, Paris Review, Boston Review, Los Angeles Review of Books, The Rumpus,* the *Academy of American Poets' Poem-a-Day, Buzzfeed Reader,* and *Poetry Magazine,* where her poem "f = [(root) (future)]" was honored with the 2019 Friends of Literature Prize. She is a recipient of fellowships from CantoMundo and Jack Jones Literary Arts, and is a doctoral candidate in English Literature and Creative Writing at the University of Southern California in Los Angeles, where she is raising her son with the help of a loyal dog.

Ronnie Garcia is a queer Puerto Rican illustrator with experience in comics, visual development, and teaching young students. With a range of storytelling experience from middle-grade to YA, their signature talent involves designing creatures of the tooth variety. When they're not drawing pictures or working with young artists, they can be found huddled in a blanket fort working on puzzles and eating fruit snacks.

Rosebud Ben-Oni is the author of *If This Is the Age We End Discovery*, winner of the 2019 Alice James Award and forthcoming in 2021; *turn around, BRXGHT XYXS* (Get Fresh Books, 2019); and *Solecism* (Virtual Artists Collective, 2013). Ben-Oni writes for *The Kenyon Review* blog and teaches at Catapult, University of California, Los Angeles, and the Speakeasy Project. She is the recipient of fellowships from the New York Foundation for the Arts, CantoMundo, and lives in Queens, New York.

Rio Burton is a freelance illustrator and comics artist located in Colorado, USA. Growing up with influences such as Studio Ghibli and Final Fantasy, she is passionate about bringing stories to life through whimsical, and sometimes dark art. She loves fantasy genres and is a sucker for anything involving wolves. When Rio isn't working on art you can find her engrossed in a good book or video game, or hiking somewhere in Colorado getting her hands dirty while hunting for fossils and minerals.

Wendy Chin-Tanner is the author of the poetry collections *Turn* (Sibling Rivalry Press, 2014), which was a finalist for the Oregon Book Award, and *Anyone Will Tell You* (Sibling Rivalry Press, 2019), and co-author of the graphic novel *American Terrorist*. She is a poetry editor at *The Nervous Breakdown* and co-publisher at A Wave Blue World. Some of her poems can be found in the *Academy of American Poets Poem-a-Day* series, *RHINO Poetry*, *Denver Quarterly*, *The Rumpus*, *Vinyl Poetry*, *The Collagist*, *North Dakota Quarterly*, and *The Mays Anthology of Oxford and Cambridge*. Her essays have been published at *Salon*, *Gay Magazine*, *xoJane*, *Cultural Weekly*, *Alternet*, and elsewhere. A trained sociologist specializing in race, identity, discourse analysis, and cultural studies, Wendy was born and raised in NYC and educated at Cambridge University, UK.

Miss Lasko-Gross is the author and illustrator of *Henni* (Honored by ALA's Amelia Bloomer List and YALSA 2016: Great Graphic Novels for Teens), Fantagraphics Books: *A Mess Of Everything* (named one of *Booklist's* top 10 graphic novels of the year) and the YALSA nominated *Escape From "Special."* She is the creator/writer of Z2 comics' scifi series *THE SWEETNESS*. Her work has also been featured in the New Yorker's Daily Shouts.

VOYAGES
THUMBNAILS BY
JEN HICKMAN

1

2

3

4

5

6

PROCESS ART

(YOU KNOW WHAT LIVING MEANS?
TITS OUT, TITS IN THE RAIN. TITS)
ROUGHS AND FINISHED ART BY LIANA KANGAS

GOOD BONES ROUGHS BY CAROLA BORELLI

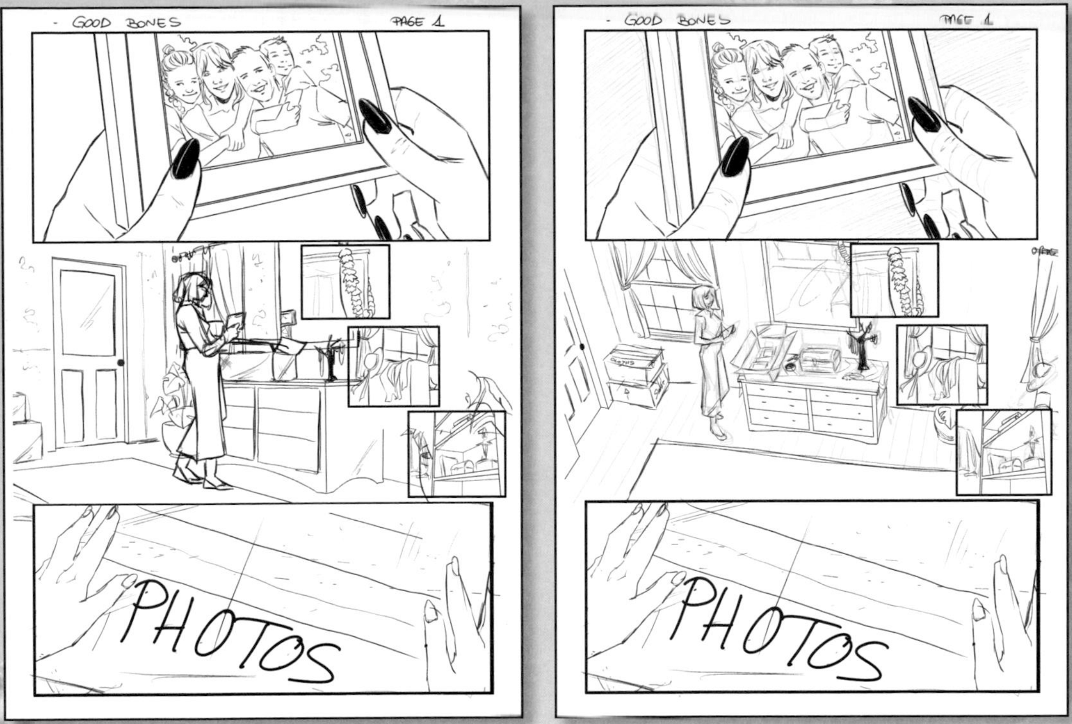
- GOOD BONES
PAGE 1
PHOTOS
- GOOD BONES
PAGE 1
PHOTOS

SOFT LANDING THUMBNAILS BY MIA CASESA

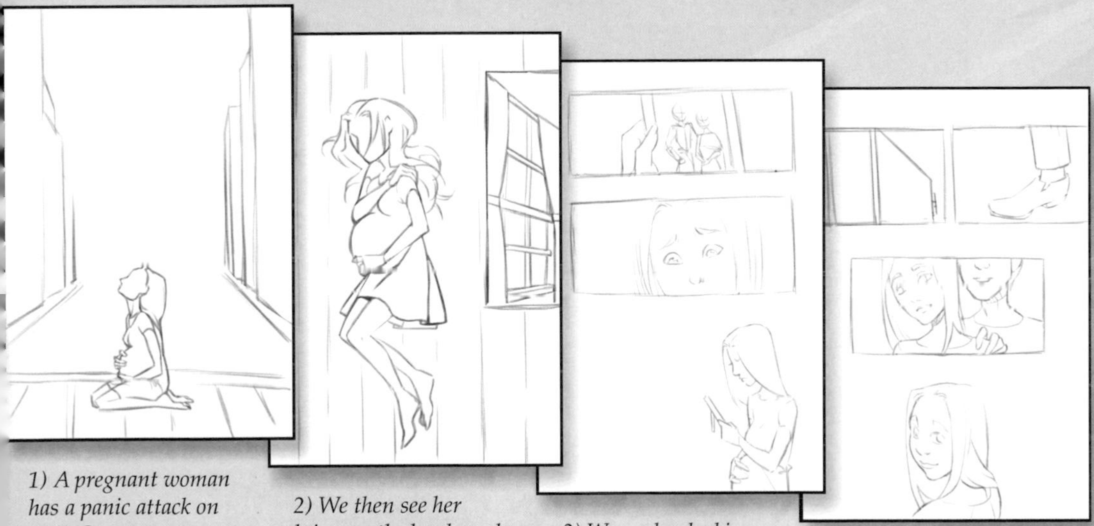

1) A pregnant woman has a panic attack on a NYC street.

2) We then see her lying on the hardwood floor of her home trying to get herself together.

3) We see her looking through a photo album of her family members in traditional Khmer dress. She is looking for answers.

4) The woman's partner, a white man, comes home. He looks concerned, but she smiles at him, says nothing, pretending that nothing is wrong, silencing herself.

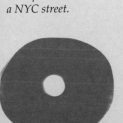

RUBBLE GIRL

1.

□1 P1 "RUBBLE GIRL"

P2 SISSOR SLIPS GIRL OH DANCING

P3 WITH RUST & KNIVES FOR LIPS

RAIN OF BLADES

□2 P1 OH SLUG GIRL HN MONEY TROUBLE DIRTY SHOWER GIRL

P2 PICK POCKET, FIRE CRACKER LAUNDRY PILE

P3 HONEY GIRL

(YUCCA BOTANICAL ILLO)

□3 P1 YUCCA MOUTH GIRL CUTTING FLOWER HEADS &

P2 SEWING CANDY SKULLS

P3 FOR SCRUBBING MEMORY'S SUGAR GIRL

P4 TEQUILA SICK + TOILET BOWL AGAIN

2

FLASH FLOOD →

FIRE PROOF   FIRE CRACKER   LAUNDRY PILE

HONEY GIRL

FABRICS IN FIRE CRACKER CURLS →

3

YUCCA MOU

CUTTING FLOWER

FALLING FLOWER HEAD

HAND FIGURE?

□4 TOP: GIRL HUNGRY GIRL YOU UNSTITCHED RAZOR GIRL BOTTOM: BLADE GIRL GRUBBY NECKED & SPITTING GIRL OR SWALLOWING HEAD DOWN GIRL STOMACH PIT

4

5

P4 DESERT BOOK / FIGURE DEAD

P3 HANDS REACH US

□5 P1 FINE GIRL GUNNING TO SIDEWALK, CATCALL GIRL

P2. ESCAPE GIRL

P3. OH PLUCKING BONES FROM GRAVES GIRL

P4. RISING & RISING

P5. GIRL TEACH ME HN TO LIVE THAT LOOSE TUMBLEDOWN GIRL

6

SMALLER?

* DO I NEED 1 MORE PANEL WITH "WIPE" OF MIRROR?

□6 P1.B I SLIT THE AGAIN.

2. AND MEND MOTHER US WHOLE.

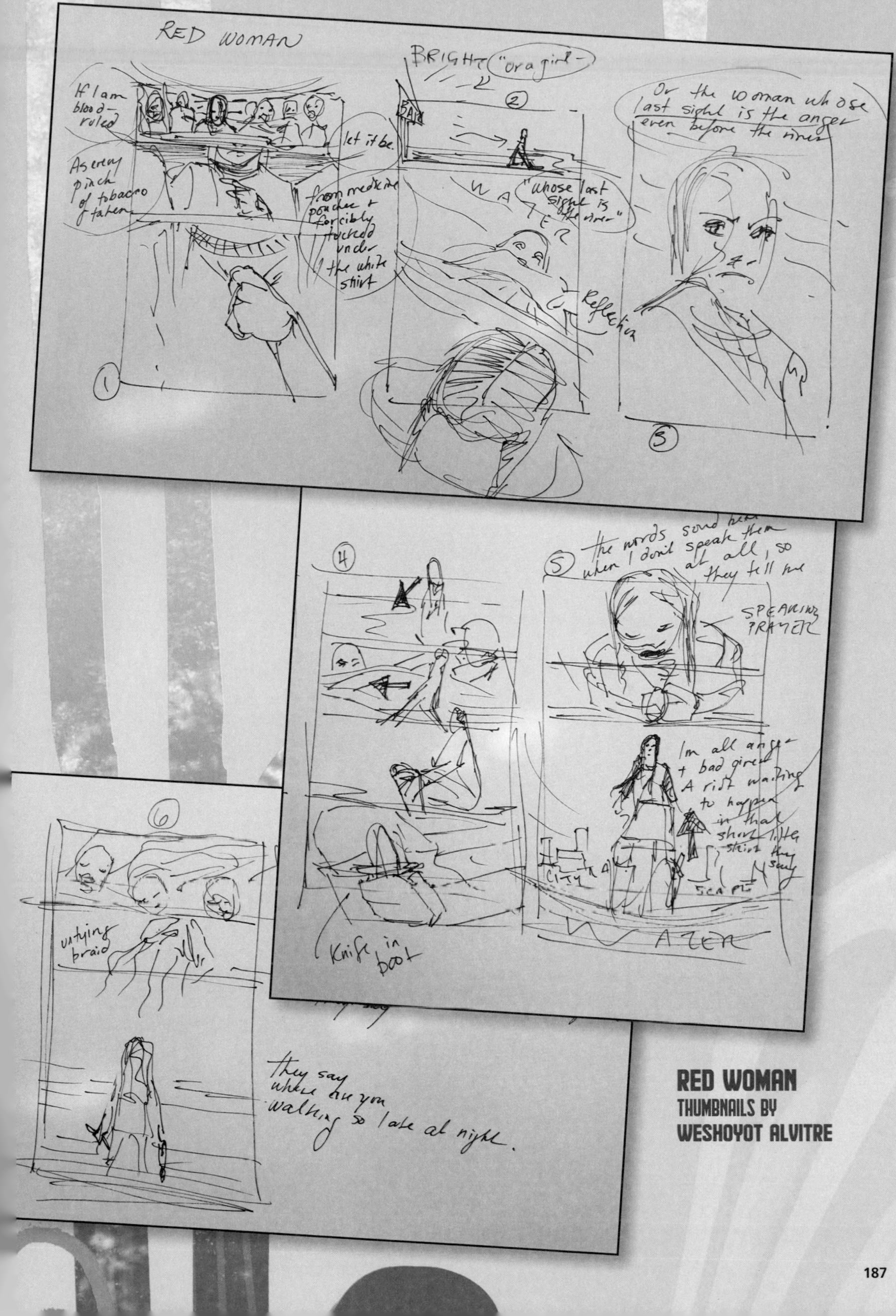
RED WOMAN
If I am blood-ruled
As every pinch of tobacco taken
let it be.
from medicine pouches + forcibly tucked under the white shirt
BRIGHT
"or a girl"
"whose last sight is the river"
W A T E R
Reflection
Or the woman whose last sight is the anger even before the river
SPEAKING PRAYER
I'm all anger + bad girl A riot waiting to happen in that short little skirt they say
CITY
WATER
knife in boot
untying braid
They say where are you walking so late at night.

RED WOMAN
THUMBNAILS BY
WESHOYOT ALVITRE

GENDER STUDIES ROUGHS BY STELLADIA

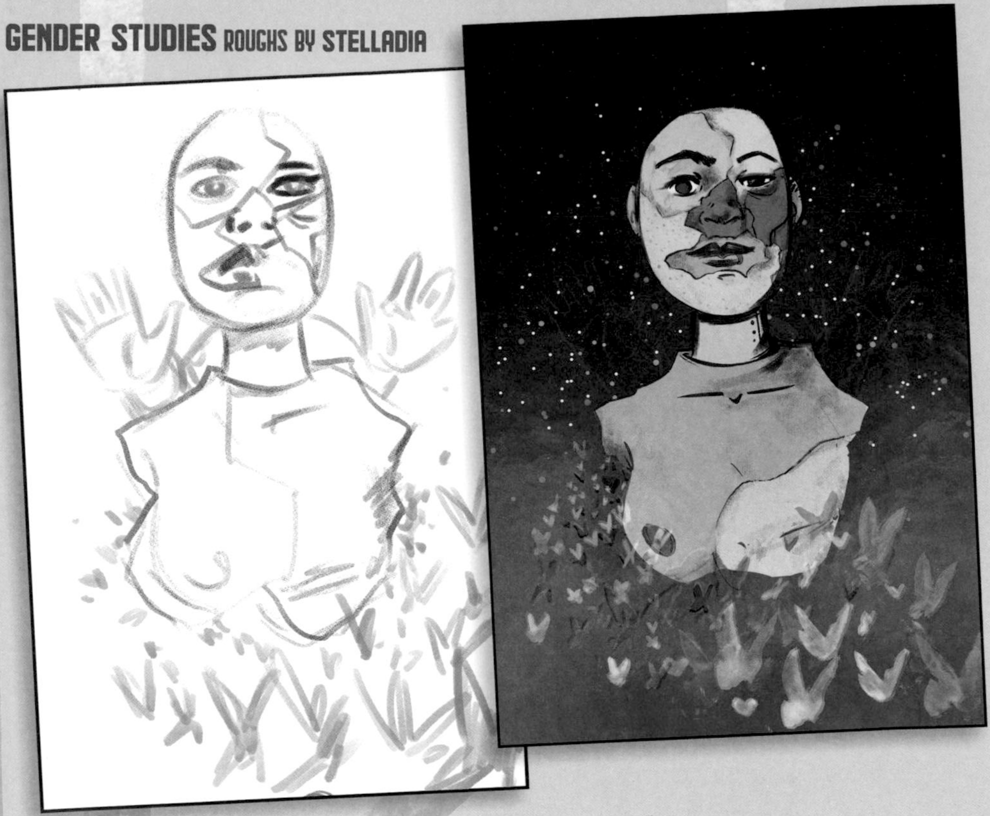

A LOVE LETTER TO THE DECADES I HAVE KISSED OR NOTES ON TURNING 5
PENCILS BY SOO LEE

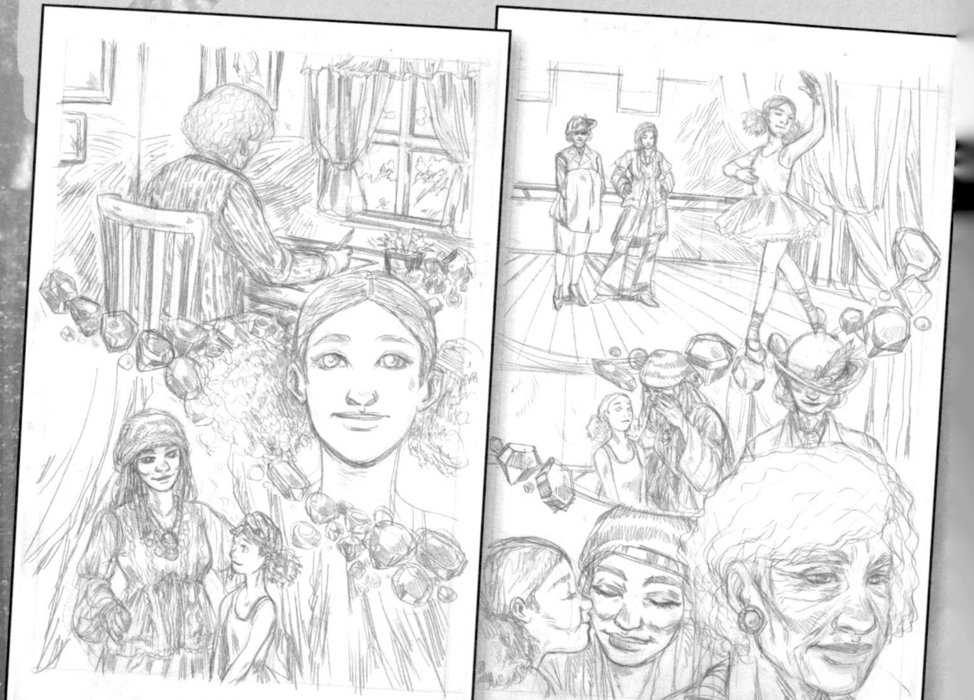

UNITS & INCREMENTS
THUMBNAIL AND INKS BY JESSICA LYNN

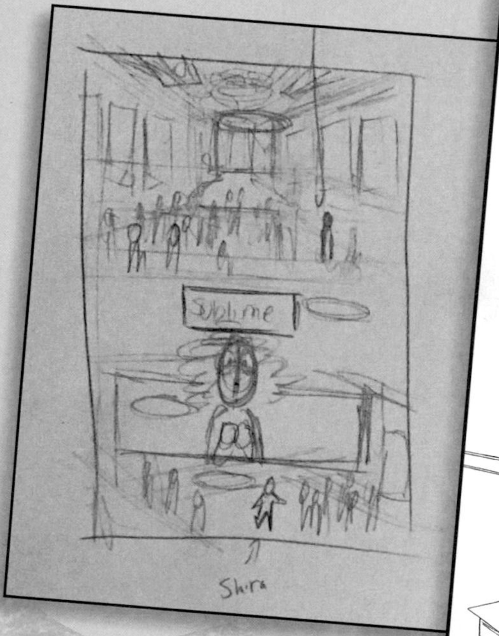
Sublime
Shira

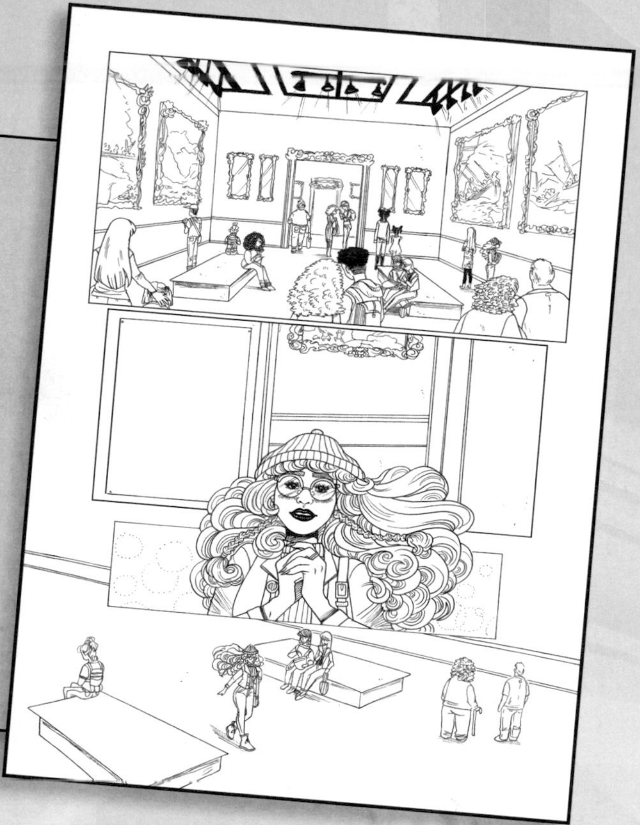

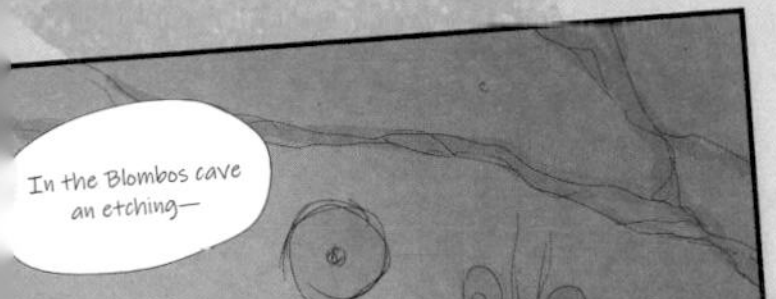
In the Blombos cave an etching—

X DIGITAL PENCILS BY ASHLEY WOODS

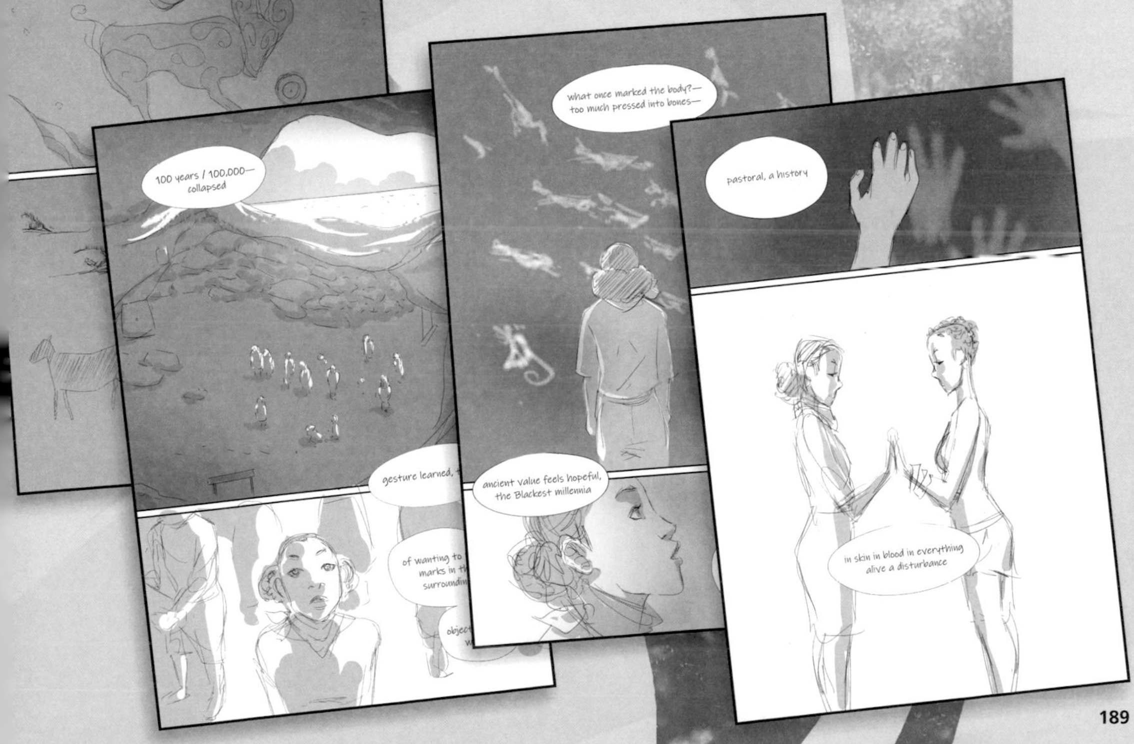
100 years / 100,000— collapsed
gesture learned,
what once marked the body?— too much pressed into bones—
ancient value feels hopeful, the Blackest millennia
pastoral, a history
in skin in blood in everything alive a disturbance

TAPESTRY ROUGHS AND INKS BY MORGAN BEEM

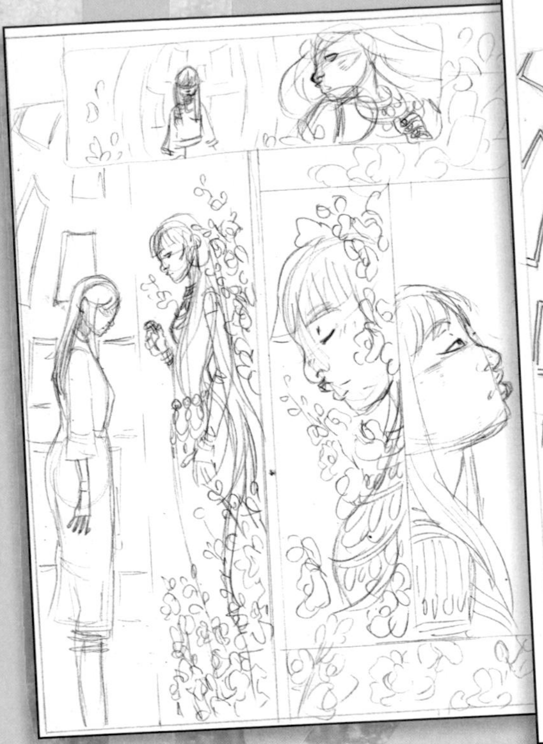

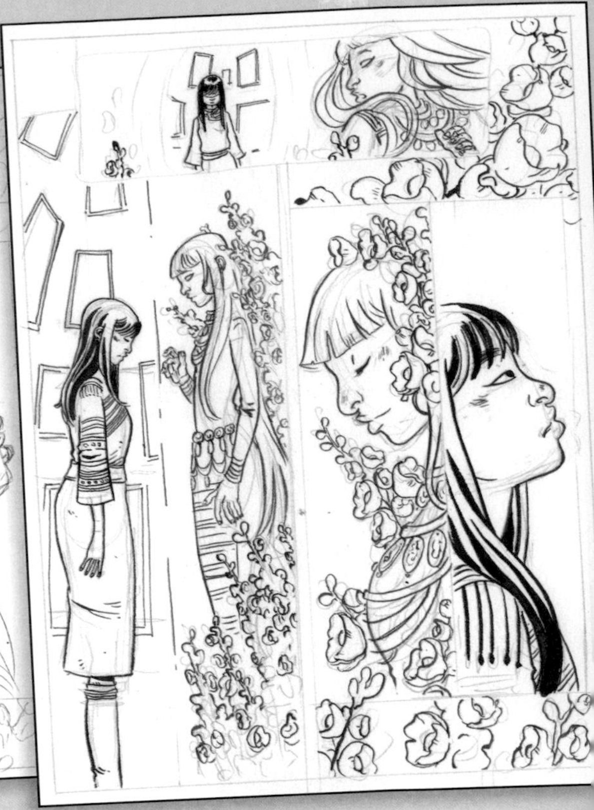

HALF GIRL THUMBNAILS AND INKS BY AYŞEGÜL SINAV

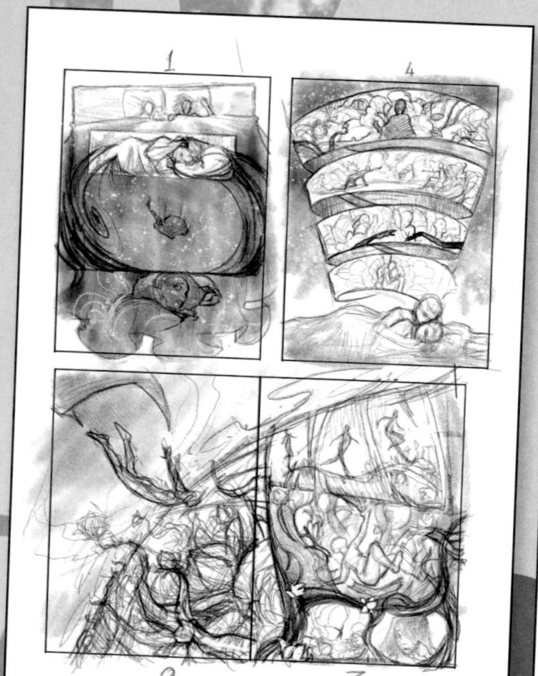
1
4
2
3

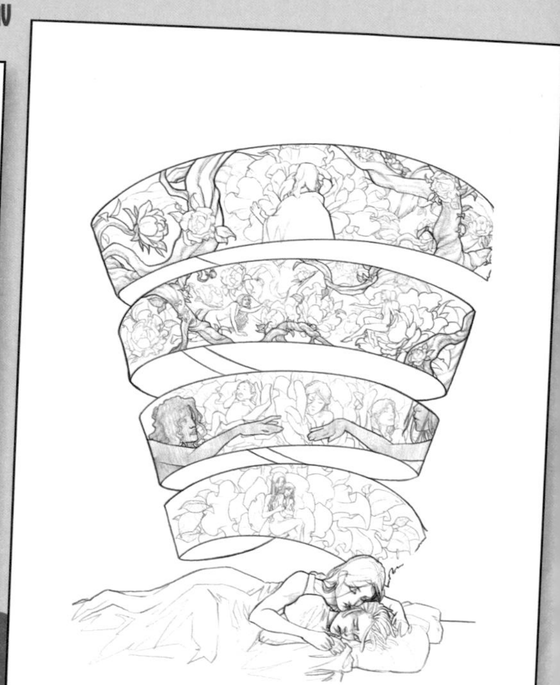

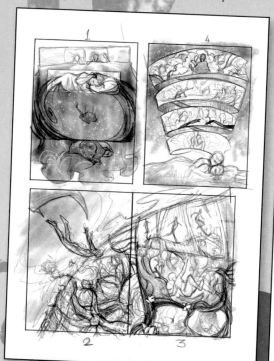

CHERRY BLOSSOMS ROUGHS BY HAZEL NEWLEVANT

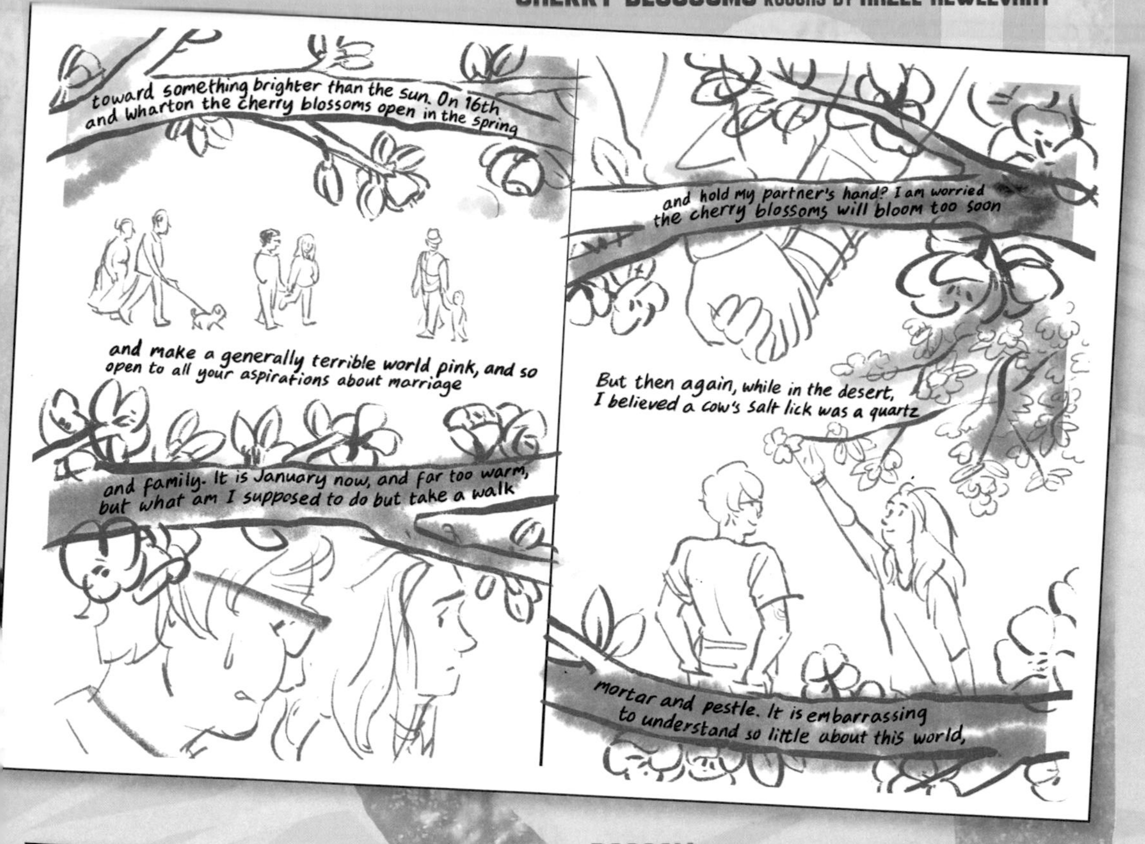

toward something brighter than the sun. On 16th and Wharton the cherry blossoms open in the spring
and make a generally terrible world pink, and so open to all your aspirations about marriage
and family. It is January now, and far too warm, but what am I supposed to do but take a walk
and hold my partner's hand? I am worried the cherry blossoms will bloom too soon
But then again, while in the desert, I believed a cow's salt lick was a quartz
mortar and pestle. It is embarrassing to understand so little about this world,

BASSAM DIGITAL PENCILSA BY EMILY PEARSON

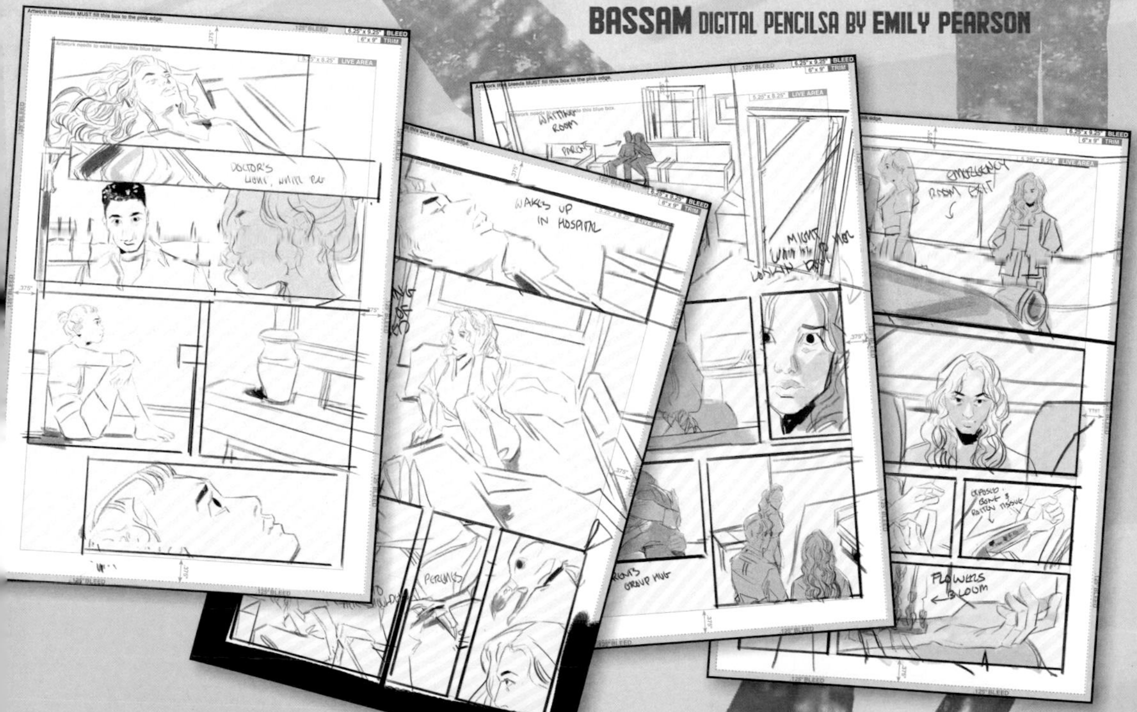

WAKES UP IN HOSPITAL
WAITING ROOM
EMERGENCY ROOM EXIT
FLOWERS BLOOM

SPEAK-HOUSE
LAYOUTS BY MARIKA CRESTA

ORIGINAL LAYOUTS

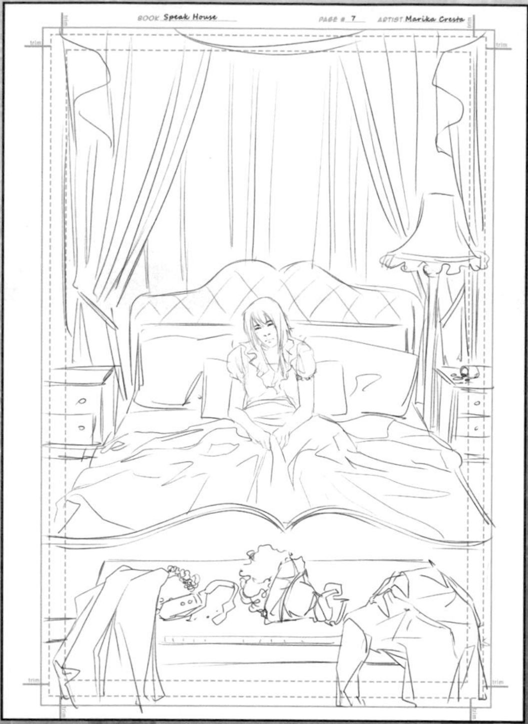
BOOK Speak House
PAGE # 7
ARTIST Marika Cresta

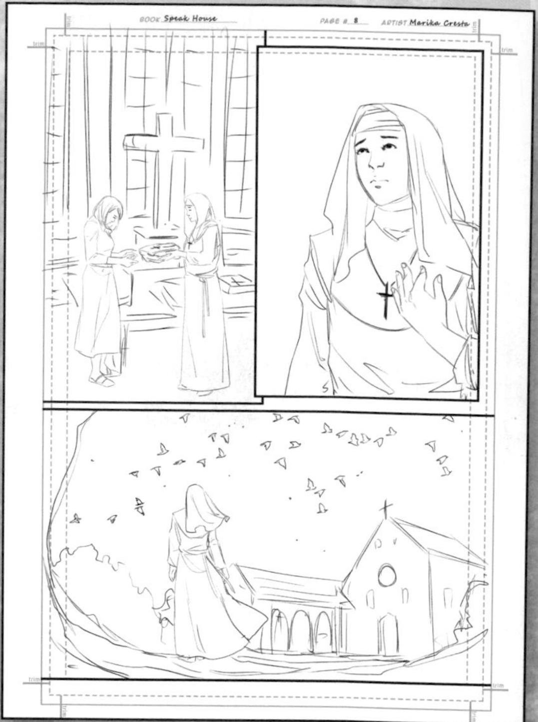
BOOK Speak House
PAGE # 8
ARTIST Marika Cresta

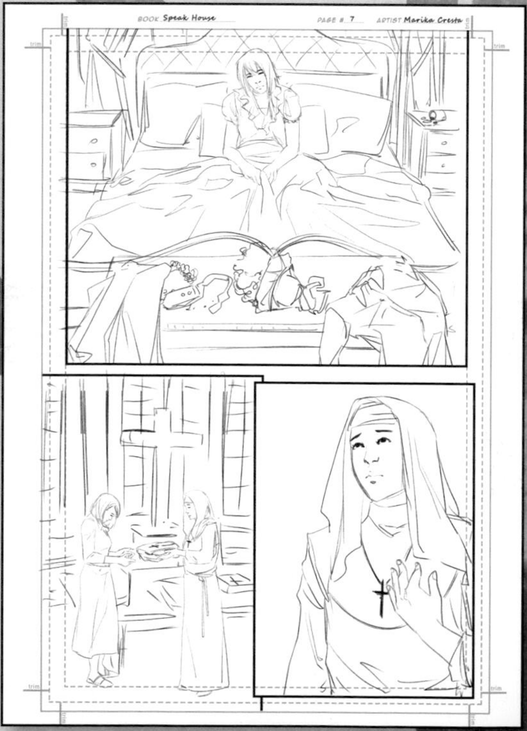
BOOK Speak House
PAGE # 7
ARTIST Marika Cresta

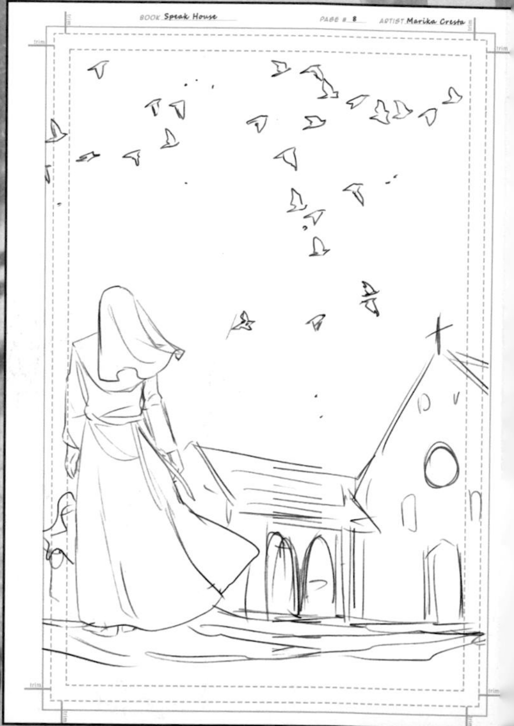
BOOK Speak House
PAGE # 8
ARTIST Marika Cresta

REVISED LAYOUTS

UNIVERSITY TOXIC

THUMBNAILS BY KAYLEE ROWENA

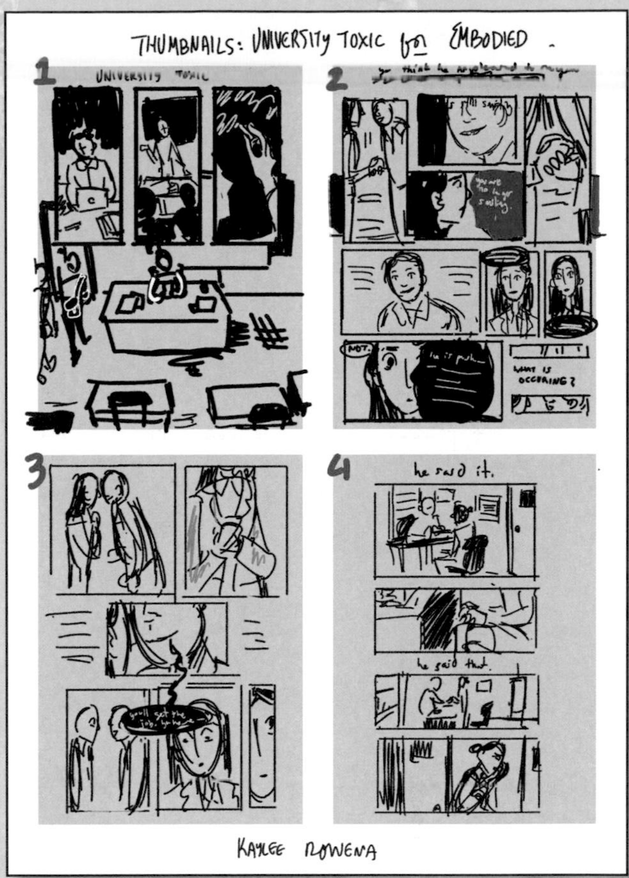
THUMBNAILS: UNIVERSITY TOXIC for EMBODIED.
1
UNIVERSITY TOXIC
2
WHAT IS OCCURRING?
3
4
he said it.
he said that.
KAYLEE ROWENA

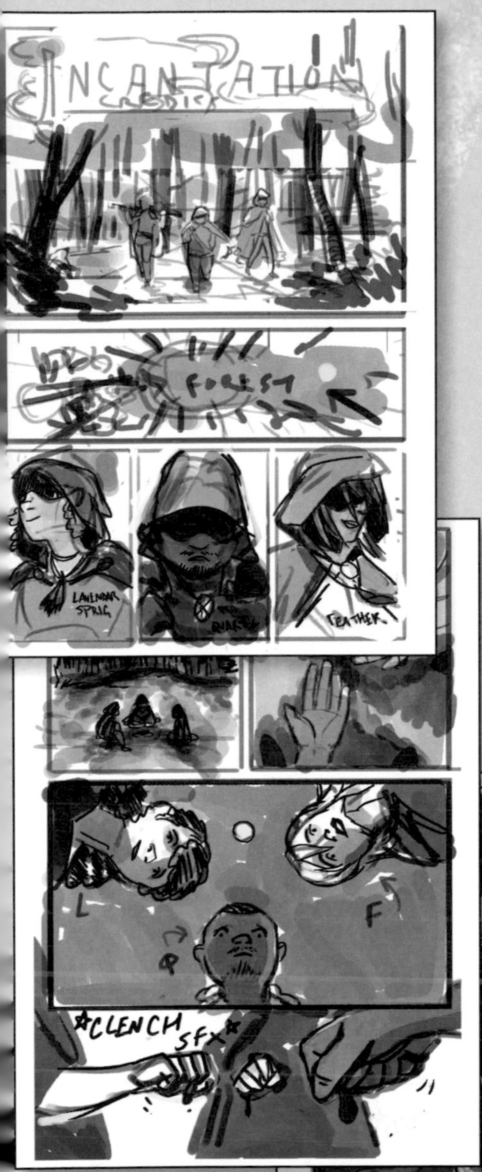
INCANTATION
CREDITS
FOREST
LAVENDAR SPRIG
FEATHER
L
F
CLENCH
SFX

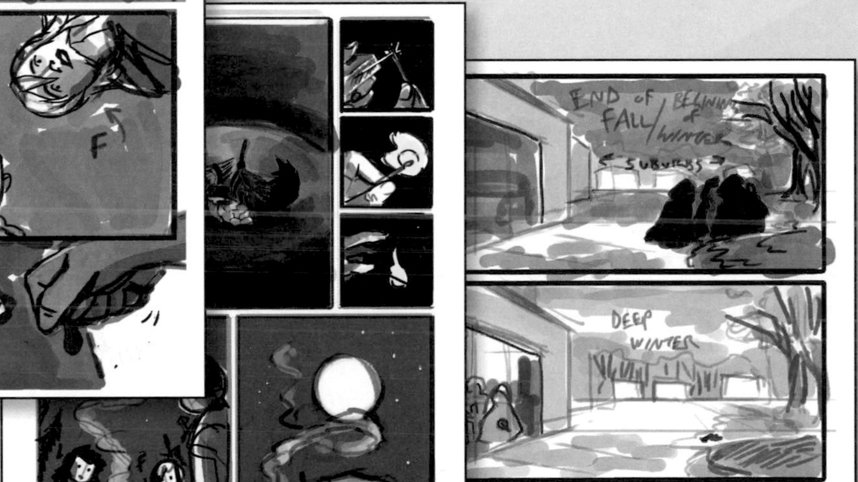
DEEP WINTER
LATE SPRING...
BLOOM
BLOOM

INCANTATION

ROUGHS BY JUDE VIGANTS

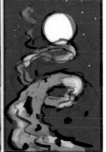

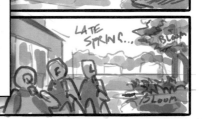

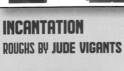

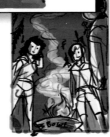

CAPITALISM RUINS EVERYTHING, EVEN WITCH CRAFT INKS BY NED BARNETT

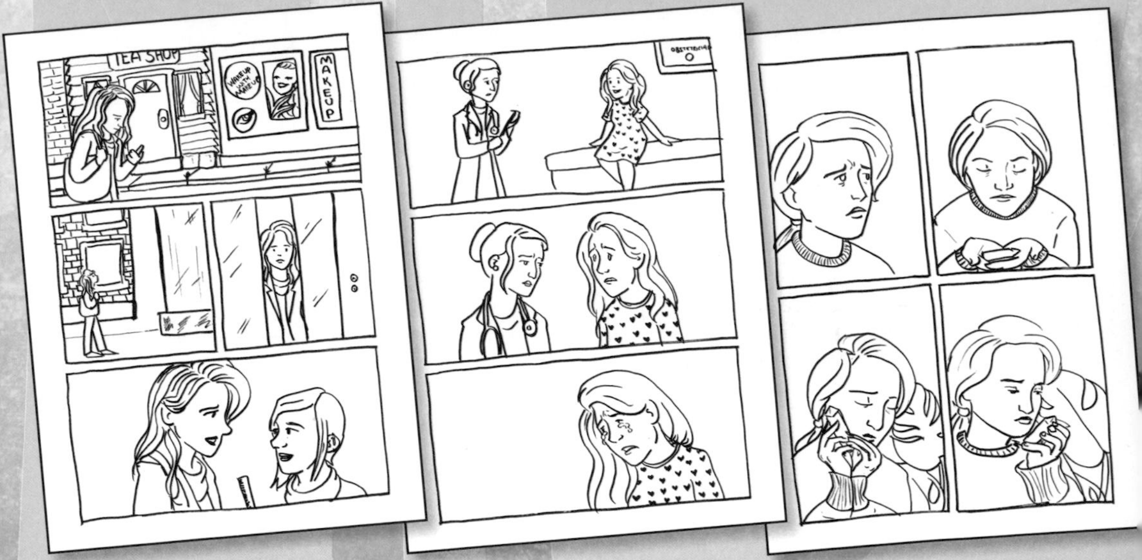
TEA SHOP
MAKEUP

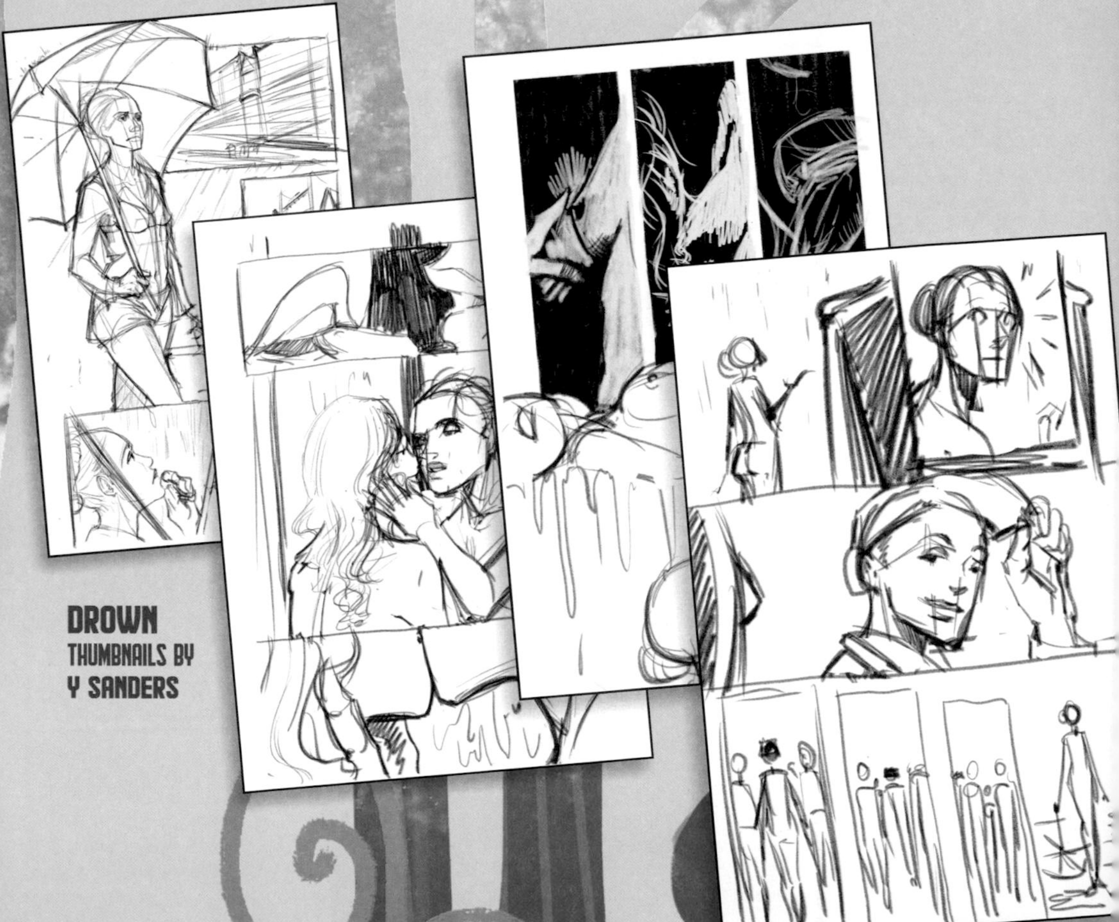

DROWN
THUMBNAILS BY
Y SANDERS

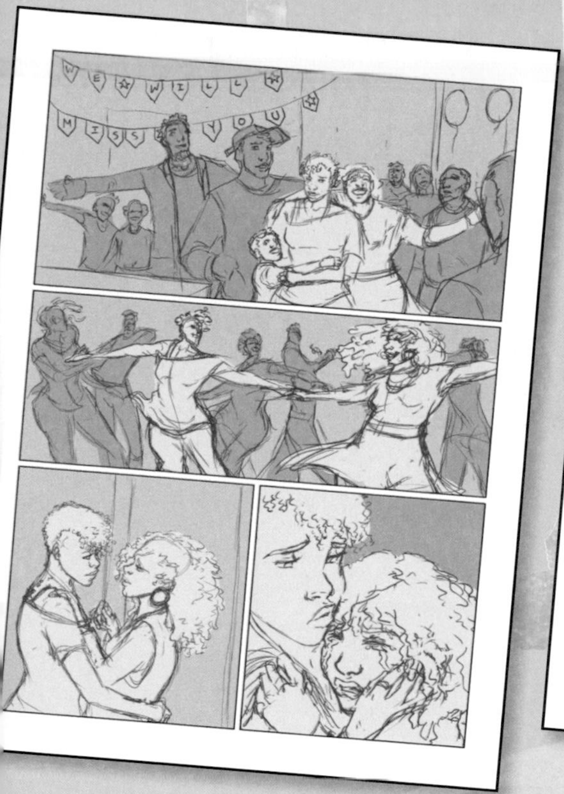
WE WILL
MISS YOU

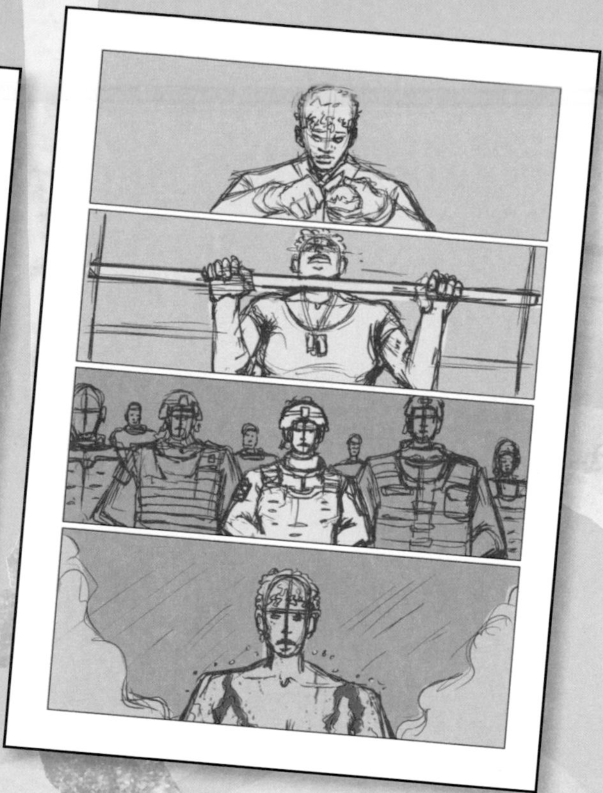

LES ANNÉES DE GUERRE

ROUGHS BY TAKEIA MARIE

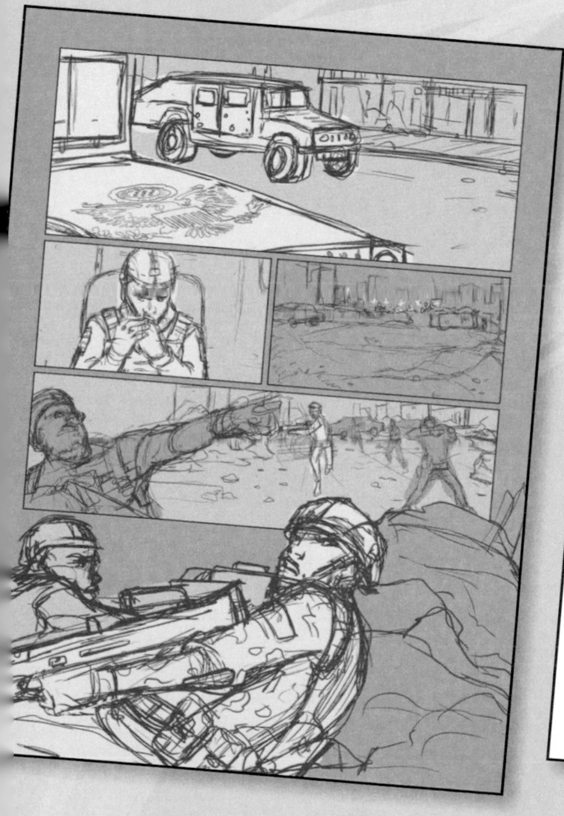

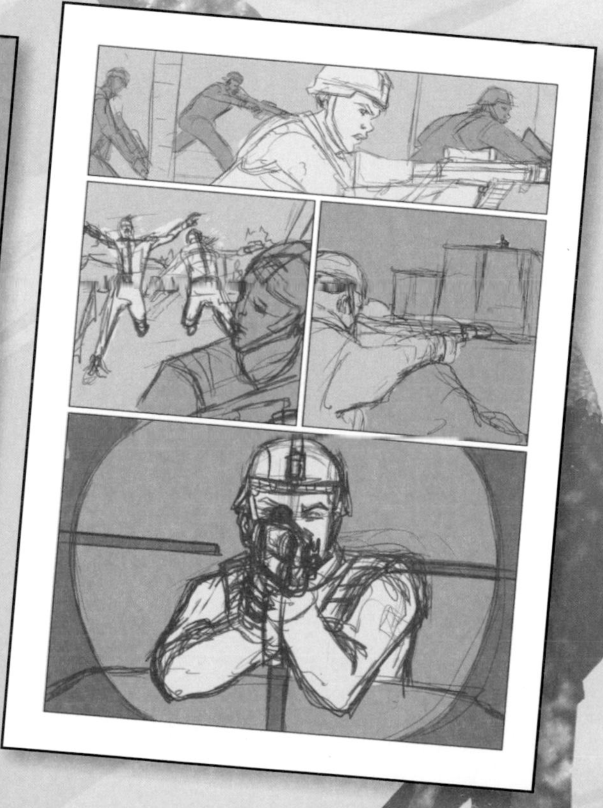

SETTLEMENT
THUMBNAILS BY
RONNIE GARCIA

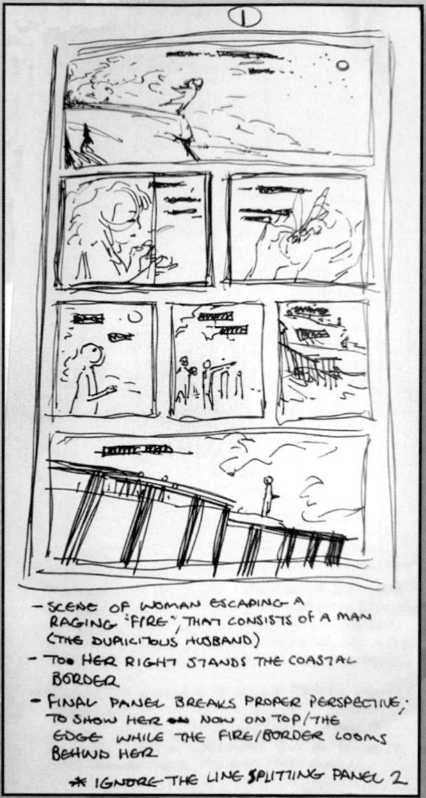
1
- SCENE OF WOMAN ESCAPING A RAGING "FIRE", THAT CONSISTS OF A MAN (THE DUPLICITOUS HUSBAND)
- TOO HER RIGHT STANDS THE COASTAL BORDER
- FINAL PANEL BREAKS PROPER PERSPECTIVE; TO SHOW HER NOW ON TOP/THE EDGE WHILE THE FIRE/BORDER LOOMS BEHIND HER
* IGNORE THE LINE SPLITTING PANEL 2

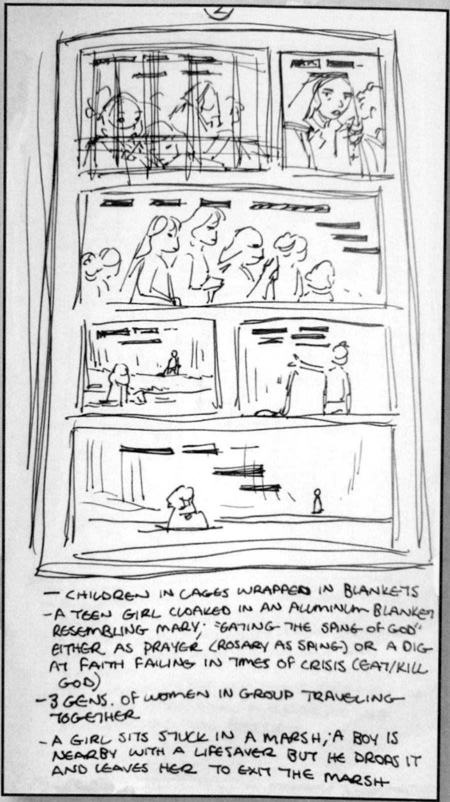
2
- CHILDREN IN CAGES WRAPPED IN BLANKETS
- A TEEN GIRL CLOAKED IN AN ALUMINUM BLANKET RESEMBLING MARY; "EATING THE SPINE OF GOD" EITHER AS PRAYER (ROSARY AS SPINE) OR A DIG AT FAITH FAILING IN TIMES OF CRISIS (EAT/KILL GOD)
- 3 GENS. OF WOMEN IN GROUP TRAVELING TOGETHER
- A GIRL SITS STUCK IN A MARSH; A BOY IS NEARBY WITH A LIFESAVER BUT HE DROPS IT AND LEAVES HER TO EXIT THE MARSH

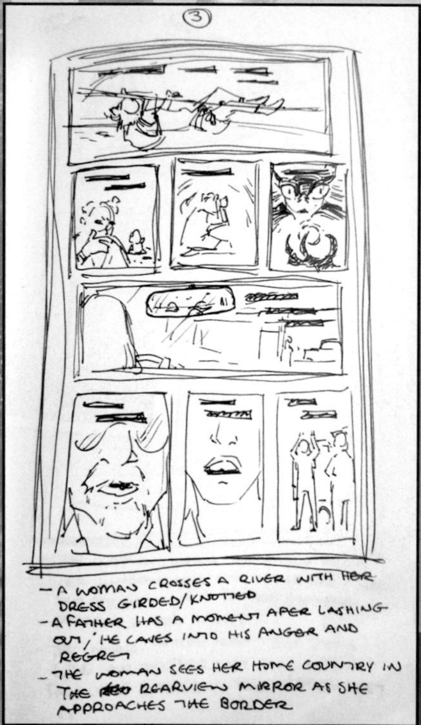
3
- A WOMAN CROSSES A RIVER WITH HER DRESS GIRDED/KNOTTED
- A FATHER HAS A MOMENT AFER LASHING OUT; HE CAVES INTO HIS ANGER AND REGRET
- THE WOMAN SEES HER HOME COUNTRY IN THE REARVIEW MIRROR AS SHE APPROACHES THE BORDER

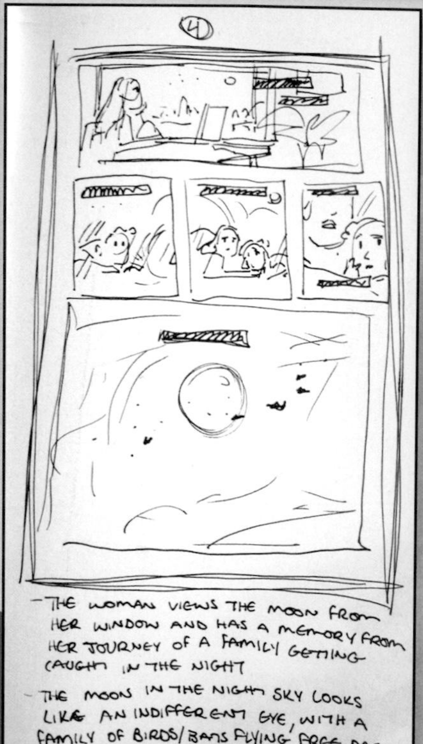
4
- THE WOMAN VIEWS THE MOON FROM HER WINDOW AND HAS A MEMORY FROM HER JOURNEY OF A FAMILY GETTING CAUGHT IN THE NIGHT
- THE MOON IN THE NIGHT SKY LOOKS LIKE AN INDIFFERENT EYE, WITH A FAMILY OF BIRDS/BATS FLYING FREE PAST

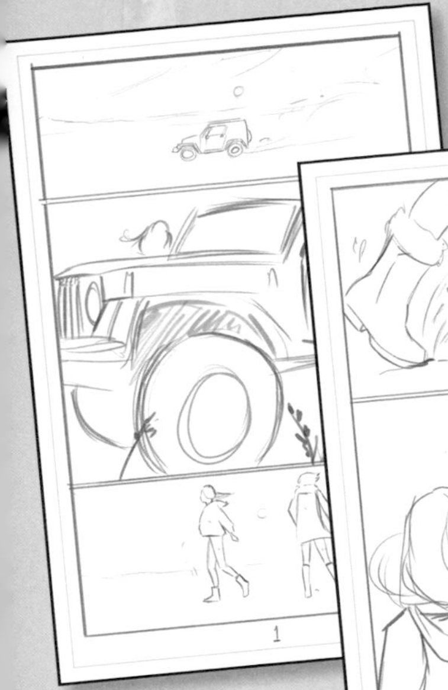

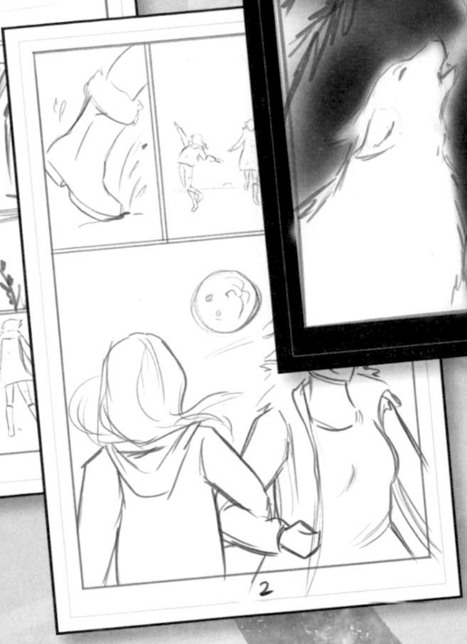

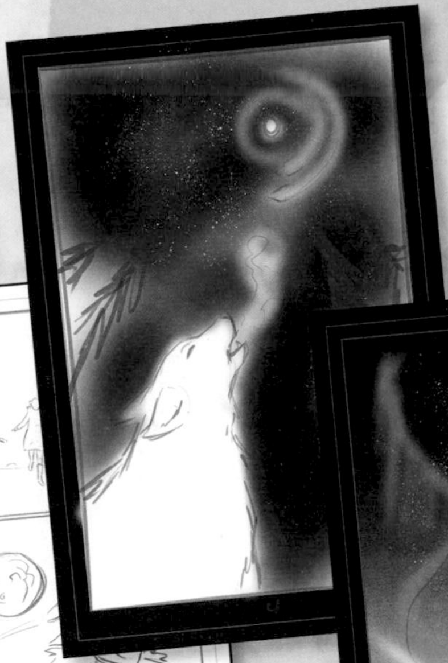

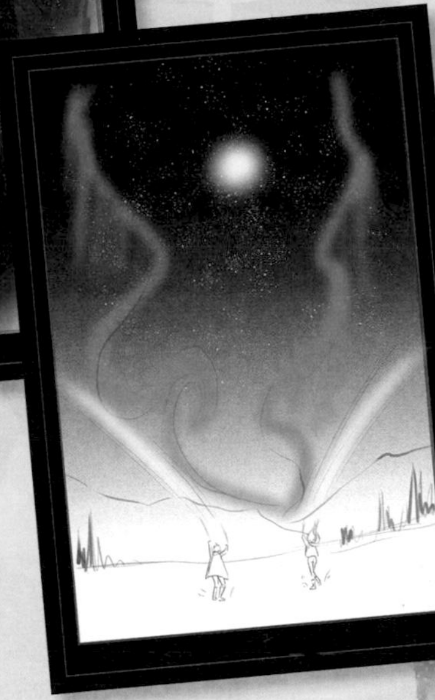

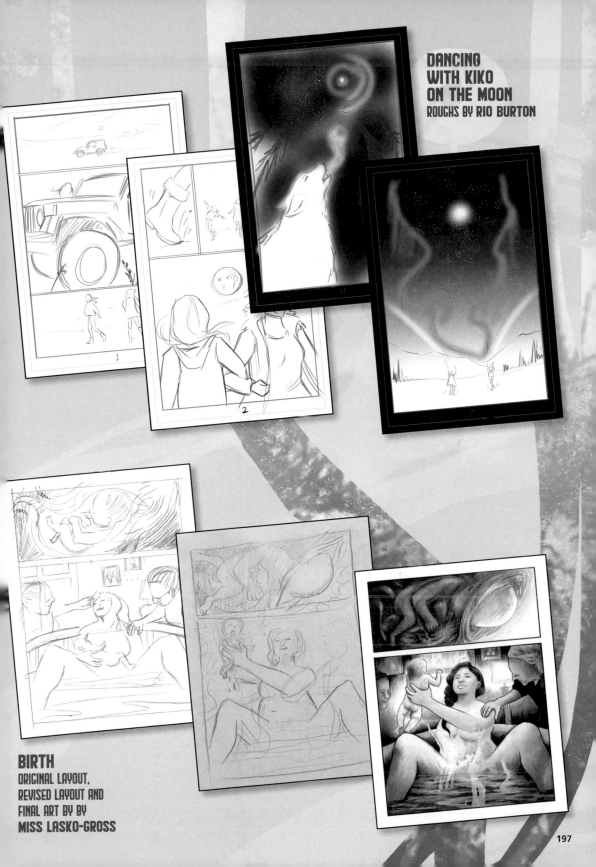

DANCING WITH KIKO ON THE MOON
ROUGHS BY RIO BURTON

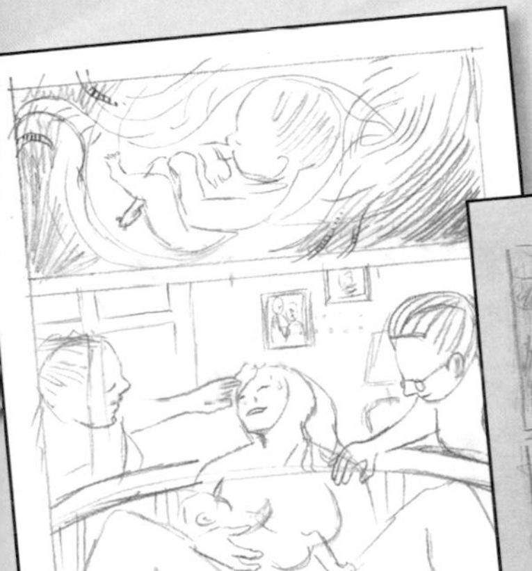

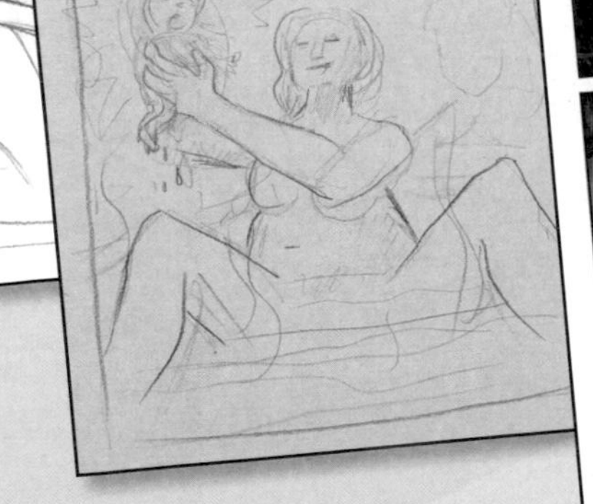

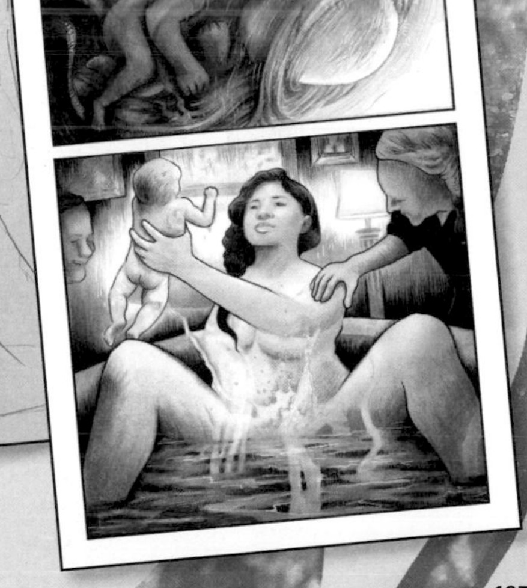

BIRTH
ORIGINAL LAYOUT, REVISED LAYOUT AND FINAL ART BY BY
MISS LASKO-GROSS

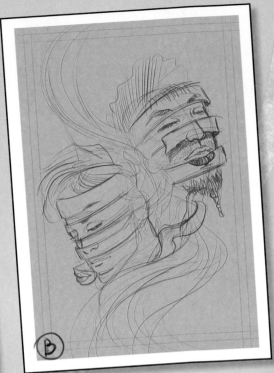

A THE IDEA IS TO DEPICT THE MULTI ASPECTS OF WOMEN AS A SORT OF LIVING TREE, EVERY BODY A BRANCH, A MULTITUDE CREATING A UNITY. FACE EXPRESSIONS ARE QUITE, RELAXED OR SERENE, AS BODY LANGUAGE SHOWING AFFECTIONS, JOY, ENERGY.
(quite weird in these times of social distancing!)

B A SORT OF FACE COMPOSITION SHOWING DIFFERENT FEATURES CREATING A RIBBON LIKE EFFECT (Escher) INTERSECTING AND OVERLAYING THE OTHER LAYERS.

C A MYRIAD OF COLOURED STREAMS REPRESENTING THE DIVERSITY OF WOMEN WHICH CREATE A "DRESS" OVER A NO-BINARY BODY. THE COLOURS CREATES ALSO A SORT OF FLOURISHING HALO AT GROUND, A METAPHORE FOR TALENTS AND ATTITUDES.

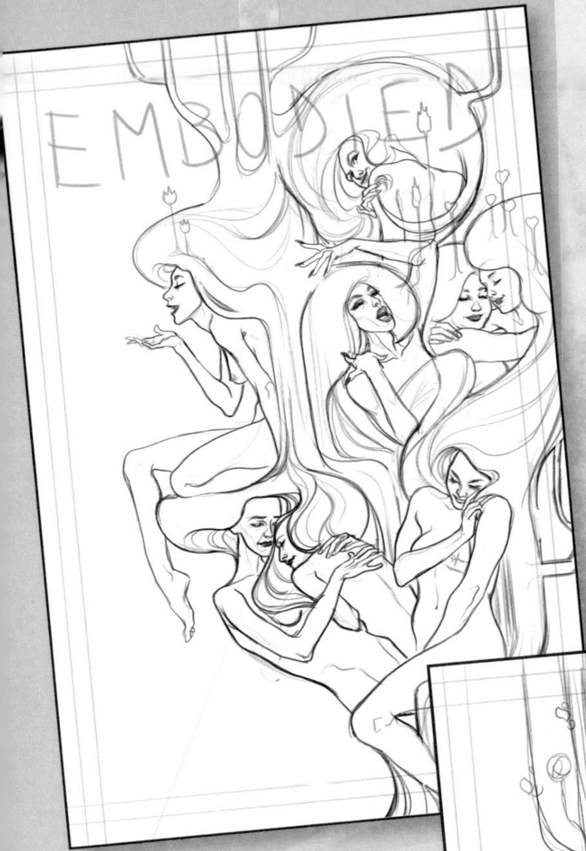
EMBODIED

COVER THUMBNAILS, NOTES & SKETCHES BY **CLAUDIA IANNICIELLO**

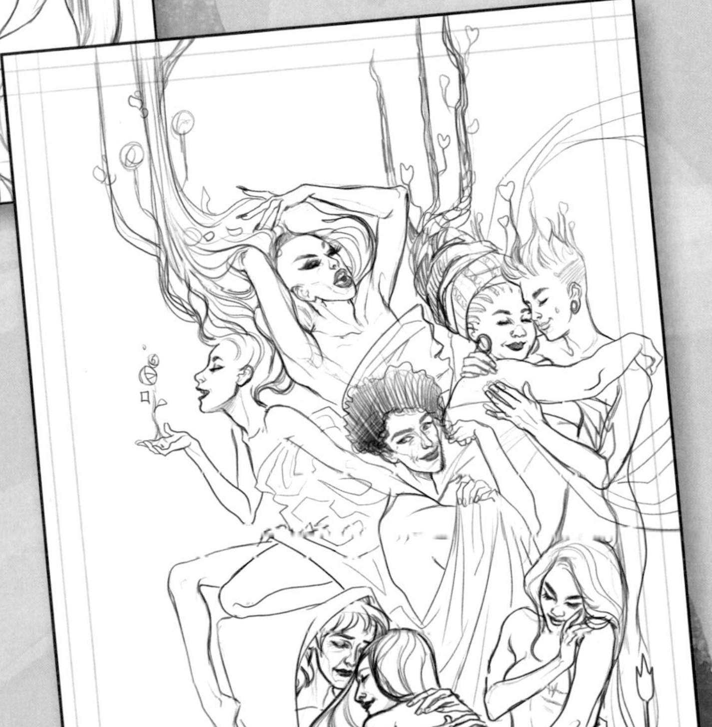

FOLLOWING PAGE:
FINISHED COVER ILLUSTRATION BY
CLAUDIA IANNICIELLO

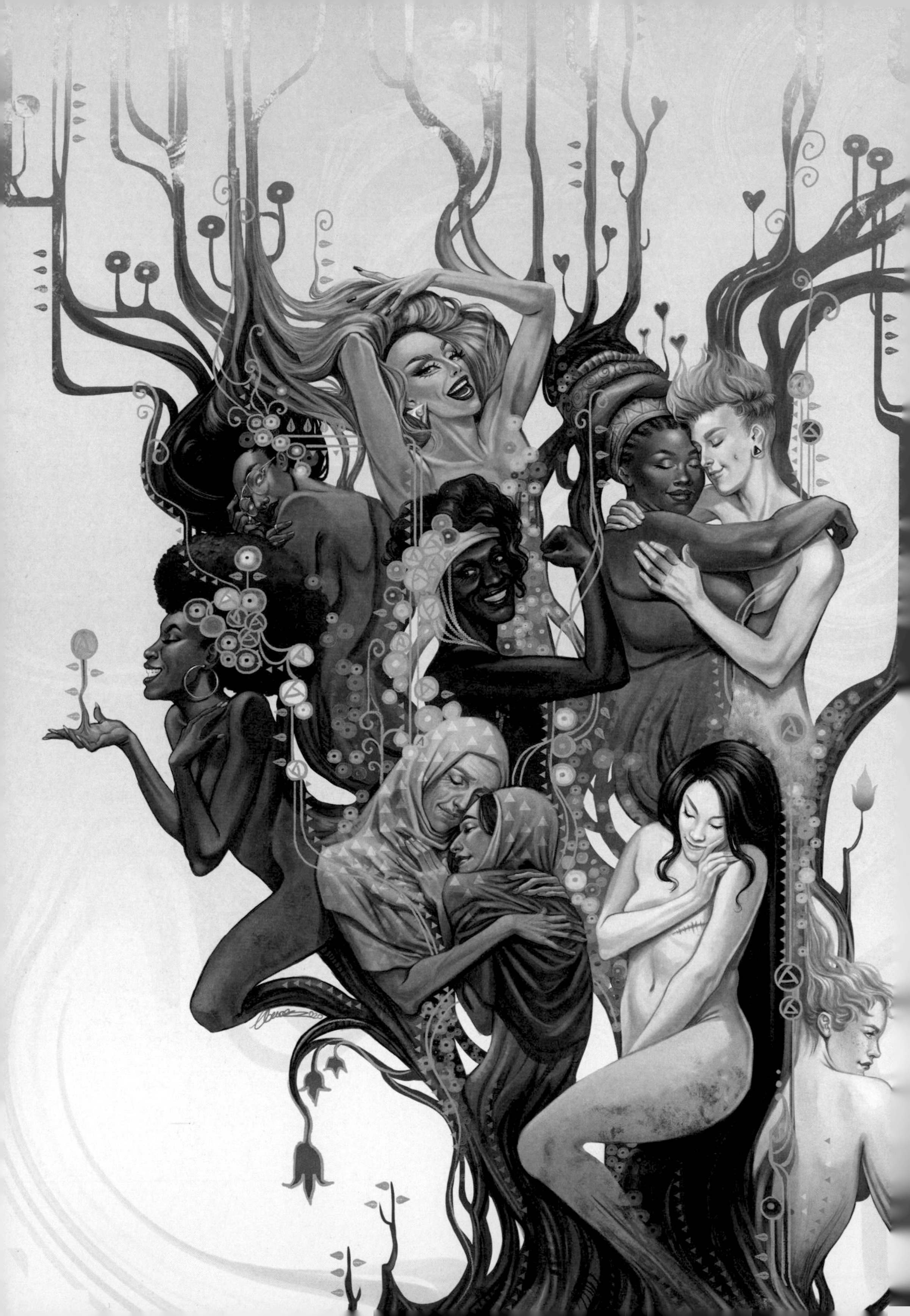